ANIMISM BEYOND THE SOUL

Studies in Social Analysis
General Editor: Martin Holbraad
University College London

Focusing on analysis as a meeting ground of the empirical and the conceptual, this series provides a platform for exploring anthropological approaches to social analysis while seeking to open new avenues of communication between anthropology and the humanities, as well as other social sciences.

ANIMISM BEYOND THE SOUL

Ontology, Reflexivity, and the Making
of Anthropological Knowledge

Edited by

Katherine Swancutt and Mireille Mazard

berghahn
NEW YORK · OXFORD
www.berghahnbooks.com

First published in 2018 by

Berghahn Books

www.berghahnbooks.com

© 2018 Berghahn Books

Originally published as a special issue of *Social Analysis*, volume 60, issue 1.

Library of Congress Cataloging-in-Publication Data

A C.I.P. cataloging record is available from the Library of Congress

British Library Cataloguing in Publication Data

A catalogue record for this book is available from the British Library.

ISBN 978-1-78533-865-6 (hardback)
ISBN 978-1-78533-866-3 (paperback)
ISBN 978-1-78533-867-0 (ebook)

CONTENTS

FOREWORD

The Anthropology of Ontology Meets the Writing Culture Debate—Is Reconciliation Possible?

Rane Willerslev

This exciting book sets out to take the 'anthropology of ontology' (also called the 'ontological turn'), along with its concern for indigenous animism, to a new level of analysis by pairing it with key issues originally raised by anthropology's influential paradigm of reflexivity, the Writing Culture debate. A few years ago, I critiqued the inclination "to neutralize the challenge" that animistic ideas present to anthropological thinking (Willerslev 2007: 12). In their introduction, the editors of this volume, Katherine Swancutt and Mireille Mazard, describe the 'reflexive feedback loop' through which native thinkers, by adopting anthropological theories of animism, cast the anthropological gaze back upon itself. Here, instead of being neutralized by anthropology, native ideas feed into and play havoc with scholarly models of animism. It is this unexpected condition of inquiry that gives rise to the editors' engagement with the 'anthropology of anthropology'.

In certain ways, this echoes the 1980s postmodern critique of anthropology and the paradigm of reflexivity that became its answer (see Clifford 1986: 17). However, the chapters in this book take the theories of the Writing Culture debate in a new and important direction by offering novel insights into wider social movements—communism, Christianity, environmentalism, Daoist revivals, socialism, post-socialism, spiritualism—that shape local thinkers', and subsequently professional anthropologists', ideas about animism. The contributors further highlight changes to animism resulting from knowledge-making practices such as techno-science, popular fiction, and autobiographical narratives, all of which can be said to lie beyond the state-of-the-art concerns of the anthropology of ontology.

The editors' argument about reflexive native thinkers also evokes the much older notion of the 'savage philosopher', a term introduced by the 'father of animism', Edward B. Tylor ([1871] 1920). I shall return to address Tylor's legacy and the reflexive native thinker in a moment. For now, I want to consider the implications of the daring route tackled by Swancutt and Mazard, which seeks to bring together the Writing Culture paradigm, the primary theory of reflexivity of the 1980s, with the theory currently in fashion in the study of animism—the anthropology of ontology.

The Reflexivity of Writing Culture versus Alterity in the Anthropology of Ontology

I consider the route 'daring' because the paradigms that the editors seek to unite are, at least on the face of it, deeply at odds. The Writing Culture paradigm does not believe in radical alterity. Rather, it suggests that we all live in a globalized world in which the high speed of communication and the wide range of intercultural connections make all the talk about absolute alterity meaningless. As George Marcus (2007: 7), one of the founding fathers of the paradigm, puts it: "[Today] few anthropologists would set out on research in the contemporary world while laying claim to this pure purpose for ethnographic inquiry of exploring cultural alterity as 'Other'." It comes as no surprise, therefore, that many of this paradigm's devotees are passionately engaged in the study of globalization (Smith and Guarnizo 1998) and the use of new digital technologies of communication (Pfaffenberger 1992), often by means of 'multi-sited' ethnographic fieldwork in urban settings (Falzon 2009).

The anthropology of ontology, by contrast, marks a return to 'ethnographic orthodoxy' through its concern for uncovering the radical alterity of others (Willerslev 2013c: 42). This radical alterity is supposed to be found primarily in small-scale communities in Amazonia (Viveiros de Castro 1992), Melanesia (Scott 2007), Mongolia (Pedersen 2011), and Siberia (Willerslev 2009, 2013c). It is within these apparently marginal communities that anthropologists hope to find alien concepts of the soul, spirits, and non-human persons that fly in the face of Western common-sense understandings of what reality entails (Candea 2011). Anthropology's greatest task, according to ontologists, is to embrace this alterity and incorporate it into its scripts, so as to alter our own ways of thinking about what constitutes the real (Holbraad 2007; Scott 2013; Viveiros de Castro 2011; Willerslev 2013b).

This fundamental difference between the two paradigms is perhaps revealed above all in their disparate take on the recurrent problem of 'cultural translation'. The Writing Culture paradigm sees the problem as one of 'representation'—that is, people impose different schemes of meanings upon the same reality, which is considered exterior to cultural representation (Burr 2003: 6). In this sense, it is presumed that there is a basic level of univocality—one that underlies what others and we are saying. The anthropology of ontology, in contrast, presupposes that an enormous gap divides indigenous ontologies from that of Euro-America. Hence, there is no common baseline that would work as a mutual referent for transcultural dialogue, since "we and they are never talking about the same things" (Viveiros de Castro 2004: 7). Cultural translation becomes in this view a matter of "controlled equivocation" (ibid.), a method of comparison that aims at keeping ontological differences in view (Willerslev 2013a: 142). Now, this is not the place to discuss which of the two paradigms is more persuasive. What is more important to Swancutt and Mazard is the prospect of bringing the paradigms together in an anthropological effort to come to grips with the shifting nature of animism. The task is difficult, and whether this collection is successful in its aim is up to the reader to judge. When perusing the chapters, I experienced a number of revelations that I will briefly share here.

Metaphysical Animism and the Native Point of View

First, by coupling the anthropology of ontology's passion for alien concepts with the Writing Culture paradigm's passion for reflexivity and global interconnectivity, animism comes to be seen as an intellectual endeavor, a product of high-level abstract thinking. In some ways, this echoes Tylor's notion of the 'savage philosopher', who attempts to provide intellectual explanations for the causal workings of the world by invoking images of spirits, souls, and the like. This take on animism as being parallel to philosophy is radically different from how it has mostly been depicted during the past two decades. The dominant view has linked animism with 'efficacy'—that is, animist beliefs have been understood to be in some fundamental sense *practical*, inseparably bound up with the hands-on concerns of everyday life (see, e.g., Humphrey and Onon 1996; Ingold 2000; Willerslev 2007). In this viewpoint, animism is not necessarily considered to be metaphysically significant with some 'higher role' that would imply providing its practitioner with a deeper insight into the mysteries of life (Willerslev 2004; 2013a: 144). Instead, animism has been understood to be primarily concerned with profane questions of cost and gain. Caroline Humphrey and James Laidlaw (1994: 11) encapsulate this notion in relation to animism's twin concept of shamanism, stating that "the question most insistently asked of [shamans is] 'Has it worked?'" Here, animism is the reverse side—indeed, the antithesis of—philosophy. This book's introduction of the 'hyper-reflexive' animist thinker is a decisive break with this view.

A few years ago I argued for a return to a Frazerian style of anthropology in the sense that metaphysical speculation, rather than the usual Malinowskian trust in empirical studies, is needed if we are to unlock the animist concept of 'soul' (Willerslev 2011). In this view, the anthropologist's speculative imagination becomes a counterpoint to empirical ethnographic research. Swancutt and Mazard make an argument that is somewhat parallel to this: they show that native metaphysics is a counterpoint to the native practice of animism. The two are not incompatible, and the existence of animism as the fabric of everyday practical life does not exclude the possibility of an 'armchair anthropology' of animism among its practitioners.

This is, in my view, one of the key insights revealed in this book. Indigenous animism is, due to the 'reflexive feedback loop', undergoing a major change in which its concern with efficacy is increasingly being replaced with metaphysical concerns. This transformation has deep-seated implications for how anthropologists can go about studying animism, since it implies novel forms of dialogue, partnership, and perhaps even co-authorship—that is, all the reflexive concerns of the 'anthropology of anthropology'.

This leads me to the next revelation, which has to do with the need to revise the status of anthropological knowledge vis-à-vis the so-called native point of view. The editors and contributors to this book are talking about parallel knowledge-making practices—those of native thinkers and those of anthropologists that feed into each other. Whether or not they regard the two types of knowledge practices as being somehow equal or even equivalent is uncertain. However, I believe it is worth pursuing a clearer answer by asking what the chapters reveal about the matter. In the face of the postmodernist crisis, Kirsten Hastrup (1993) makes the thorny argument that anthropological knowledge is fundamentally different from, and by no standards reducible to, the native point of view. She states that the "native point of view is part of ethnography, but the goal of scholarship is not just to record the world as seen from a particular point of view ... As science, anthropology aims at general truth, which lies beyond any particular narrative" (ibid.: 176). She adds that "there is no way in which one can claim privileged access to *anthropological* knowledge—except by being native to anthropology" (ibid.: 181; original emphasis).

Hastrup has a point all right, but as this volume quite clearly illustrates, the categories of both 'native' and 'anthropologist' are not unambiguous, straightforward, or uniform. Modern-day anthropology is not immune from being bamboozled by the sophistication of native animist thinking, just as native thinkers are not 'theory free', devoid of metaphysical thought. If we miss out on the complexity of the relationship between native thinkers and the various theories, cosmologies, or ideologies that shape their ways of understanding animism, then we are missing out on the complexity of the present day's native point of view. This is true even in the most remote corners of the world. What are the implications of this for the status of anthropological knowledge versus the native point of view? The implications, I venture to argue, are substantial. Several of the chapters in this collection confront us with cases of interactions that blur the finite and fixed idea of the professional anthropologist as being someone manifestly different from the native.

Swancutt's chapter on the Nuosu discusses a native anthropologist named Tuosat, who cannot by any academic standards (even by the strict criteria endorsed by Hastrup) be denied the legitimacy of being a professional anthropologist. The same goes for Olga Ulturgasheva. An Eveny from a small remote Siberian village who was trained in anthropology at Cambridge, her research monograph details ethnographic fieldwork that she conducted in her native community (see Ulturgasheva 2012). Likewise for Kathleen Richardson, who, as an anthropologist, writes about her own native Euro-American society. On another level, Diana Espírito Santo analyzes how her interlocutors, including those spirits in the Cuban or Brazilian cosmos who set in motion their own processes of self-becoming, influence her place in fieldwork dialogues and recursive processes of anthropological theory making. Furthermore, we meet in this volume native thinkers, such as Ayima and Ahuo in Mazard's chapter, who are not and do not pretend to be anthropologists, yet they debate with high sophistication about the metaphysical commonalities and divergences between animistic and Christian cosmologies.

All of this means that the native point of view is rife with intellectual vigor— so much so that it seems meaningless to reduce it to a particular culturally situated point of view, as opposed to the anthropologist's generalized scientific view (cf. Hastrup 1993: 176). Whether or not all of these new hyper-reflexive native voices are equivalent to anthropological knowledge (although some clearly are) also seems to be a moot point. What is critical is that we need to take their metaphysics seriously and allow them not only to influence but also to rejuvenate our theories of animism.

Finally, in many of the chapters I read a meta-message that I find highly pertinent. While the majority of the authors are firmly committed to the anthropology of ontology, they all signify that this paradigm, if it is to provide a viable route for the future of anthropology, needs to take seriously (just as it takes indigenous animism seriously) the insights about globalization and reflexivity that grew out of the Writing Culture debate. If not, there is a real risk that the 'radical orthodoxy' of the anthropology of ontology will end up on the historical junkyard of failed anthropological doctrines. What makes this book unique is that it is the first serious attempt at merging the two arguably most influential theoretical paradigms of contemporary anthropology, and this, I want to stress, has important implications for how anthropology will develop in the future.

Rane Willerslev is Director of the National Museum of Denmark. He is the author of *Soul Hunters* (2007) and *On the Run in Siberia* (2012). His main field of research has been among Siberia's indigenous peoples (Yukaghirs and Chukchi), and he has recently started conducting fieldwork among the Ik of northern Uganda. While the overall bulk of his work has been within the anthropology of religion, addressing themes such as the 'new animism', his publications cover a wide spectrum of classical and more current anthropological interests, including experimental methodology, human security, and the interface between anthropology, biology, and archaeology.

References

Burr, Vivien. 2003. *Social Constructionism*. 2nd ed. New York: Routledge.

Candea, Matei. 2011. "Endo/Exo." *Common Knowledge* 17 (1): 146–150.

Clifford, James. 1986. "Introduction: Partial Truths." In *Writing Culture: The Poetics and Politics of Ethnography*, ed. James Clifford and George E. Marcus, 1–26. Berkeley: University of California Press.

Falzon, Mark-Anthony, ed. 2009. *Multi-sited Ethnography: Theory, Praxis and Locality in Contemporary Research*. Burlington: Ashgate.

Hastrup, Kirsten. 1993. "The Native Voice—and the Anthropological Vision." *Social Anthropology* 1 (2): 173–186.

Holbraad, Martin. 2007. "The Power of Powder: Multiplicity and Motion in the Divinatory Cosmology of Cuban Ifá (or *Mana*, Again)." In *Thinking Through Things: Theorising Artefacts Ethnographically*, ed. Amiria Henare, Martin Holbraad, and Sari Wastell, 189–225. London: Routledge.

Humphrey, Caroline, and James Laidlaw. 1994. *The Archetypal Actions of Ritual: A Theory of Ritual Illustrated by the Jain Rite of Worship*. Oxford: Clarendon Press.

Humphrey, Caroline, with Urgunge Onon. 1996. *Shamans and Elders: Experience, Knowledge, and Power among the Daur Mongols*. Oxford: Clarendon Press.

Ingold, Tim. 2000. *The Perception of the Environment: Essays on Livelihood, Dwelling and Skill*. London: Routledge.

Marcus, George E. 2007. "Collaborative Imaginaries." *Taiwan Journal of Anthropology* 5 (1): 1–17.

Pedersen, Morten Axel. 2011. *Not Quite Shamans: Spirit Worlds and Political Lives in Northern Mongolia*. Ithaca, NY: Cornell University Press.

Pfaffenberger, Bryan. 1992. "Social Anthropology of Technology." *Annual Review of Anthropology* 21: 491–516.

Scott, Michael W. 2007. *The Severed Snake: Matrilineages, Making Place, and a Melanesian Christianity in Southeast Solomon Islands*. Durham, NC: Carolina Academic Press.

Scott, Michael W. 2013. "What I'm Reading: The Anthropology of Ontology (Religious Science?)" *Journal of the Royal Anthropological Institute* 19 (4): 859–872.

Smith, Michael P., and Luis E. Guarnizo, eds. 1998. *Transnationalism from Below*. New Brunswick, NJ: Transaction Publishers.

Tylor, Edward B. (1871) 1920. *Primitive Culture: Researches into the Development of Mythology, Philosophy, Religion, Language, Art, and Custom*. Vols. 1 and 2. London: John Murray.

Ulturgasheva, Olga. 2012. *Narrating the Future in Siberia: Childhood, Adolescence and Autobiography among Young Eveny*. New York: Berghahn Books.

Viveiros de Castro, Eduardo. 1992. *From the Enemy's Point of View: Humanity and Divinity in an Amazonian Society*. Trans. Catherine V. Howard. Chicago: University of Chicago Press.

Viveiros de Castro, Eduardo. 2004. "Perspectival Anthropology and the Method of Controlled Equivocation." *Tipití* 2 (1): 3–22.

Viveiros de Castro, Eduardo. 2011. "Zeno and the Art of Anthropology: Of Lies, Beliefs, Paradoxes, and Other Truths." Trans. Antonia Walford. *Common Knowledge* 17 (1): 128–145.

Willerslev, Rane. 2004. "Spirits as Ready to Hand: A Phenomenological Study of Yukaghir Spiritual Knowledge and Dreaming." *Anthropological Theory* 4 (4): 395–418.

Willerslev, Rane. 2007. *Soul Hunters: Hunting, Animism, and Personhood among the Siberian Yukaghirs*. Berkeley: University of California Press.

Willerslev, Rane. 2009. "The Optimal Sacrifice: A Study of Voluntary Death among the Siberian Chukchi." *American Ethnologist* 36 (4): 693–704.

Willerslev, Rane. 2011. "Frazer Strikes Back from the Armchair: A New Search for the Animist Soul." *Journal of the Royal Anthropological Institute* (n.s.) 17 (3): 504–526.

Willerslev, Rane. 2013a. "God on Trial: Human Sacrifice, Trickery and Faith." *HAU: Journal of Ethnographic Theory* 3 (1): 140–154.

Willerslev, Rane 2013b. "Rebirth and the Death Drive: Rethinking Freud's 'Mourning and Melancholia' through a Siberian Time Perspective." In *Taming Time, Timing Death: Social Technologies and Ritual*, ed. Dorthe R. Christensen and Rane Willerslev, 79–98. London: Ashgate.

Willerslev, Rane. 2013c. "Taking Animism Seriously, but Perhaps Not Too Seriously?" *Religion and Society: Advances in Research* 4 (1): 41–57.

INTRODUCTION
Anthropological Knowledge Making, the Reflexive Feedback Loop, and Conceptualizations of the Soul

Katherine Swancutt and Mireille Mazard

In recent decades, anthropologists have been increasingly concerned with the epistemological foundations of their discipline. Moving away from the certainties of the early twentieth century, theories of culture have evolved to explain the situatedness and complexity of anthropological knowledge-making practices. Roy Wagner (1981) argued that fieldwork entails a self-transformation, wherein culture itself is revealed as an object to describe and invent. George Marcus (1986: 168) saw anthropology as "[d]ialogic interchanges between ethnographer and other," pointing out the need to "take account of the manner in which world-historical political economy constitutes their subjects." These and other accounts have disclosed the context for the production of ethnography and theory, the conditions of fieldwork, the relationships between anthropologists and research participants, and the importance of attending to the culture of anthropology itself (see Asad 1983; Bamo et al. 2007; Geertz 1973). Yet little

Notes for this section begin on page 15.

attention has been paid to an increasingly important aspect of contemporary anthropological research, that is, the impact of anthropological ideas on the cultures we study. Anthropological fieldwork is not today, and probably never was, an expedition to a faraway island entirely isolated from the rest of the globe. In field sites across the world, researchers enter into dialogue with people who have absorbed and reinterpreted ideas about their own social lives through influences such as colonialism, religious evangelism, and even contact with the researchers themselves. Without an awareness of how native conceptualizations have changed in response to anthropological theory and other abstractions, we fail to grasp fully what it means to do anthropology today.

Our point of departure is 'animism', the *locus classicus* of anthropological theory. We situate our inquiry at the crossroads of 'native' and 'non-native' scholarship on animism and the soul, exploring how indigenous thinkers have adopted what we propose to call a 'hyper-reflexive' point of view. Whereas reflexivity is a reference point for postmodern anthropology, the concept of 'hyper-reflexivity' describes the circulation of ideas through multiple sites, as the subjects of ethnographic inquiry appropriate and reinvent the abstract formulations of anthropology and other systems of thought. How would anthropological theories of the soul (and of other phenomena commonly identified as 'animistic') evolve if anthropologists were to take into account the influence that their own practice, theory, and epistemology are having on native ontologies, and vice versa? How might we envision animism through the lens of the 'anthropology of anthropology'? Each of the case studies in this book offers its own answer to these questions. Thus, we take as our starting point an anthropology that is directly implicated in the world it purports to describe.

This book benefits from being situated amid the vibrant re-emergence of animism as a field of anthropological inquiry over the past 20 years, largely under the auspices of Claude Lévi-Strauss's oeuvre. Descola (1992, 1996, 2005), Bird-David (1999), and Ingold (2006) have reclaimed animism as a complex and varied mode of engagement with the world. Terence Turner (1988, 2009), Scott (2007), Willerslev (2011), and others have suggested new theoretical frameworks for understanding cultural difference through the study of animistic groups. Viveiros de Castro's (1998, 2004, 2007) theory of perspectivism has provoked debates far beyond Amazonia (Brightman et al. 2012; Pedersen et al. 2007). Each of these studies shows that animism is very much alive and in flux today. Yet, as Pedersen and Willerslev (2012: 467–469) point out, ethnographies still often rely on received categories such as 'soul' and 'body' that are indebted to the heritage of Judeo-Christian thought, but that leave unanswered questions about what kinds of soul(s) or bodies can actually be said to animate different beings. Beyond the singular or transcendent soul, animistic ontologies offer alternative imaginings and configurations of agency and personhood and even of what it means to be human.

Throughout the case studies in this book, souls take a multiplicity of forms. The diversity of terms for souls and soul-like entities is a deliberate editorial choice on our part. In cross-cultural publications like this one, there is a temptation to draw on the same language of interpretation in order to allow a closer comparison of concepts. If our contributors all employed the same terms, such as 'soul', it would create an appearance of homogeneity, subsuming ontological difference under a single theory—animism in the singular. Our contributors, then, employ various words to translate soul concepts, such as 'soul-spider' (Swancutt), 'soul attributes' (Mazard), and 'forerunner' (Ulturgasheva). Our use of these multiple terms stems from our commitment to an open-ended dialogue with our collaborators in the field. We feel that this demonstrates the diversity of animisms across cultures—and the importance of writing 'animisms' in the plural form in anthropological theory. At its best, anthropology is open to changing its theoretical models and its ethnographic language. In this spirit of openness, native thinkers and native practices can enrich our theoretical models of animism.

Taken as a whole, this book offers multiple perspectives on what we call the 'reflexive feedback loop'. This is a mode of anthropological transmission in which professional visitors—fieldworkers, missionaries, ideologues—transmit elements of their theoretical perspectives to native thinkers. These thinkers, in turn, offer anthropologizing perspectives back to us, indirectly reflecting the diverse ethnographic influences that shape anthropologists' views. At the core of this process, culture is reinvented through a reflexive entanglement of theory and practice. It is no accident that animism can be found at the center of this Möbius-like loop. Central as it already was to some of the earliest anthropological theory, animism became an oppositional idea in evangelical religious movements and socialist activism among indigenous peoples, both of which are explored in this volume. In laying bare the dialogic nature of ethnography, we show that, at an even more radical level, animism has been reinvented by the process of anthropological fieldwork itself.

As the contributors to this book show, the reflexive feedback loop has been a major vehicle through which anthropology's Judeo-Christian heritage (Asad 1983) has filtered into indigenous cosmologies, introducing (among other things) views that the 'transcendent' soul is interior to the body. That these views are often too rigid for the ethnographic terrain they enter has been shown by the numerous studies that contravene them.

Hyper-reflexivity refers to the mutually constitutive relationship between native ontologies and the various abstract practices, concepts, or even 'traditions' that comprise them. These can include not only animistic rites, Christian liturgy, and Marxist materialism, but also ethnographic methodology, environmentalism, spiritualism, technoscience, and contemporary anthropological thought. Laura Mulvey (1975) introduced the 'male gaze' to feminist critical theory, showing the internalization of this gaze in the portrayal of female characters on screen. In some cases, hyper-reflexivity involves a kind of 'ethnographic gaze' similar to the 'male gaze', wherein native thinkers re-present their social lives as an object for the consumption of the anthropologist. They may undergo a process parallel to the anthropologist's experience of 'inventing' culture, as Wagner (1981: 4) would have it—that is, creating 'culture' as a conceptual object. But whereas the on-screen characters of Mulvey's study cannot talk back, the native thinkers discussed in this book do actually turn the ethnographic gaze back onto itself. The borrowing goes in both directions. It is not simply that anthropologists become aware of their role in the field, or that the subjects of anthropological inquiry become aware of themselves as such. Rather, the dynamics of participant observation—and the social transformations that occur in the presence of conceptual flows—can reconfigure reflexivity for anthropologists and native thinkers alike.

There is more than one way in which native ontologies and these practices, concepts, and traditions may come to be assembled. Thus, while hyper-reflexivity is a recurrent term and theme in this book, we have—as with our discussion of souls and animisms in the plural—encouraged our contributors to shape their parlance in response to their ethnographic contexts. In Vanessa Grotti and Marc Brightman's contribution, for instance, the hyper-reflexive dynamic finds its most apt expression in the term 'double reflexivity', which among native Amazonians, as they suggest, "is both internal to the self and constituted through relationships between interlocutors." Diana Espírito Santo offers the term 'deep reflexivity' to specifically denote the self-generating capacities of the cosmos in both her Cuban and Brazilian ethnography, where not just persons or spirits but the cosmos itself is capable of being reflexive. Because of the flow of practices and epistemologies, as well as the responsiveness of field sites to what is written about them, cultural relativism alone cannot account for the complex processes at work and, indeed, the reinvention of 'native' ontologies that may be happening before our very eyes.

Anthropologists may, without realizing it, not only create the context for reflexive fieldwork findings, but actively influence the outcome of events through their participation. For instance, Mireille Mazard (2011) has shown that speech practices from the Mao era continue to shape Nusu elders' autobiographical narratives of starvation and political turmoil in China, even decades after Mao's death. When interviewing elders about their life histories, she unwittingly created a context for them to revive speech forms that harkened back to political meetings of the 1960s, when autobiographies of suffering constituted valuable political capital. The elders' forms of remembrance reveal an awareness of the political implications of the spoken word, as well as its potential effects in the spirit world. Even in their sincerest outpourings of emotion, Nusu narratives are never 'raw' or uncultivated (ibid.: 167–168). As "act[s] of self-definition that [place] the subject in the framework of national history" (ibid.: 174), they must be understood through the lens of hyper-reflexivity.

Similarly, Katherine Swancutt (2012c: 43–47) found herself creating a context for hyper-reflexivity when she played the card game solitaire to relax during her research with Buryat Mongols, unaware that they considered it a form of divination. Not convinced that she was just playing a game, her Buryat fieldwork family (and thereafter, other fieldwork friends) became convinced that she possessed divinatory expertise. As they insisted that she share this expertise throughout her stay and on her return visits, she chose to study techniques from an American divining manual (ibid.: 44–45). The divinatory collaborations between Swancutt and the Buryats she knew influenced not just how the Buryats handled a range of misfortunes, but also how Swancutt ultimately understood them "from both sides of the divining table" (ibid.: 42). Revealingly, the reflexive feedback loop in Swancutt's study shaped the Buryat production of innovative magical remedies, since the Buryats solicited not only Swancutt's divinations but also her insights into their own divinations and harnessed these in their efforts to resolve misfortunes (ibid.: 85–91).

Cases like these, which are not at all uncommon in anthropology, highlight how ethnography is produced in real time in the field through hyper-reflexive anthropological (inter)actions. By observing how, in tandem with their interlocutors, anthropologists create and respond to the dynamics of the reflexive feedback loop, this book challenges portrayals of animism as a phenomenon that occurs in a time-space vacuum (Descola 2005; Harvey 2005). Instead, our contributors show that animistic cosmologies, settings, practices, concepts, and sometimes even persons shapeshift in response to highly reflexive forms of cultural invention.

Hyper-reflexivity, we argue, pervades the anthropological encounter, and examples abound outside of this publication. Bamo Ayi, Stevan Harrell, and Ma Lunzy (2007) describe in detail their decades-long collaborative fieldwork in China and the United States, which provides rich evidence for the blurring of boundaries between anthropological and native knowledge making. Meanwhile, Marjorie Balzer (2011) offers an illuminating discussion of shamans in contemporary Siberia, whose high degree of education and exposure to anthropological concepts strongly influences shamanic practices.[1]

In this book, notions of hyper-reflexivity are deployed to illuminate the complexities of the anthropological encounter. The contributors highlight how indigenous peoples in a wide variety of ethnographic locales articulate their own compass of personhood and agency through the anthropologically astute discussions they hold with us and among themselves. These dialogues explore how different forms and views on animism enter the reflexive feedback loop. Moreover, a number of the authors show that whole subfields of our discipline—notably, the anthropology of Christian discourse on the conceptualization of souls and spirit worlds—may acquire transformational, even authorial capacities, shaping autobiographical speech and dialogues with deities and spirits (Chua 2012: 512–513, 520; Keane 1997a: 675–677, 684, 690; 1997b: 58–64).

Each contributor highlights the prominent role of religious, social, or even popular culture movements in the production of hyper-reflexivity. We explore the transformational capacities of Chinese, Cuban, and Soviet communism; evangelical Christianity; spiritualism and Daoism; environmentalism; and popular fiction. The reflexive feedback loop extends itself through time, as concepts flow in multiple directions. A common feature of all the chapters in this book is their close attention to the passage of time, often involving long-term ethnography and repeat visits to the field. Some of our contributors examine the uses of history in hyper-reflexive processes, illuminating highly personal forms of history, as in Grotti and Brightman's autobiographies of Christian converts or Ulturgasheva's narratives of Eveny youths. Hyper-reflexivity, we argue, changes the conditions of anthropological inquiry.

The authors in this book take three interrelated approaches to the study of animism, which, we submit, are key to uncovering the mutually constitutive relationships between native views on the soul and anthropological reflexivity. These approaches are (1) engaging in anthropology in a way that showcases ethnographic variability; (2) cutting across conceptual boundaries to explore how 'soul theory' is interconnected with those concepts and practices that underpin personhood; and (3) revealing how agency is attributed to spirits and souls, as well as the circumstances in which they can be considered persons unto themselves.

Approach I: Showcasing Ethnographic Variability

Showcasing ethnographic variability is the classic anthropological method for uncovering new concepts and practices that are introduced into our storehouse of knowledge on ontologies or ways of being in the world (Corsín-Jiménez and Willerslev 2007: 527–529; Henare et al. 2007: 8). Whole studies have recently been devoted to expanding our understanding of specifically animistic ontologies by way of ethnographic comparison (Brightman et al. 2012; Fausto 2007) or the comparative study of perspectivism (Pedersen et al. 2007). These studies throw light on the relationship between ethnography and anthropological theory making.

Our focus on the 'anthropology of anthropology' adds a further dimension to this comparative endeavor. Namely, it entails understanding that the ethnographic variability we find in the field is, to some degree, the product of the reflexive feedback loop between native thinkers, professional anthropologists, and the numerous epistemologies that inform anthropological perspectives on the human condition. These dynamic modes of co-authorship have been, we suggest, important catalysts to the 'invention of culture' outlined some decades ago by Wagner (1981: 17–20). Through joint efforts at anthropologizing what is often referred to as 'ethnography', anthropologists and their interlocutors simultaneously create and become the conduits through which concepts, practices, traditions, and so forth move across cultures. This kind of collaboration has increased what Balzer (2011: 15–16) calls the "multiple diverse yet intersecting roles that anthropologists can potentially integrate in studying constructions of the sacred and the politics of identity."

As our varied anthropological 'roles' extend across a lifetime of work, so the reflexive feedback loop further draws in our ethnographic experience. Repeat visits to the field give rise to what Piers Vitebsky (2012: 184) calls "our joint quests and agendas and our mutual dependencies, [from which] there arises a certain mythic founding time from the beginning of our relationship." We suggest that, over time, these relationships open up new avenues for the ethnographic materials that anthropologists gather and the ways in which they—and their interlocutors—anthropologize their findings. Moreover, we propose that the reflexive feedback loop gives these joint endeavors "an unforeseen force of their own" (Vitebsky 2008: 258).

Anthropologists constantly create new pathways and vantage points for gathering their ethnographic materials. Vitebsky's (2012) return visits to the Sora of eastern India and the Eveny of Siberia are remarkable illustrations of this. His dialogues with Sora and Eveny friends have resuscitated funeral chants and provoked shamanic journeys to the underworld. More generally, these peoples have shared living memories with an anthropologist who has preserved them when no one else would (ibid.: 183–191, 195–200; see also Vitebsky 2008: 250–258). Vitebsky recalls that his dialogues with his Sora friend Monosi Raika created a new path in the latter's thinking (pers. comm., 21 May 2012). When Vitebsky originally conducted fieldwork among the Sora, his research focused on shamanship, then a vital religious practice (see Vitebsky 1993). In the years between this early work and Vitebsky's later research, many Sora, including Raika, converted to Baptist Christianity and broke off their customary relations with the dead (Vitebsky 2008, 2012). Raika came to believe that Sora *sonums* (spirits of the dead) only oppressed and demanded things from people rather than helping them. Vitebsky enjoined Raika to study Sora texts and kinship, and through this study Raika was persuaded that Sora ancestors do in fact play a productive role, giving back their soul force to their descendants. Together, Vitebsky and Raika (2011) co-authored and even privately printed copies of their Sora-language handbook of indigenous knowledge in India, with the express purpose of distributing them to local Sora (pers. comm., 28 January 2016). In cases like this, the reflexive feedback loop catalyzes the circulation of concepts, practices, and traditions—including the tradition of anthropological myth-making in a Malinowskian style, and the 'semi-conversion' of both native thinkers and anthropologists.

Edith Turner's postscript to this book speaks to the hyper-reflexive anthropology that we propose here by revealing the feedback loop that has brought a veteran fieldworker's experiences with healing practices among animistic groups into dialogue with indigenous healers in Alaska and Africa. Turner's remarkable career points to some of the possibilities that can emerge from long-term engagement with research participants as peers rather than 'informants'. Reflecting on some of the key transformations in her fieldwork relationships (some of which included her collaboration with Victor Turner) from 1954 to the present, Turner's postscript offers us a concrete case where the person of the anthropologist becomes the fulcrum of comparison as she describes to an Iñupiat healer her own experiences of African healing decades earlier. Turner calls for an anthropology that is radically open to the other's world, even to the point of subsuming the anthropologist's perspective. Not every anthropologist will pursue this path, but we encourage the reader to view Turner's postscript as a study in the 'anthropology of anthropology', which prompts us to think reflexively about how a lifetime of collaborations can merge the vocations of professional anthropologists and native thinkers.

Approach II: Cutting across Conceptual Boundaries

The hyper-reflexive approach detailed above leads to our next point: the possibility of renewing anthropological theory through the exploration of native ontologies and, by that token, challenging the tenets of our own anthropological ontologies. In step with anthropology's recent ontological turn, this book explores the transformative power of ethnographic research as process and as discourse. Each of the chapters throws new light on familiar dualisms (e.g., body/soul, nature/culture, material/spiritual) that were influential in the development of the anthropology of religion in general and of animism in particular. In some cases, these dualisms are demonstrated ethnographically, while in others they are not. Our concern is not to argue that anthropologists should adopt a dualistic, non-dualistic, or poly-ontological approach per se, a theme that is always ethnographically contingent and debated in much detail elsewhere (Venkatesan et al. 2013; see also Scott 2013). We wish to suggest instead that anthropology requires a more thorough engagement with the co-authorship that we embark on when 'doing ethnography' through fieldwork or 'doing anthropology' in any context. Ideally, this co-authorship would be formulated through anthropological efforts at engaging with the world as the locals do, using the approach Michael Scott refers to as 'methodological non-dualism', which critically pivots around locals' conceptualizations and practices, whether they be dualist, non-dualist, or pluralist (see Venkatesan et al. 2013: 303–308).

Our contributors' ethnographic case studies underline the importance of attending to the context for ethnographic translations of native conceptualizations and practices. As suggested by the early literature on animism (Frazer 1957; Tylor [1871] 1920), the 'soul' or 'spirit' has sometimes been taken for granted as a subject of ethnographic inquiry among animistic peoples. Yet many ethnographic regions do not offer evidence for a stable, monadic human soul of purely spiritual constitution. This mythical creature is rarely evident in ethnographic or anthropological works. Instead, each of our contributors shows that a person's 'soul aspects'—which may take the form of trickster-like spirit entities, doppelgängers, traveling spirits, and so on—reveal the contingency of our familiar conceptual categories. Lacking stability, these souls and soul-like entities may emerge as latent aspects of the self that appear only in the act of projecting oneself into the future (as in Ulturgasheva's Eveny ethnography) or in moments of affective crisis (as in Mazard's chapter on the Nusu). Neither transcendental nor beholden to the body, they may possess material qualities while eluding the laws of physics. We find several examples of terms for soul entities that employ word roots meaning 'body' or 'person', rather than word roots meaning 'spirit', as with certain Nusu terms for spectral doppelgängers (e.g., *yisu*, envy personified, literally ending in the word 'person'). Their appetites, too, may be bodily in kind. The soul-spiders of Swancutt's (2012a, 2012b, 2012d) Nuosu ethnography are sometimes visible, sometimes invisible fragments of the self that, when lost, may be lured back by tasty morsels of meat and other comforts of the home, or whose loss may doom a person to weaken and die. We look at animism beyond the soul to imagine multiple possibilities for exploring the spiritual or invisible dimensions of personhood, their transformative elements, and their ethnographic situatedness.

'Personhood' and 'dividuality' are therefore useful concepts for this book, since the ethnographies of several contributors do not evidence a one-to-one relationship between the person and his or her soul(s). Soul attributes bear different degrees of their owners' personhood within them and may, at times, act as persons in their own right. In the contributions by Espírito Santo, Ulturgasheva, and Mazard, we find soul aspects acting as fragmentary selves that nonetheless retain the complete agency to make life choices, especially in cases where they share the affective (or emotional) states of their owners. One of the key problems raised by animism is the phenomenon of incomplete versus complete personhood and/or agency, which, we suggest, can be fully addressed only by analyzing the dynamic co-authorship of native epistemologies on the soul(s) and professional anthropological fieldwork, discourse, and theory making on animism.

Another commonality between the contributions to this book is their emphasis on the multiplicity and mutability of souls and hence of selves. The ability to transform one's soul aspect may be regarded as a particularity of shamans and other powerful beings. Yet, as Mazard shows among the Nusu and as other chapters demonstrate, metamorphosis or transformation is often at the core of animistic personhood. In Espírito Santo's ethnography, the tricksterish *muertos* of Cuban spiritism shift in shape and purpose to accompany changes in the lives of their owners (and the life of the anthropologist as well), while in Ulturgasheva's chapter, we find Eveny forerunners 'doubling' their owners and thereby duplicating their futures within the present or the past.

Metamorphosis is underpinned by specific conceptualizations and techniques of the body and soul that may enable us to redefine the boundaries of animism as theory and as practice. Kathleen Richardson's study of robotics in this book shows the power of 'technological animism' even in the absence of souls and soul theory, whereby robots are endowed with human-like qualities and treated as persons, evoking Freud's sense of 'the uncanny' when they become too imperfectly human. As Richardson shows, experts in the field of technoscience who strive to animate their robots at prominent laboratories—like those at the Massachusetts Institute of Technology (MIT)—raise questions that are directly salient to philosophers and anthropologists: what is the significance of the body to the soul, the soul to the person, or the person to the body?

Beyond this, there is the question of how technological animism, or any kind of animism for that matter, hinges upon the transformation of concepts (such as 'the uncanny') that travel between various animistic settings and intellectual traditions. Alberto Corsín-Jiménez and Rane Willerslev (2007: 527–528) offer illuminating insights into how anthropologists—and especially those working on animism—can reflexively identify anthropological "concepts that can cross boundaries, that can move and change shapes between and across contexts." They propose that indigenous concepts, such as souls or shadows, are mutable and undergo metamorphosis. When traversing what they call the "hidden side" of the visible world (ibid.: 528), the person evinces shapeshifting and unpredictable yet unique-in-the-moment qualities that emerge in what we call their 'soul aspect'. Aparecida Vilaça's (2005) description of 'chronically unstable bodies' in Amazonia articulates the same transformative qualities. But more crucially, as regards the subject matter of this book, Corsín-Jiménez and Willerslev reveal that the chronic instability observed for the soul/body also permeates the anthropological/native concepts exchanged through dialogues during fieldwork. Consider these provocative questions posed by Corsín-Jiménez and

Willerslev (2007: 528): "What would our [anthropological] concepts look like if they were to (say) move or transform like spirits? And what use would this concept-spirit, or concept-transformation, have for anthropological theory at large?" To answer these questions, we must consider how the reflexive feedback loop informs our views on animism.

Approach III: Attributing Agency to Spirits and Souls

We have arrived at the crux of this publication's contribution to anthropology and the study of animism. The contributors to this book have taken up the idea that anthropological concepts move and transform like spirits, thus bearing within them the capacity to transform our disciplinary thought. Moreover, the emphasis that they place on the instability of souls and soul-like entities suggests that these may acquire agency or even 'become' persons unto themselves, during the very moments in which we—often in collaboration with fieldwork friends—anthropologize them.

Fieldwork, as we have suggested above, brings into dialogue professional anthropologists, native thinkers, and anthropological concepts influenced by a wealth of earlier ethnographies. Anthropologists share their know-how with their interlocutors during fieldwork and, increasingly often these days, through their published works, which native thinkers may harness in the service of reshaping and transforming anthropologists' views—and even their publications. Our fieldwork visits thus often prompt native thinkers to speak reflexively to us, covering topics such as how culture is produced. For instance, Terence Turner (1991: 310) has commented that his role as an anthropologist shifted from documenting Kayapo culture to becoming a "cultural instrument" of the Kayapo people in their political struggles. Over the course of his many years of engagement with the Kayapo, he observed their adoption of the Portuguese term *cultura* to externalize the idea of 'culture'. The Kayapo reflexively reappropriated an abstract conceptualization of their way of life, in part, through collaboration with Turner, an anthropologist.

Faced with this 'native reflexivity', the anthropologist may grasp the opportunity of entering into what Vitebsky terms 'joint quests' that lead to an 'unforeseen force'. But what would this unforeseen force be? None other than the opportunity for native thinkers' ontologies—already exposed to anthropology and its foundations in numerous ethnographies and epistemologies—to re-enter our minds, selves, notebooks, published findings, and professional perspectives on the human condition. When looking honestly into the 'hall of mirrors' that comprises the reflexive feedback loop, then, we come to see how anthropological perspectives are continually reshaped and refracted through accretions of various epistemologies. We also find that the reflexive feedback loop has its 'hidden side', in Corsín-Jiménez and Willerslev's sense of the term, since it enables the reshaping of native epistemologies through time. As native thinkers hold dialogues with us, they may take on certain anthropological perspectives, frequently of their own initiative and choice. These anthropological perspectives may transform or destabilize their soul aspects, as shown by several chapters in this book. Of course, this raises the paradox that 'native' epistemologies may be presented to us as 'authentic' or 'timeless' aspects of a reified culture when in fact they are the products of mimesis and cultural invention, as our contributors show. We propose that when whole epistemologies (and not just the native conceptualizations contained within them) take on lives of their own, they should—like spirits—be granted the status of 'subjects', ontologically speaking.

Two important points arise from this discussion. First, if we accept that, in our hyper-reflexive world, native epistemologies have already entered our catch-all of anthropological concepts—traveling with us to numerous places and inspiring fieldwork dialogues and publications—then we should consider how these same epistemologies bear within them the agency to influence an enormous range of native thinkers on an ontological level. Second—and this is a related point—when native epistemologies take on lives of their own, they become capable of delivering what Scott (2012: 120) calls "an openended cycle of tales," which, like "cargoistic discourses as powerful elements in the semiotic process of ethnogenesis," reveal as much about native thinking as they do about anthropology. What native thinkers tell us, and what comes to be considered as our 'fieldwork findings', is largely produced as a cycle of tales within the reflexive feedback loop. Even classic anthropological concepts, like the soul, shapeshift over time in response to this hidden side of reflexivity, much as notions of the soul have changed, we suggest, in response to missionary contact. And in anthropology, the feedback loop is two-directional, since anthropologists are often as eagerly indoctrinated as any native thinker might be. The reflexive feedback loop thus puts a new spin on the making of anthropological practice and concepts, not to mention the new spin it puts on the soul(s) and the body (or bodies), the ontological turn, animism, perspectivism, and so on.

In a nutshell, our point is this: anthropological concepts and native epistemologies are jointly redefining the ontological make-up of what we call 'animism' or 'the soul'. The soul is highly unstable and mutually created by the many contexts through which it emerges, as Corsín-Jiménez and Willerslev (2007) suggest. These multiple contexts are composed of both the visible and hidden sides of people, places, practices, concepts, traditions, fieldwork, publications, and relationships.

The Chapters

The complexity and multiplicity of soul beliefs is at the heart of Mazard's chapter on the Nusu 'algebra of souls'. Mazard proposes the idea of algebra to encapsulate the way that the Nusu think of personhood through soul attributes in terms of "fractions (fragmentary selves), doubles, and latent possibilities." To the Nusu, the number and state of a person's soul attributes is not fixed but shifts in response to unforeseen events, shocks such as death or major illness, and vivid emotional states. Today, as more and more Nusu are converting to Protestant Christianity, Nusu assumptions concerning ontology and personhood are in conflict with Christian doctrine, which proposes the concept of a single, stable, transcendent soul. In death rituals, this conflict comes to a head in practices surrounding the soul aspects of the deceased. Mazard draws on Scott's (2007) notion of 'poly-ontology' to show that different types of beings, and even aspects of the self, may occupy different ontological realms in Nusu cosmology. An example is funerals, where fire and other agents of metamorphosis ensure the transfer of deceased souls from the realm of the living to the 'shadow realm', or *mhade*. There is a hyper-reflexivity inherent in the Nusu engagement with Christianity as its practitioners are intensely aware of the doctrinal ramifications of certain ritual actions. Adding further dimensions of hyper-reflexivity, Nusu animism is being reinvented through interactions with ethnologists, creating a reflexive feedback loop between those practicing animism and those researching and documenting their ritual practices.

Espírito Santo examines the gods and ghosts of spiritualist cults in Cuba and Brazil. Inspired by Don Handelman's (2004) work on 'ritual in its own right', she argues that the trickster-like spirit beings of her study represent 'self-organizing' aspects of the cosmos. In both the Cuban and Brazilian cults, "people perceive spirits to be aware of themselves," suggesting the possibility that the "metamorphic cosmos" might have "wielded its modes of 'deep reflexivity' since its inception." Espírito Santo's descriptions of spirit mediumship and interactions with ritual specialists show how spirits can acquire agency as independent beings, fragmentary selves, or even latent aspects of their human owners. An Espiritismo practitioner's spirits embody aspects of his or her personhood, reflect upon it, even structure it, and may also provoke or invite transformations of the practitioner's self. Here is another manifestation of the reflexive feedback loop occurring in the interactions between religious practitioners and their spirit companions, as "spirits and persons enfold each other in the production of their respective selves or personhoods." Espiritismo and Umbanda present us with an animate cosmos that exceeds human agency or the human capacity for self-determination; here the animate is multiple, always in the process of unfolding, revealing new directions, connections, and refractions of sociality and the self.

Ulturgasheva's contribution explores the unforeseen force of collaborations between native thinkers and anthropologists. Her ethnography of the Eveny in a Siberian village spans six years, providing a diachronic perspective on the Eveny *djuluchen*, a 'traveling spirit' or 'forerunner'. During her initial research, Ulturgasheva asked Eveny adolescents to imagine what their future lives would look like. On her return six years later, she found to her surprise that their predictions had been entirely fulfilled by virtue of their *djuluchen*, which project personhood forward in time. The *djuluchen* is a latent aspect of the self, appearing when one formulates a wish or vision of the future. Not only humans but also certain wolves and reindeer have the ability to put forth forerunners. Drawing on Deleuze's concept of 'actualization in progress', Ulturgasheva argues that the *djuluchen* initiates a "kinetic distribution" of the Eveny person, who remains stretched between present and future geographies and chronologies, until he or she "catches up with this forward-traveling spirit." For the Eveny, personhood is dynamic, a "process of unfolding, splitting, doubling, and departing." As it turns out, Ulturgasheva's request for adolescents to discuss their future lives had the unforeseen effect of encouraging them to project their *djuluchen* toward their life dreams, creating a reflexive feedback loop in the flow of agency and ideas. Her findings illustrate the importance of attending to the collaborative nature of the encounter between anthropologists and their research participants.

Swancutt's chapter on the Nuosu 'art of capture' brings into dialogue a native anthropologist, an ethno-historian, and a village-based native thinker in Southwest China, each of whom wields mischievously reflexive ideas about animism. Swancutt shows that Nuosu use hidden jokes to comment reflexively on both animistic ideas and the very concept of animism. Recently, the Chinese environmentalist movement has reclaimed what the Nuosu anthropologist in Swancutt's chapter terms the 'ideology of animism'. This ideology reframes Nuosu people as guardians of the landscape, while employing rhetoric about the soul—anthropological in tone—to encourage tree-planting activities. In this vein, the Chinese government has made funds available to support 'animistic' tree-planting campaigns in Nuosu villages. Swancutt's ethnography explores the Nuosu engagement with this and other reinventions of their animistic ideas, hinging on the art of capture. This 'art' is a distinctively Nuosu means of engaging with others, which ranges from the capture of slaves in combat to the capture of souls in ritual. As Swancutt reveals, Nuosu thinkers—such as the three who feature prominently in her case studies—are reinventing the art of capture for a new political era, deploying their reflexive intellectual engagement with animism to lure in new resources (Chinese development funds) and new collaborators (foreign anthropologists). By means of the reflexive feedback loop, these Nuosu thinkers draw on the characterizations of their beliefs in anthropology and government discourse to re-present animism back to their interlocutors.

Grotti and Brightman examine the self-constitution of Christian subjects in their ethnography of autobiographical accounts among the Trio of Suriname and other Amazonian groups. The genre of 'missionary autobiography' operates a *mise en scène* of a person's engagement with animistic spirits, his or her rejection of those spirits, and the renewal of his or her identity through Christianity. Through these narratives, Trio Christians reflexively enter into dialogue with the tropes of religious conversion. As Grotti and Brightman explain, native Amazonian storytelling enables master interlocutors, such as talented shamans, to display "a form of 'double reflexivity'." This double reflexivity is internal and self-affirming, yet constituted through relationships with anthropologists, missionaries, and others. The narration of autobiography causes the person not only to traverse different bodies or souls, but also to momentarily experience being a 'master' of spirits "without completely losing his original social perspective." Consequently, master storytellers present anthropologists with life histories that often transcend the ordinary bounds of self-other relations. Trio storytelling thus transforms concepts, persons, the mastery of skill, and even the ontological status of alterity.

Richardson's study of technological animism takes the concept of animism out of its traditional, small-scale religious setting and reconfigures it in the realm of scientific research. Her chapter examines the ways that scientists, members of the public, and works of popular fiction "attribute human-like qualities to non-humans." Working with Japanese and American scientists at MIT, Richardson shows that roboticists are heavily influenced by fictional representations of human-like machines, such as Japan's Astro Boy. Thus, in a reflexive feedback loop, there is a direct mutual influence between science fiction and new technological developments. This influence takes the form of creative inspiration and animistic danger, since automata have the potential to destabilize "the boundaries between human and machine, living and dead, animate and inanimate." From this destabilization emerges a phenomenon that Japanese roboticist Masahiro Mori, drawing on Freud, called the 'uncanny valley'. Roboticists are intensely aware of the alluring yet frightening potential for their creations to develop human-like qualities. Like certain other non-human persons found in the ethnographies of this book, it is the partial, liminal personhood of robots that makes them frightening, even terrifying at times. The reflexive relationship of technology to fiction, and of philosophy to technology, provides a fertile environment for rethinking animism, personhood, and agency.

Conclusion

At the start of this introduction, we asked how we might envision animism through the lens of the 'anthropology of anthropology'. This book gives a timely answer to that question. Each of the contributors offers compelling case studies that demonstrate how animistic practices, concepts, traditions, ontologies, and so forth are co-authored—and even co-anthropologized—in highly reflexive ways by anthropologists and their interlocutors. These chapters show that native epistemologies, which inform anthropological notions and travel with us during fieldwork, underpin our dialogues with interlocutors. Beyond this, they suggest ways in which native thinkers might be influenced by anthropological concepts and, equally, how they might subtly or dramatically transform those same concepts before 'returning' them to us. This hidden side of the reflexive feedback loop is what animates our quest for a sustained engagement with hyper-reflexivity in anthropology. It is through this unique initiative that we wish to mobilize an open-ended discussion within the 'anthropology of anthropology' for some time to come.

Acknowledgments

The idea for this book arose from conversations on animism, anthropology, and hyper-reflexivity in China between the editors since late 2010. In the spirit of cross-cultural comparison, we decided to extend this conversation, inviting our team of contributors to showcase the unique relationship between animism and hyper-reflexivity in their ethnographies. We would like to thank Knut Rio, our contributors, and the anonymous reviewers for their generous and stimulating suggestions.

Katherine Swancutt is a Senior Lecturer in the Anthropology of Religion in the Department of Theology and Religious Studies, King's College London. She is the author of *Fortune and the Cursed: The Sliding Scale of Time in Mongolian Divination* (2012). Her main area of interest is Inner Asia, and she has conducted fieldwork among Buryat Mongols, Deed Mongols, and, more recently, the Nuosu of Southwest China. A major theme running through her work has been the rise of innovative religious practices, especially among animistic or shamanic groups. Currently, she is taking her work in several related directions that reveal the links between imagination and ethno-theology in China, from the study of fame and the production of ethnographic dreams to the internationalization of indigenous peoples through native and foreign scholarship.

Mireille Mazard is an independent researcher who recently completed a post-doctoral fellowship at the Max Planck Institute for Religious and Ethnic Diversity. Her areas of interest are ethno-politics and identity among the Nusu of Southwest China. She is currently writing a monograph about Nusu religious and political transformations, which explores their engagement with Christian and Communist ideologies in creating new ontological frameworks for experiencing the world.

Notes

1. It is beyond the scope of this publication to discuss the connections between hyper-reflexivity and native anthropology in detail. However, we hope that this challenge will be taken up in further scholarship.

References

Asad, Talal. 1983. "Anthropological Conceptions of Religion: Reflections on Geertz." *Man* (n.s.) 18 (2): 237–259.

Balzer, Marjorie M. 2011. *Shamans, Spirituality, and Cultural Revitalization: Explorations in Siberia and Beyond.* New York: Palgrave Macmillan.

Bamo Ayi, Stevan Harrell, and Ma Lunzy, eds. 2007. *Fieldwork Connections: The Fabric of Ethnographic Collaboration in China and America.* Seattle: University of Washington Press.

Bird-David, Nurit. 1999. "'Animism' Revisited: Personhood, Environment, and Relational Epistemology." *Current Anthropology* 40 (S1): S67–S91.

Brightman, Marc, Vanessa E. Grotti, and Olga Ulturgasheva, ed. 2012. *Animism in Rainforest and Tundra: Personhood, Animals, Plants and Things in Contemporary Amazonia and Siberia.* New York: Berghahn Books.

Chua, Liana. 2012. "Conversion, Continuity, and Moral Dilemmas among Christian Bidayuhs in Malaysian Borneo." *American Ethnologist* 39 (3): 511–526.

Corsín-Jiménez, Alberto, and Rane Willerslev. 2007. "'An Anthropological Concept of the Concept': Reversibility among the Siberian Yukaghirs." *Journal of the Royal Anthropological Institute* 13 (3): 527–544.

Descola, Philippe. 1992. "Societies of Nature and the Nature of Society." In *Conceptualizing Society*, ed. Adam Kuper, 107–126. London: Routledge.

Descola, Philippe. 1996. "Constructing Natures: Symbolic Ecology and Social Practice." In *Nature and Society: Anthropological Perspectives*, ed. Philippe Descola and Gisli Pálsson, 82–102. London: Routledge.

Descola, Philippe. 2005. *Par-delà nature et culture*. Paris: Gallimard.

Fausto, Carlos. 2007. "Feasting on People: Eating Animals and Humans in Amazonia." *Current Anthropology* 48 (4): 497–530.

Frazer, James G. 1957. *The Golden Bough: A Study in Magic and Religion*. Abridged ed., vols. 1 and 2. London: St. Martin's Press.

Geertz, Clifford. 1973. "Thick Description: Toward an Interpretive Theory of Culture." In *The Interpretation of Cultures: Selected Essays*, 3–30. New York: Basic Books.

Handelman, Don. 2004. "Introduction: Why Ritual in Its Own Right? How So?" *Social Analysis* 48 (2): 1–32.

Harvey, Graham. 2005. *Animism: Respecting the Living World*. London: C. Hurst.

Henare, Amiria, Martin Holbraad, and Sari Wastell, eds. 2007. "Introduction: Thinking through Things." In *Thinking through Things: Theorising Artefacts Ethnographically*, 1–31. London: Routledge.

Ingold, Tim. 2006. "Rethinking the Animate, Re-animating Thought." *Ethnos* 71 (1): 9–20.

Keane, Webb. 1997a. "From Fetishism to Sincerity: On Agency, the Speaking Subject, and Their Historicity in the Context of Religious Conversion." *Comparative Studies in Society and History* 39 (4): 674–693.

Keane, Webb. 1997b. "Religious Language." *Annual Review of Anthropology* 26: 47–71.

Marcus, George E. 1986. "Contemporary Problems of Ethnography in the Modern World System." In *Writing Culture: The Poetics and Politics of Ethnography*, ed. James Clifford and George E. Marcus, 165–193. Berkeley: University of California Press.

Mazard, Mireille. 2011. "Powerful Speech: Remembering the Long Cultural Revolution in Yunnan." *Inner Asia* 13: 157–178.

Mulvey, Laura. 1975. "Visual Pleasure and Narrative Cinema." *Screen* 16 (3): 6–18.

Pedersen, Morten Axel, Rebecca Empson, and Caroline Humphrey. 2007. "Editorial Introduction: Inner Asian Perspectivisms." *Inner Asia* 9 (2): 141–152. Special issue titled "Perspectivism."

Pedersen, Morten Axel, and Rane Willerslev. 2012. "'The Soul of the Soul Is the Body': Rethinking the Concept of Soul through North Asian Ethnography." *Common Knowledge* 18 (3): 464–486.

Scott, Michael W. 2007. *The Severed Snake: Matrilineages, Making Place, and a Melanesian Christianity in Southeast Solomon Islands*. Durham, NC: Carolina Academic Press.

Scott, Michael W. 2012. "The Matter of Makira: Colonialism, Competition, and the Production of Gendered Peoples in Contemporary Solomon Islands and Medieval Britain." *History and Anthropology* 23 (1): 115–148.

Scott, Michael W. 2013. "The Anthropology of Ontology (Religious Science?)." *Journal of the Royal Anthropological Institute* 19 (4): 859–872.

Swancutt, Katherine. 2012a. "The Captive Guest: Spider Webs of Hospitality among the Nuosu of Southwest China." *Journal of the Royal Anthropological Institute* 18 (S1): S103–S116.

Swancutt, Katherine. 2012b. "Fame, Fate-Fortune, and Tokens of Value among the Nuosu of Southwest China." *Social Analysis* 56 (2): 56–72.

Swancutt, Katherine. 2012c. *Fortune and the Cursed: The Sliding Scale of Time in Mongolian Divination*. New York: Berghahn Books.

Swancutt, Katherine. 2012d. "Masked Predation, Hierarchy and the Scaling of Extractive Relations in Inner Asia and Beyond." In Brightman et al. 2012, 175–194.

Turner, Terence. 1988. "Ethno-Ethnohistory: Myth and History in Native South American Representations of Contact with Western Society." In *Rethinking History and Myth: Indigenous South American Perspectives on the Past*, ed. Jonathan D. Hill, 235–281. Chicago: University of Illinois Press.

Turner, Terence. 1991. "Representing, Resisting, Rethinking: Historical Transformations of Kayapo Culture and Anthropological Consciousness." In *Colonial Situations: Essays on the Contextualization of Ethnographic Knowledge*, ed. George W. Stocking, Jr., 285–313. Madison: University of Wisconsin Press.

Turner, Terence. 2009. "The Crisis of Late Structuralism. Perspectivism and Animism: Rethinking Culture, Nature, Spirit, and Bodiliness." *Tipití* 7 (1): 3–42.

Tylor, Edward B. (1871) 1920. *Primitive Culture: Researches into the Development of Mythology, Philosophy, Religion, Language, Art and Custom*. Vols. 1 and 2. London: John Murray.

Venkatesan, Soumhya, Keir Martin, Michael W. Scott, Christopher Pinney, Nikolai Ssorin-Chaikov, Joanna Cook, and Marilyn Strathern. 2013. "The Group for Debates in Anthropological Theory (GDAT), the University of Manchester." *Critique of Anthropology* 33 (3): 300–360.

Vilaça, Aparecida. 2005. "Chronically Unstable Bodies: Reflections on Amazonian Corporalities." *Journal of the Royal Anthropological Institute* 11 (3): 445–464.

Vitebsky, Piers. 1993. *Dialogues with the Dead: The Discussion of Mortality Among the Sora of Eastern India*. Cambridge: Cambridge University Press.

Vitebsky, Piers. 2008. "Loving and Forgetting: Moments of Inarticulacy in Tribal India." *Journal of the Royal Anthropological Institute* 14 (2): 243–261.

Vitebsky, Piers. 2012. "Repeated Returns and Special Friends: From Mythic Encounter to Shared History." In *Returns to the Field*, ed. Signe Howell and Aud Talle, 180–202. Bloomington: Indiana University Press.

Vitebsky, Piers, and Monosi Raika. 2011. *Jujunji do Yuyunji a Banuddin: Sora Jattin a Sanskruti. Sora Beran Batte, Aboi Tanub* [Indigenous Knowledge: A Handbook of Sora Culture. In Sora, Part I]. Visakhapatnam: Privately printed.

Viveiros de Castro, Eduardo. 1998. "Cosmological Deixis and Amerindian Perspectivism." *Journal of the Royal Anthropological Institute* 4 (3): 469–488.

Viveiros de Castro, Eduardo. 2004. "Exchanging Perspectives: The Transformation of Objects into Subjects in Amerindian Ontologies." *Common Knowledge* 10 (3): 463–484.

Viveiros de Castro, Eduardo. 2007. "The Crystal Forest: Notes on the Ontology of Amazonian Spirits." *Inner Asia* 9 (2): 153–172.

Wagner, Roy. 1981. *The Invention of Culture*. Rev. and expand. ed. Chicago: University of Chicago Press.

Willerslev, Rane. 2011. "Frazer Strikes Back from the Armchair: A New Search for the Animist Soul." *Journal of the Royal Anthropological Institute* 17 (3): 504–526.

Chapter 1

THE ALGEBRA OF SOULS
Ontological Multiplicity and the Transformation of Animism in Southwest China

Mireille Mazard

In a large, almost empty conference room inside the rundown Liuku Hotel, Lañi, an elderly Nusu man, slowly climbs steps up to the theatrical stage at the front of the room.[1] He is wearing a handmade woven jacket with narrow blue-and-white stripes, a self-consciously 'ethnic' garment (Ch. *minzu fuzhuang*). A machete hangs at his waist. Lañi seizes the machete, still in its holster, and strikes it nine times on the stage floor. He is miming the way a Nusu shaman would open the ground of the burial plot to open the path for the deceased into the 'shadow realm', or *mhade*.[2]

In the ritual unfolding of a Nusu funeral, the *yān-hla* (soul or doppelgänger) emerges from latency into full personhood, supplanting the corporeal existence of the deceased. Through transformations enacted in death and fire, the deceased and his or her belongings become ontologically other. This process of metamorphosis entails a geographical movement as well, as they set off for the land of the dead (*mhade*). Lañi, onstage, is demonstrating the beginning of this journey for a group of researchers who traveled from Kunming, the capital city of Yunnan in Southwest China, to the province's remote northwestern frontier to study endangered traditions of ethnic minority music and dance. In his home village of Khrada, however, Lañi ceased his ritual activities decades ago when he converted to Christianity.

The cleavage between the living and the dead, mapped out in separate geographies and enacted in the ritualized transformation of the person, reflects the poly-ontological character of Nusu animism, which I explore in this chapter. For Lañi and other Nusu participants in the research encounter, it is echoed in a further ontological divide, between themselves and the researchers documenting their cultural artifacts. More than a matter of linguistic or social differences, for Nusu, different ethnicities, like different states of being, are essentially and irreducibly different, but interactions can occur across ontological divides. The key to this is metamorphosis.

Metamorphosis and Animism

This chapter takes metamorphosis as a starting point to explore poly-ontological animism among the Nusu in Southwest China. The transformation of persons and ideas enables productive exchanges across boundaries in a fundamentally plural socio-cosmic order. In looking at animism, my focus is on how Nusu understand the invisible dimensions of personhood. Dualistic paradigms—viewing the body as 'clothing' for the soul, for instance (Viveiros de Castro 1998: 471)—are inadequate to describe Nusu ways of thinking about the self, whose 'soul attributes' possess corporeal as well as spiritual qualities.

The anthropology of animism has long enjoyed a mutual rapport with Euro-American philosophy. Exchanges between these disciplines have infused new energy and ideas into theoretical models on both sides. Consider Deleuze and Guattari's (1980) exploration of non-dualism, for instance, or Viveiros de Castro's (1998) description of Amazonian perspectivism. Yet in the heady meeting of anthropological and philosophical minds, there is a risk of making flesh-and-soul animists into pure thought exercises (Starn 2011: 193). Michael Scott argues that our theoretical models require careful calibration as they "are not context-free universal decoders" (see Venkatesan et al. 2013: 306). By situating Nusu animism in the ethnographic encounter, I hope to depict the subtlety of their soul theories, showing that animists engage in philosophical explorations that reflect back on anthropological beliefs.

The ethnonym 'Nusu' refers to roughly 8,000 people who speak a Tibeto-Burman language and live primarily in Nujiang, a steep mountainous prefecture bordering Myanmar in the west and the Tibetan Autonomous Region in the north. Due to its geographical proximity to these two politically sensitive regions, Nujiang was militarized and subject to intense ideological scrutiny from the Chinese Communist Party during the Mao era. I conducted 12 months of fieldwork in Nujiang in 2006 and 2008 and additional fieldwork among Nusu living in Kunming during the same period. I spent most of my time in the villages of Khrada and Uvri, which cling to the sides of the Nu mountain range. This location is regarded as a remote and exotic frontier, attracting visitors in search of untouched natural wonderland, but in fact it saw radical transformations during and after the Mao era. The tree line has shifted, new roads crisscross the river gorge, and a massive, controversial dam project is underway (Litzinger 2007). The greatest shift is perhaps in the area's ideological points of reference.

Historically, Nusu ritual life centered on shamanic practitioners called *yüigu* or *yüigusu*, meaning 'a person who makes sacrifices to the *yüi*', the miscellaneous term for spectral beings such as spirits of the forest and human ghosts (see He Shutao 2000: 845–847). In their rituals, shamans divined the spectral causes of illnesses and offered animals as sacrifices across ontological boundaries. From the 1940s to the mid-1950s, Nusu came into contact with evangelists from the neighboring Lisu ethnic group and began converting to Christianity in large numbers (Mazard 2014). This coincided with the beginnings of Chinese ethnographic research in Yunnan, which defined animism in terms of *yuanshi zongjiao* (primitive religion) (Yunnansheng Bianji Weiyuanhu 1981: 113). People in Southwest China came to understand their ritual practices as 'backward' (*luohou*) and insufficient (see Swancutt, this volume). From 1958 onward, episodes of political turmoil interfered with shamanic and Christian practices, as well as with ethnological projects. The intense politicization of discourse during the Mao era—and the violence surrounding it—made Nusu people intensely aware of the ideological implications of discourse and ritual life (Mazard 2011).

This brings us to the concept of hyper-reflexivity developed in this book, which is essential to understanding the transfers of people, objects, and ideas between 'natives' and 'anthropologists', to employ a well-worn dualism. Reflexivity has infiltrated animism and anthropology alike as Nusu thinkers engage with outsiders whom they consider ontologically other. The encounter between animism and two powerful ideologies in Southwest China, that is, socialism and Christianity, has opened up unstable philosophical ground for Nusu people, who are now questioning and redefining their beliefs. Metamorphosis—in this case, the metamorphosis of animism itself—allows exchanges to occur across ontological boundaries, and anthropology is implicated in the transformation.

The 'Algebra of Souls'

Nusu assume that their social interactions take place in a context of plurality, in which ordinary people experience only one facet of a poly-ontological social order. I draw the idea of poly-ontology from Michael Scott's (2007) work on the Arosi of the Solomon Islands. Scott deploys this concept to resolve the contradictions between Marilyn Strathern's (1988) relational, anti-essentialist model of Melanesian sociality and the forms of essentialism that Scott (2007) discerns among the Arosi. Arosi differences are grounded in a "cosmos in which the parts precede the whole" (ibid.: 10), and their cosmogenesis stories point to an "original plurality" (ibid.). Moving on from the anecdote above about a staged ritual in the Liuku Hotel, I argue that Lañi and other Nusu participants view their transactions with the researchers through the lens of poly-ontology, as participants in two separate realms that can communicate only through a carefully managed transformation of words and ideas.

For Nusu, multiple forms of being comprise the inhabitants of multiple, communicating ontological realms. These include multiple 'types' that a mono-ontological outsider, such as a non-Nusu anthropologist, might identify as ethnicities, souls, soul attributes, 'gods' or 'ghosts', each associated with its own geographies and capacities. This conceptual framework has implications for our theory of personhood. Rather than being a monadic individual, or even a relational dividual (Strathern 1988), a person can, under certain conditions, evince different aspects of the self, with multiple ontological identities. Seen from another perspective, ontologically different persons can converge into one identity.

I employ the term 'algebra of souls' to describe the Nusu understanding of personhood because it suggests the complexity and transformability of this poly-ontological order and of other forms of animism as well. In mathematics, algebra offers a language for resolving the co-existence of known and unknown elements. An algebraic equation, static on the page, illustrates the movement and transformation of terms. Nusu personhood is reckoned complexly, as in algebra. Some of its attributes remain unknown or possibly in flux, while ontological shifts may bring unresolved elements to the fore. Nusu think of soul attributes in terms of fractions (fragmentary selves), doubles, and latent possibilities. Unforeseen events, shocks such as death or major illness, and vivid emotional states can unbalance the equation of self and shift the number and state of one's soul attributes. In algebra, equivalent values may take different forms on two sides of an equation, and something similar is at work in Nusu ways of understanding persons, whose multiple attributes, some of them spectral, may co-exist on two sides of an ontological divide. To illustrate this, let us first examine the work of Nusu funerals.

Crossing Ontological Divides

Nusu mortuary rituals involve the management of people and objects transitioning from the realm of the living into the afterlife. For non-Christians, this afterlife is *mhade*, the shadow realm, where the dead go about their business much as they did when alive, pursuing the same occupations and daily chores. In *mhade*, as in the realm of the living, people cultivate crops to feed themselves. The dead, like the living, can be wealthy or poor. Items belonging to the dead are sent to *mhade* to ensure their comfort and to prevent the *yān-hla* (soul or doppelgänger) from being drawn back to the family home to use favored items, unable to see the difference between the living world and the shadow realm, unaware that he or she is dead.

During the days following a burial, the deceased still return to their former homes to partake in meals with the living in spectral form. Their presence is often sensed in disembodied perceptions, such as through the sound of chopsticks scraping against a bowl. Funerals end with the *yān-hla lōng*, the 'soul-awaiting day', when the deceased's presence should be felt for the last time. This occurs on the seventh day for women and on the ninth day for men, counting either from death or burial, depending on the family and village. Mueggler (2014a: 200) has also documented the custom of holding seven- and nine-day vigils elsewhere in northwest Yunnan. Wellens (2010: 251n14) notes that "[t]he symbolic association of the number seven with female and nine with male is widespread" among speakers of Tibeto-Burman languages. In Nusu communities, one explanation for the seven- and nine-day vigils is that women and men possess so many souls, a point I return to below.

Managing the belongings of the deceased is a way to maintain souls in their proper place after death. They are detached from the household and their former social relations, as these items form a link that may bring them into dangerous proximity with the living. There are several ways to achieve the transition from the realm of the living into the shadow realm. Items can be buried directly with the deceased or placed on or adjacent to the tomb. It is common to see porcelain bowls and liquor bottles holding the remnants of rice and a strong grain alcohol (Ch. *baijiu*) placed on the lip of a tomb. Some families also place food next to the deceased during the wake, to sustain them in their transition to the afterlife, as I saw done for a young Christian woman from Uvri village who died at the age of 27 after a sudden illness.[3] In addition, fire acts as a means of transport between this world and *mhade*. Mourners may burn common-use items that are too bulky to fit inside the tomb, such as bedclothes and mattresses. A former shaman also told me that the practice of tomb burial replaced the earlier custom of cremation, which has historically been practiced among ethnic minority groups in Yunnan (Mueggler 2014b: 20–22). Perhaps the deceased themselves once reached the afterlife through means of fire.

Fire can transform objects into a form that the dead can receive. Charcoal or charred wood is money in the shadow realm, and it may be placed in the tomb with food and other important items. When I first asked my Nusu friend Ayima about the significance of charcoal, I employed the term 'symbolize' (Ch. *xiangzheng*). "Does charcoal symbolize money?" I asked. Ayima corrected me: "Charcoal does not symbolize money. It *is* money for the deceased." Some families prefer to buy Chinese paper money at the lowland market and burn it after burial. In each case, fire acts as a transformative element. More broadly, in Nusu social life, fire is an agent of destruction and transformation. Yet it also enables social relations of a certain kind. In swidden agriculture, fire destroys vegetation in order to fertilize crops. It enacts creative destruction, initiating cycles of productivity and reproduction: fields lie fallow when their fertility decreases before new vegetation is burned off to make them fertile again. In the household, the fire is at the center of comings and goings in the social space surrounding the hearth. Visiting friends and relatives are told to *mi hla*, draw close to the fire, where people share gossip and tall tales, drink liquor and eat *amödjioguei* (maize porridge), pop corn and roast tidbits of meat in the burning embers.

Fire anchors the *gra*, the cooking tripod and embodied presence of founding ancestors within the house, the link between the living and the dead. The three legs of the *gra* represent generations of ancestors: *aya*, *abaw*, and *api* (grandmother, grandfather, and great-grandparents). The *gra* is fed bits of food—lumps of maize and rice that are placed at the top of each of its three legs. Nusu do not practice 'ancestor worship' in the sense that anthropologists have employed the term among Han Chinese. Yet ancestors are, in a sense, present in the *gra* that encompasses the fire. Among the Premi, who also speak a Tibeto-Burman language, Wellens (2010: 120) finds that "the hearth and fireplace with its iron tripod … make up the locus of worshipping the 'ancestors' (*bap'u*) and divine beings of the mountains, water, wind, heaven, and earth." For the Nusu, the ancestors persist through the hearth, not as known and named persons, but as generic and unnamed elders in a de-individuating remembrance that doubles as an act of forgetting (Carsten 1995; Vitebsky 2008: 245). Elsewhere in northwest Yunnan, effigies take the place of the dead and are gradually moved away from the living, eventually to be discarded (see Mueggler 2001: 71–72).

Acts of giving to the dead, which maintain their relations with the living, also simultaneously contribute to dissolving their social relations. The deceased belong to their own ontological plane, whose geography communicates with that of the living, but whose essence remains fundamentally incompatible—the living cannot live off scraps or swap charcoal money for goods at the market. The *yān-hla* is continuous in life and in death, yet living and dead persons are essentially different categories of being, not just different in outer appearance, in spite of shared attributes of personhood. This essential difference is echoed in the ontological divisions between human and non-human persons, the living and the shadow realm, Nusu and non-Nusu.

Plural Selves

Nusu refer to souls of the living and the dead indiscriminately as *yān-hla*. However, the *yān-hla* may become separated from the living self even in life, and in death it entirely supplants it. The *yān-hla* is only one of several alternative, fragmentary selves that partake in the identity of their owner, while sometimes exhibiting their own agency. I suggest that we think of Nusu *yān-hla* and other kinds of doppelgängers (Hultkrantz 1953; Willerslev 2007) and fragmentary selves as soul attributes, latent and malleable components of the person that, in becoming manifest, may acquire their own agency, acting without their owners' knowledge. An important corollary to this is that a Nusu person may be perceived as a different ontological type, endowed with different capacities, when certain of her or his soul attributes are present or absent.

One good example of how a Nusu person may become a different ontological type can be found in the difference between women and men, who possess different numbers of souls. Women, who have only seven, can never become *yüigu* (shamans), although they can acquire the skill to perform certain rituals. The two additional souls possessed by men endow them with the full potential to become *yüigu*. Meanwhile, men and women endowed with second sight, that is, seers or *mia-vr-su* (people who see through), possess a predatory soul attribute, the *kösu*, which can attack and consume human victims. Fear, envy, bereavement, and other affective crisis states can furthermore trigger the inception or appearance of an otherwise latent soul attribute. If one should suffer an emotional disturbance, such as the death of a loved one, the *yān-hla* can separate from the body-self and wander away: its owner overcome with grief, the *yān-hla* seeks out the deceased in the shadow realm. The owner of the soul remains in possession of his or her wits and personality, but will gradually weaken and die if not reunited with it, similar to soul loss in Chinese folk belief (Harrell 1979: 524–527). Nor can a *yān-hla* survive for long in the realm of the living without its corporeal owner, which disappears from the living world within a few years of its owner's death. Non-Christian families sometimes leave food and alcohol at their relatives' tombs for some time following the death, typically three years, after which it is not necessary. Even very unhappy or confused ghosts leave the realm of the living after a few years, at most five to seven, I was told. This illustrates the ontological rift between the living and the dead, the impossibility of co-existence due to an essential multiplicity (Scott 2007). By contrast, among other native societies in Southwest China, such as the Nuosu (Swancutt 2012: 67–69) and the Lòlop'ò (Mueggler 2001: 250–284), ghosts can interact with the living for many years after death, whether as benevolent ancestors or malevolent predators.

For the Nusu, human and non-human persons can be multiplied or split into 'algebraic' soul fractions in soul loss and in other affective states. The *yisu* is a soul attribute that emerges from envy. It appears when a person intensely desires an item that belongs to someone else. The *yisu* attacks the target of envy, sickening his body-self and consuming his *yān-hla*. To prevent this, a person will sometimes offer up a belonging as a gift—whether a bracelet, jacket, or penknife—as soon as someone else expresses admiration for it, however innocuously. However, the emergence and attack of an *yisu* cannot always be avoided, as it can be triggered simply by another's youth and beauty. Because he or she has no knowledge of its actions, the person who has given rise to the *yisu* is not considered morally responsible for it in the same way that one is morally responsible for a deliberate curse, which would have a similar effect on the victim. This is something like the view of witchcraft in Evans-Pritchard's (1937) classic study of the Azande.

The difficulty of translating concepts like *yān-hla* and *yisu*, Pedersen and Willerslev (2012) argue, lies in their 'fuzziness'. We could gloss them as 'corporeal souls', but this is a hybrid term for what are discrete and coherent entities. Pedersen and Willerslev (ibid.: 465) maintain that "in the 'animist' concept of 'soul', we find the same fuzzy boundaries between self and other, human and inhuman, inner and outer, that are said to characterize postmodernity in the advanced and sophisticated, globalizing West." Their observation reflects a recurrent theme in the recent anthropology of animism: its capacity to confound dualistic concepts such as the notion of an exterior body and an interior soul (see also Vilaça 2005). I would go further, arguing that the notion of 'fuzziness' does not denote any lack of lucidity in animist thought. Rather, it points to the unsatisfactoriness of 'non-fuzzy' concepts such as 'body' and 'soul'. Nusu have no difficulty understanding the human-inhuman nature of personhood, or the spiritual-material qualities of their soul attributes. There is nothing inherently 'fuzzy' to them in the idea that a spectral being consumes a person's flesh when it attacks his or her soul, or that one self can emerge from another self that contains the possibility of yet other latent selves.

Soul attributes such as the *yisu* possess varying degrees of agency and personhood. They sometimes act as true doppelgängers, separating from the consciousness and moral core of their originators, even attacking their loved ones. The terms *yisu* and *kösu* build on the linguistic root *su*, meaning 'person' or 'people', underlining the potential to achieve personhood. Other kinds of *su*— for example, what an anthropologist might refer to as other 'ethnic groups'—are endowed with different ontological attributes. The Bai (Miwa, in Nusu) are the originators of a predatory emanation that attacks Nusu children. Spectral beings, such as the *mikhru* who inhabit mountains and forests, possess their own predatory, metamorphic qualities. The essential difference of non-human personhood is situated in its corporeal-spiritual attributes, such as the ability of *mikhru* and certain other non-humans to transform or disguise their appearance at will, or to imbue foods from the forest with their displaced agency. Thus, the distinction between different types of beings lies not so much in their interiority as it does in their latency, in the kinds of soul attributes they possess. The presence or latent possibility of their existence marks both intra- and inter-species differences in personhood (cf. Swancutt 2007: 242–243).

Dividual Souls

Since the reflexive turn in late-twentieth-century anthropology, early theories of animism have been critiqued for their social evolutionism and the Judeo-Christian assumptions they brought to the study of soul beliefs (Harvey 2006: 3–12; Willerslev 2011). Nevertheless, early anthropological studies sometimes touched on the non-dualistic, complex nature of animistic personhood—what I call its 'algebraic' qualities. In *Primitive Culture*, Tylor ([1871] 1920) endows souls with material as well as spiritual qualities and with the potential to exhibit independent agency while acting as the double of their owner (see Pedersen and Willerslev 2012: 466). Durkheim ([1912] 2001: 49) draws attention to these qualities in *The Elementary Forms of Religious Life*. In *The Uncanny*, Freud ([1919] 2003: 142–143) describes spectral doppelgängers as a "defence against annihilation" that nevertheless become "object[s] of terror." He sees them as liminal beings between life and death, as Richardson notes in her ethnography of technological animism (this volume). However, the theoretical potential of these descriptions remained latent until the recent revival of anthropological interest in animism. New ethnographies have challenged us to explore animistic personhood in its full complexity.

In the Nusu socio-cosmic order, a shaman (*yüigu*) develops the ability to negotiate ontological boundaries and the 'algebraic' qualities of animistic personhood:
human/non-human, visible/invisible, living/dead, and, by extension, Nusu/
non-Nusu. Ordinary people cannot address spectral beings like the *mikhru*. Shamans possess the linguistic skills to do so, typically claiming the ability to speak
numerous languages and to communicate with spectral beings in their language
of origin. Shamans can ritually retrieve lost souls and identify the beings responsible for soul attacks. They address sacrifices to spectral beings, who consume
invisible aspects of the animal offering and leave the flesh for the humans to eat.
Shamans also know how to open paths into the afterlife, and some can transform
into snakes. They manage the transformations that occur at ontological boundaries, which enable communication between different ontological categories. Perhaps for all of these reasons, very few Nusu men who perform rituals today call
themselves 'shamans'. People speak of shamanism mostly in the past.

In Nusu funerals, the cremation and entombment of items belonging to the
deceased is important because of the malleability of human souls and their
movement and transformation between this realm and the shadow realm. Christians, however, learn new doctrines concerning personhood and the afterlife. In
this view, the soul is monadic and acquires a transcendence that is supposed
to protect it from the predations of spectral beings on earth and ensure its swift
transport to the afterlife. Nusu Christians speak of the 'eternal soul' as a single
entity that does not leave the body until death. This 'eternal soul' is the locus
of Christian disciplinary practices (e.g., the avoidance of alcohol and cigarettes)
that are intended to guarantee the practitioners' proper standing in relation to
God and, hence, their ability to reach Heaven after death. Conversion to Christianity thus involves "the cultivation of a conscious, reflexive self ... that must
serve as its own moral regulator," as Chua (2012: 517) notes for the Bidayuh of
Malaysian Borneo. Yet church doctrine often proves difficult to reconcile with
what Nusu Christians already know about souls, creating dissonance between
what they say they do and what they feel 'should' be done to ensure the proper
transformation of persons and objects into the shape they must take in the
afterlife. Layou's funeral in late 2007 displayed some of these compromises with
religious orthodoxy.

From Multiplicity to Dualism

Layou had been sick for some time when he died in 2007, and his funeral was
a lively affair. In his youth, he had been a successful *yüigu*, but he converted
to Protestantism around the time of the Communist takeover and had already
been a Christian for many years by the time of his death. When the Commu-
nists initiated campaigns against religion in 1958 (Mazard 2011), the family was
one of the few in Khrada to hold secret worship meetings in their homes. Layou
went on to become a popular and respected preacher in his old age, trading
his former skill in ritual for success of another kind. Preachers, like *yüigu*, are
expected to 'speak well', that is, to possess the gift of charismatic speech.

I went to Layou's funeral with his grandson Youlin, who was my host in Nujiang. A significant number of the inhabitants of Khrada and many of Layou's family members who had traveled from other towns and villages were also in attendance. After the wake, a procession transported Layou's body to the gravesite some distance from his home, in the semi-forest at the northwestern edge of the village. We saw a group of young men putting the final touches to the raised concrete tomb, freshly built. The men pulled the coffin up into the vault while, in light rain, the church-goers in the audience opened their hymnals and began to sing. Layou's kin then placed his favorite belongings in the tomb. Youlin proferred his grandfather's chipped enamel tea mug and a few other forgotten items that he had rushed back to the house to fetch. A couple of mourners started a fire to burn the items too bulky to place in the tomb—Layou's mattress and some of his bedding and clothing. The damp weather delayed the fire at first. As mourners filed back downhill to the funeral feast, a few people remained behind to finish sealing the tomb and ensure that the reluctant fire fully consumed the belongings of the deceased.

The careful way that Layou's relatives dealt with his personal belongings reflects the untidy reality of a Christian funeral set in the context of animist ontological assumptions. By the time Layou died, I had been living in Khrada for several months and had participated in a number of funerals in varying shades of Christianity. Subscribing to the anthropological teaching that my task as an ethnographer was to discern consistent ritual patterns across varied and often messy real-life ritual events, I had endeavored to develop an idea of the 'normal' structure of a Nusu funeral. I expected to find a clear division between Christian and non-Christian funerals, reflecting the differences that Nusu Christians strive to assert in their everyday lives. But while the religious identity of the deceased was never ambiguous, I found that I could not conclusively sort funerals into Christian and non-Christian types. Christian doctrine certainly opposes the burial or burning of personal items belonging to the deceased, as it suggests that the mourners do not trust in the transcendence of the soul. Burning Layou's items was an ambiguous act. Perhaps it was intended to send the items to *mhade*, the afterlife, with different connotations for Christians and non-Christians. Or perhaps it was only to ensure that the belongings did not remain where the soul of the deceased might return to fetch them. In any case, it was certainly not an orthodox Christian act.

I returned to Layou's house nine days after his burial for the *yān-hla lōng* (soul-awaiting day). Most of the out-of-towners had already left, but many of the original mourners from Khrada and some other relatives and friends of the deceased filled the house during the day and night of the ritual. There was more drinking, pork, and card games, as there had been during the wake. Later I mentioned the event to my friend Ayima, and she flatly contradicted me: "That's impossible! Christian funerals can only last three days. That's the rule." Christians are not supposed to await the soul's return, since they should believe that departed souls cannot return to the realm of the living after death. There is, in other words, a transition from 'spectral attributes' (with their latent multiplicity) to a unique, transcendent, morally constituted soul. This lays the blueprint for a clear body-soul dualism: the body is vulnerable to disease and death, while the soul is not.

In practice, however, Nusu Christians act as if souls and selves remain multiple, 'unstable' (Vilaça 2005), subject to fragmentation and metamorphosis. Yazhu, my first host mother, is a prominent member of the Khrada church and is married to a well-known local preacher and evangelist. Like many other Christians in Khrada, Yazhu describes events such as soul loss and attacks by spectral beings (*yüi*) as matters of simple fact. She often warned me against walking the mountain roads at night because of the presence of 'bad people'. Eventually, when I failed to take the hint, she clarified that she meant *yüi*, which she has encountered in various spots around Khrada. She refused to let her daughter take her grandson, then a year old, to the forest higher up on the mountain, a popular spot for young people's hunting and leisure expeditions, because of the known presence of *mikhru*, to which infants are particularly vulnerable—in spite of the fact that Yazhu proclaims her belief in prayer as an infallible protection against *yüi*. Yazhu related vividly the encounters she has had with disembodied souls, such as her mother-in-law's *yān-hla*, which visited her shortly before her mother-in-law's death. As is often the case, this 'soul encounter' (Chua 2011) manifested itself as fragmentary sensations: a sound as if her mother-in-law were knocking on the door and a sense of her invisible presence.

Such somatic experiences of *yüi* confront Nusu Christians with the question of how to reconcile their empirical reality with contradictory religious doctrine, a question that leads to an inherently reflexive approach to both the new and the old. As Webb Keane (1997: 677) observes: "[M]issionary activity and religious conversion have been a constant inducement to self-revelation and reflection. Missionization demands an enormous amount of talk, as preachers, converts, and the unconverted are compelled to explain themselves to others, to explain others to themselves, and even to explain themselves to themselves."

Consider the dialogue below, which follows the death of an Uvri man who had been attacked and slowly driven insane by a *mikhru* over a period of several years. The *mikhru* eventually killed him in the forest and left behind his partially consumed corpse. As is typical in such cases, the people who told me about the event made no distinction between the *mikhru* consuming the man's body and consuming his soul, since they are part of the same process. However, for two Christians, Ayima and her cousin Ahuo, this raised an ontological problem, since the soul is supposed to transcend material existence. Employing Chinese terms for soul attributes (see Harrell 1979), Ahuo concedes that the *hun*, which could be translated into English as the 'living soul' (or 'vital principle'), might be consumed by a *mikhru*. But, he argues, this would not affect the fate of one's *ling*, one's eternal soul.

Ahuo: What the superstitious say is that they [the *mikhru*] seize our soul … they attack our soul! That way, an illness appears in our physical body … That's what the superstitious say … But what we Biblicals say is, we humans can't live anymore after our soul is gone from inside our physical body. It will die. Because, when [a *mikhru*] has gone away with our soul, that's how it is—

Ayima: [interrupts him in disagreement]

Ahuo: But that's how it is! In Chinese, 'departed soul' [*ling*] and 'living soul' [*hun*] are two different things, right?

Ayima: Yes.

Ahuo: That's right ... Maybe what [*mikhru*] take is our 'living soul'. A 'departed soul' [means] a person can die, that's what it says in the Bible. Whatever the Bible says is the truth.

Faced with doubt, Ahuo cuts short his exposition on the soul and falls back on a statement about the Bible's infallibility that Ayima cannot challenge. Ahuo explicitly locates the soul inside the body and refers to non-Christians as 'superstitious'. The nature of the soul, its identity (single or plural), and its relationship to the body remain in question. This ontological uncertainty underlines the failure of Christian doctrine to account for what Nusu already understand about the soul. This discussion, like Yazhu's accounts of her 'soul encounters', directly touches on the question of soul ontology, indicating the incomplete success of missionary attempts to establish body-soul dualism through ritual and doctrinal measures, and the resulting reflexivity and 'post-modernist' multiplication (Gerholm 1988) in Nusu beliefs.

The soul-awaiting ritual, burning of personal items, and other practices that I witnessed during and after the funeral of a prominent preacher challenge the church's doctrine that the soul, after death, immediately and irreversibly departs from the body to take its place in one of two afterlives (heaven or hell), both understood as morally transcendent domains. Nusu Christians are called upon to forswear practices like the *yān-hla lōng* that refer to a divisible personhood, an overlap between the body and its soul attributes, and a fluid interconnection between the living and the shadow realm. But then they must grapple with body-soul dualism, which, to them, has become a 'fuzzy' framework of interpretation.

"We Don't Call It Primitive Religion Anymore"

Perhaps it is because Nusu view the world as poly-ontological that they are predisposed to reformulate their socio-cosmic assumptions when they interact with those whom they see as ontological outsiders, including representatives of the Chinese state. Ethnographies of ethnicity and religion in China have brought to light the complexity of the relationship between the Chinese body politic and nationalities such as the Yao (Litzinger 2000), Dai (Davis 2005), Tibetans (Makley 2007), and Premi (Wellens 2010). Following in the vein of post-colonial theory, this research has shown that power is best understood not as an externally applied force, in the sense of 'oppression', but rather as a deeply embedded aspect of social relations. Ethnic minorities have been "active agents in the reimagining of the post-Mao Chinese nation" (Litzinger 1998: 241) and in their own reform-era cultural reinvention (ibid.; see also Gros 2012; Schein 2000), including the reinvention of religious life (Litzinger 1998).

Over the past sixty-odd years, there have been several shifts in Chinese state policies toward ethnic minority (*shaoshu minzu*) religions in Southwest China (see Swancutt, this volume).[4] In the mid- to late twentieth century, Nusu rituals were officially classed as 'primitive religion' (Ch. *yuanshi zongjiao*) and then attacked as 'feudal superstition' (Ch. *fengjian mixin*) before being re-evaluated in the 1980s onward as 'nature religion' (Ch. *ziran zongjiao*) and 'animism' (Ch. *wanwu you ling*), or the teaching that "everything has a soul" (Swancutt, this volume). Through these recent discursive shifts, Chinese ethnologists have moved away from the social evolutionism of Marxist-Leninist anthropology to seek ways of recognizing and even respecting indigenous religion. The political sensitivity that continues to surround manifestations of indigenous culture within the People's Republic of China has fostered the careful cultivation of state discourse among both anthropologists (Mullaney 2004) and cultural representatives of ethnic minorities, such as tour guides, folk performers, and native intellectuals.

As members of the Nu nationality, one of China's smallest officially recognized ethnic groups or *xiaoshao* (small minorities), Nusu lack the clout of larger groups who have mustered their political representation and intellectual elites to create official spaces for their reinvented religious identities in the post-Mao reform era. Litzinger (1998), for instance, documents the revitalization of the deity Pan Wang as a Yao cultural icon, while Swancutt (this volume) examines the role of Nuosu ritualists and intellectuals in state-sponsored research on Nuosu religion. Yet Nusu are also active participants in the reinvention of animism, albeit on a smaller scale.

In 2006 to 2008, the researchers whom I met and collaborated with in Yunnan were intensely aware of the politically 'sensitive' (Ch. *mingan*) nature of projects concerning minority ritual and religion. Fieldwork in Nujiang was already considered *mingan* because of the controversy surrounding a series of planned hydroelectric dams all along the Nujiang river from the Tibetan border to the fringes of Kachin State (Litzinger 2007). The term 'sensitive' metonymically suggests topics that must be approached with caution, often indirectly. In spite of its sensitivity, however, Nusu animism has been reinvented—in the field by its practitioners, as well as in ethnographies and video recordings. Practitioners and researchers alike must navigate difficult political waters with a tricksterish skill, transforming the meanings of terms to disguise sensitive ideas (Mullaney 2004), redefining identities, and carving out cosmological spaces at the margins of a hegemonic apparatus of state. A shamanic ritual might be enacted and recorded as a 'folk dance', for instance, as was the case with the video recording session at the Liuku Hotel.

Let us then return to the event described in the opening paragraphs of this chapter—the ritual performed onstage in the Liuku Hotel. The recording session was organized by a team of Chinese researchers who traveled from Yunnan's capital city to the province's remote northwest in late 2007, ostensibly to record the 'folk songs' and 'folk dances' of the ethnic minorities of Nujiang Prefecture. They devoted several days to the Nusu participants, who, like all the performers, were asked to dress in 'traditional' outfits to represent their nationality. At one of the recording sessions, Lañi and another elderly Nusu man demonstrated a soul-calling chant. Lañi later acted out the mortuary ritual where he struck the machete on the ground to open the path for the *yān-hla* into the afterlife. Onstage, he was pretending to be a shaman. He was also pretending *not* to be a shaman. In front of the stage, brandishing a video camera, microphones, and a boom stand, the researchers pretended that this was not a ritual—and that it was *not* not a ritual. Both parties were navigating ambiguous boundaries of being and becoming, action and mimicry.

Lañi was in his mid-eighties when I interviewed him in December 2007, a month after the recording session. When he was a young man, his first wife was sick for three years. His father, who was a shaman, conducted sacrifices of pigs, chickens, and two heads of cattle, but she did not recover. Afterward, Lañi thought that perhaps the sacrifice had not been carried out well, or perhaps they were too poor to do enough. He became a shaman sometime later, and then, at a point that remained unclear in our interview, he converted to Christianity. His second wife was a Christian as well. In the 1980s, she became a follower of a millenarian religious leader in Khrada and remained so until her death in 2008. Millenarians differed from other Christians in Khrada, eschewing the use of medicine in favor of prayer. Their religious differences were a cause of unhappiness for both spouses, leading to domestic strife. Lañi's wife would argue with him, pressuring him to convert. By 2007, then, when Lañi acted the part of the shaman for the recording session, he had not been a shaman for quite some time, and Christian religious debates loomed large in his personal life. Nevertheless, people in Khrada knew that Lañi had passed on some of his knowledge and skill to one of his daughters and that she was active as a ritualist, perhaps putting into question his identity as a non-shaman. The recording session placed him in the equally tenuous role of a politically neutral shamanic folk dancer.

After Lañi's recording session, I asked Zhou, the Chinese team's leader, about the place of animism in his research on the Nusu. I employed the term 'primitive religion' (Ch. *yuanshi zongjiao*), which is commonly used among anthropologists and other visitors when discussing indigenous cosmologies in Yunnan. Zhou quickly corrected me: "We don't call it primitive religion anymore. Now we use the term 'nature religion' [Ch. *ziran zongjiao*]." Skirting the sensitive topic altogether, Zhou explained that he wanted the recordings to become a permanent document of Nujiang's folk music and dance. He also planned to introduce cultural elements into the university admissions procedure for ethnic minority candidates. His idea was to mandate that all such candidates must recite at least one of the 'folk songs' belonging to their nationality in order to pass the admission test. The songs would be checked against a list drawn from research projects like theirs. He complained that the Nusu performers were almost all old men and women, and he expressed concern that these traditions might disappear in Nujiang's current phase of development. Indirectly, the team leader was drawing a connection between the preservation of animism and the strengthening of minority identity.

The researchers could not address the cultural life of shamanic rituals or their animistic connotations. They staged Lañi's rituals in the guise of a performance, devoid of ritual intentions or effects, like the denatured rituals that occur in the Beijing Ethnic Culture Park as demonstrations of ethnic minority traditions (Makley 2010). Yet this was a way for them to mark out a space for ritual and to preserve it as an aspect of minority identity. Approaching animism from the perspective of 'folk dance' allowed the researchers to create possibilities for its study and documentation in a political context where it remained officially banned.

Amid these ambiguities, one of the Nusu participants was tasked with navigating between the shamanic and ethnological realms. Youlin, whose grandfather Layou was buried a few weeks earlier, was invited to organize the performers and act as interpreter for them and the researchers. Youlin supports his family through a variety of sources: he farms, operates one of Khrada's hostels, acts as a tourist guide, performs as a singer and dancer in county events, and holds office as a village councilor for the administrative village of Laomudeng. In most of his roles, Youlin acts as a gatekeeper between outside visitors and the village (or image) of Khrada and its Nusu inhabitants, adeptly molding himself to visitors' expectations. He honed his intercultural skills during his first job at a cultural park similar to the one described by Makley (2010) in her analysis of post-Mao 'national exhibitionism'. At a time when Southwest China is banking on its cultural capital for economic development, Youlin displays "a trickster-like ability to negotiate between the new market system and the old parallel culture of socialism" (Pedersen and Højer 2008: 82).

During the 2007 research project in Liuku, Youlin acted as a kind of 'cultural shaman', mediating between Nusu and non-Nusu. Most importantly, he translated the text and content of Lañi's shamanic 'dances' into Chinese-language description—into a cultural form that he knew would be both acceptable and comprehensible to the researchers. This meant that the researchers were never confronted with the differences between the socio-cosmic assumptions underlying the ritual performances and the understanding of animism that they brought with them into the field. Like the *yüigu* who speak to spectral beings, or the kin who bury coal as money for the deceased, Youlin deployed transformative techniques to make interaction possible across ontological divides. Metamorphosis—whether of forms or ideas—is the fundamental precondition of exchange in any poly-ontological world. As Scott (2007: 18) puts it: "[A]ctors engaged with poly-ontological assumptions must create unifying relations among multiple pre-existing categories of being. In so doing … they must also find ways to preserve their distinctive identities without rupturing the ties they have formed and reverting to primordial disjunction." Whereas Nusu shamans enact transformative exchanges with spectral beings, Youlin and other masterful cultural interpreters perform such exchanges with ethnologists, whom the Nusu situate in another ontological domain.

Conclusion

The 'algebra of souls' describes a socio-cosmic order in which personhood is subject to plurality and fragmentation. Unknown aspects continuously emerge from and propel the person throughout her or his lifetime, engaging visible and invisible aspects of self. Nusu persons are "irreducibly plural and capable of transformation," as Carlos Fausto (2011: 581; my translation) says of the powerful beings depicted in the ritual masks of the Upper Xingu. Among the Nusu, this applies to ordinary men and women as well as to shamans, seers, and spectral entities. Human and non-human persons possess a "non-dual plurality" (ibid.), containing unknown fractions and doubles, multiplying and shifting in a non-dualistic matrix.

To this dynamic uncertainty is added the complexity of other perspectives on the animistic self, resulting from Nusu participation in Christian and socialist representations of their reality. Animistic ideas are reformulated in and through Christianity, as well as in political and anthropological encounters. When Lañi and others provide researchers with cultural prestations, they are acutely aware that these have ideological implications (Mazard 2011). Ideas move hyper-reflexively across ontological boundaries. I view Nusu rituals, whether staged or 'real', as ontological statements formulated in this sensitive context.

As Nusu animism has become hyper-reflexive, a new ontological uncertainty has emerged, beyond the uncertainty of soul algebra. Christian doctrine asserts the unity and transcendence of the soul, which Nusu understand as partly corporeal and dangerously divisible. Socialist modernity competes with sacrifice and prayer, and ethnology reinvents animism through its theoretical trajectory. Nusu people who participate in these competing representations in various ways therefore understand their practices and beliefs from points of view that are already reflexive, implicitly responding to the cosmological and ideological implications of ritual discourse. Their rituals are organized around multiple negotiations and transformations between domains: the realm of the living and the shadow realm, shamanic practices and the values of Christianity, political history and anthropological classifications. Nusu situate these multiple realms of meaning in a poly-ontological order. The key to their co-existence lies in metamorphosis, a necessary condition of exchange across ontological divides.

Acknowledgments

The ethnography presented in this chapter was made possible by grants from the Firebird Foundation and the University of Cambridge. Many thanks are due to Ayima, Youlin, Lañi, and other Nusu hosts and friends who showed me the meaning of patience and generosity. Material that eventually made its way into this chapter was first presented in a talk entitled "Ghosts of Ritual" at the Magic Circle seminar, held at the Scott Polar Research Institute, University of Cambridge. I wish to thank Piers Vitebsky, the organizer of the seminar, for his valuable feedback and the anonymous reviewers for their comments on the chapter. In addition, Katherine Swancutt, co-editor of this book, suggested new lines of thought and gave encouragement throughout the writing process. Erik Mueggler's work in northwest Yunnan provided inspiration, particularly with regard to the importance of ghosts.

Mireille Mazard is an independent researcher who recently completed a post-doctoral fellowship at the Max Planck Institute for Religious and Ethnic Diversity. Her areas of interest are ethno-politics and identity among the Nusu of Southwest China. She is currently writing a monograph about Nusu religious and political transformations, which explores their engagement with Christian and Communist ideologies in creating new ontological frameworks for experiencing the world.

Notes

1. I employ pseudonyms for Nusu names throughout the text.
2. Unless otherwise indicated, all non-English terms are in Nusu.
3. The bowl of rice and meager serving of meat placed by her head when she was lain out for the wake would have attracted disapproval among the Christians of Khrada, who are perhaps more sensitive to church prohibitions on such practices.
4. See also Mullaney (2011) on the history of the term *minzu* and its connotations in Chinese ethnology.

References

Carsten, Janet. 1995. "The Politics of Forgetting: Migration, Kinship and Memory on the Periphery of the Southeast Asian State." *Journal of the Royal Anthropological Institute* 1 (2): 317–335.

Chua, Liana. 2011. "Soul Encounters: Emotions, Corporeality, and the Matter of Belief in a Bornean Village." *Social Analysis* 55 (3): 1–17.

Chua, Liana. 2012. "Conversion, Continuity, and Moral Dilemmas among Christian Bidayuhs in Malaysian Borneo." *American Ethnologist* 39 (3): 511–526.

Davis, Sara L. M. 2005. *Song and Silence: Ethnic Revival on China's Southwest Borders.* New York: Columbia University Press.

Deleuze, Gilles, and Félix Guattari. 1980. *Capitalisme et schizophrénie 2: Mille plateaux.* Paris: Éditions de Minuit.

Durkheim, Émile. (1912) 2001. *The Elementary Forms of Religious Life.* Trans. Carol Cosman. Oxford: Oxford University Press.

Evans-Pritchard, E. E. 1937. *Witchcraft, Oracles and Magic among the Azande.* Oxford: Oxford University Press.

Fausto, Carlos. 2011. "Le masque de l'animiste: Chimères et poupées russes en Amérique indigène." Trans. Emmanuel de Vienne. *Gradhiva* 13: 48–67.

Freud, Sigmund. (1919) 2003. *The Uncanny.* Trans. David McLintock; intro. Hugh Haughton. London: Penguin.

Gerholm, Tomas. 1988. "On Ritual: A Postmodernist View." *Ethnos* 53 (3–4): 190–203.

Gros, Stéphane. 2012. *La Part manquante: Échanges et pouvoirs chez les Drung du Yunnan.* Nanterre: Société d'ethnologie.

Harrell, Stevan. 1979. "The Concept of Soul in Chinese Folk Religion." *Journal of Asian Studies* 38 (3): 519–528.

Harvey, Graham. 2006. *Animism: Respecting the Living World.* New York: Columbia University Press.

The Algebra of Souls | 35

He Shutao. 2000. "Nuzujuan." [Nu Nationality Chapter] In *Zhongguo Ge Minzu Yuan-shi Zongjiao Ziliao Jicheng: Naxizu, Qiangzu, Dulongzu Juan, Lisuzu, Nuzujuan* [Collected Materials on Primitive Religions of All Chinese Nationalities: Naxi, Qiang, Dulong, Lisu, and Nu Nationality Chapters], ed. He Zhiwu, Qian Anduan, and Cai Jiaqi, 826–938. Beijing: Zhongguo shehui kexue chubanshe.

Hultkrantz, Åke. 1953. *Conceptions of the Soul among North American Indians: A Study in Religious Ethnology.* Stockholm: Ethnographical Museum of Sweden.

Keane, Webb. 1997. "From Fetishism to Sincerity: On Agency, the Speaking Subject, and Their Historicity in the Context of Religious Conversion." *Comparative Studies in Society and History* 39 (4): 674–693.

Litzinger, Ralph A. 1998. "Memory Work: Reconstituting the Ethnic in Post-Mao China." *Cultural Anthropology* 13 (2): 224–255.

Litzinger, Ralph A. 2000. *Other Chinas: The Yao and the Politics of National Belonging.* Durham, NC: Duke University Press.

Litzinger, Ralph A. 2007. "In Search of the Grassroots: Hydroelectric Politics in North-west Yunnan." In *Grassroots Political Reform in Contemporary China*, ed. Elizabeth J. Perry and Merle Goldman, 282–299. Cambridge, MA: Harvard University Press.

Makley, Charlene. 2007. *The Violence of Liberation: Gender and Tibetan Buddhist Revival in Post-Mao China.* Berkeley: University of California Press.

Makley, Charlene. 2010. "Minzu, Market and the Mandala: National Exhibitionism and Tibetan Buddhist Revival in Post-Mao China." In *Faiths on Display: Religion, Tourism, and the Chinese State*, ed. Tim Oakes and Donald S. Sutton, 127–156. Plymouth: Rowman & Littlefield.

Mazard, Mireille. 2011. "Powerful Speech: Remembering the Long Cultural Revolution in Yunnan." *Inner Asia* 13: 157–178.

Mazard, Mireille. 2014. "The Art of (Not) Looking Back: Reconsidering Lisu Migrations and 'Zomia.'" In *Globalising Migration History: The Eurasian Experience (16th–21st centuries)*, ed. Jan Lucassen and Leo Lucassen, 215–246. Leiden: Brill.

Mueggler, Erik. 2001. *The Age of Wild Ghosts: Memory, Violence, and Place in Southwest China.* Berkeley: University of California Press.

Mueggler, Erik. 2014a. "'Cats Give Funerals to Rats': Making the Dead Modern with Lament." *Journal of the Royal Anthropological Institute* 20 (2): 197–217.

Mueggler, Erik. 2014b. "Corpse, Stone, Door, Text." *Journal of Asian Studies* 73 (1): 17–41.

Mullaney, Thomas. 2004. "Ethnic Classification Writ Large: The 1954 Yunnan Province Ethnic Classification Project and Its Foundations in Republican-Era Taxonomic Thought." *China Information* 18 (2): 207–241.

Mullaney, Thomas. 2011. *Coming to Terms with the Nation: Ethnic Classification in Modern China.* Berkeley: University of California Press.

Pedersen, Morten Axel, and Lars Højer. 2008. "Lost in Transition: Fuzzy Property and Leaky Selves in Ulaanbaatar." *Ethnos* 73 (1): 73–96.

Pedersen, Morten Axel, and Rane Willerslev. 2012. "'The Soul of the Soul Is the Body': Rethinking the Concept of Soul through North Asian Ethnography." *Common Knowledge* 18 (3): 464–486.

Schein, Louisa. 2000. *Minority Rules: The Miao and the Feminine in China's Cultural Politics.* Durham, NC: Duke University Press.

Scott, Michael W. 2007. *The Severed Snake: Matrilineages, Making Place, and a Melanesian Christianity in Southeast Solomon Islands.* Durham, NC: Carolina Academic Press.

Starn, Orin. 2011. "Here Come the Anthros (Again): The Strange Marriage of Anthropology and Native America." *Cultural Anthropology* 26 (2): 179–204.

Strathern, Marilyn. 1988. *The Gender of the Gift: Problems with Women and Problems with Society in Melanesia*. Berkeley: University of California Press.

Swancutt, Katherine. 2007. "The Ontological Spiral: Virtuosity and Transparency in Mongolian Games." *Inner Asia* 9: 237–259.

Swancutt, Katherine. 2012. "Fame, Fate-Fortune, and Tokens of Value among the Nuosu of Southwest China." *Social Analysis* 56 (2): 56–72.

Tylor, Edward B. (1871) 1920. *Primitive Culture: Researches into the Development of Mythology, Philosophy, Religion, Language, Art and Custom*. Vols. 1 and 2. London: John Murray.

Venkatesan, Soumhya, Keir Martin, Michael W. Scott, Christopher Pinney, Nikolai Ssorin-Chaikov, Joanna Cook, and Marilyn Strathern. 2013. "The Group for Debates in Anthropological Theory (GDAT), the University of Manchester: The 2011 Annual Debate—Non-dualism is Philosophy Not Ethnography." *Critique of Anthropology* 33 (3): 300–360.

Vilaça, Aparecida. 2005. "Chronically Unstable Bodies: Reflections on Amazonian Corporalities." *Journal of the Royal Anthropological Institute* 11 (3): 445–464.

Vitebsky, Piers. 2008. "Loving and Forgetting: Moments of Inarticulacy in Tribal India." *Journal of the Royal Anthropological Institute* 14 (2): 243–261.

Viveiros de Castro, Eduardo. 1998. "Cosmological Deixis and Amerindian Perspectivism." *Journal of the Royal Anthropological Institute* 4 (3): 469–488.

Wellens, Koen. 2010. *Religious Revival in the Tibetan Borderlands: The Premi of Southwest China*. Seattle: University of Washington Press.

Willerslev, Rane. 2007. *Soul Hunters: Hunting, Animism, and Personhood among the Siberian Yukaghirs*. Berkeley: University of California Press.

Willerslev, Rane. 2011. "Frazer Strikes Back from the Armchair: A New Search for the Animist Soul." *Journal of the Royal Anthropological Institute* (n.s.) 17 (3): 504–526.

Yunnansheng Bianji Weiyuanhu, ed. 1981. *Nuzu shehui lishi diaocha* [Investigations on the Social History of the Nu]. Kunming: Yunnan minzu chubanshe.

Chapter 2

RECURSIVITY AND THE SELF-REFLEXIVE COSMOS
Tricksters in Cuban and Brazilian Spirit Mediumship Practices

Diana Espírito Santo

A classic example of a non-human shapeshifter is the 'trickster', who appears in myriad cross-cultural guises and stories from India to Latin America and in forms as diverse as Mercury, Hermes, Krishna, Raven, Coyote, and Eshu. Cosmologies that include tricksters destabilize readings of ontological configurations as ordered or unambiguous, while challenging the anthropologist's bias toward describing cultural representations as coherent and homogeneous. Studies of shamanic, animist, and/or perspectivistic cultures have made progress in relating understandings of interspecies metamorphosis to concepts of self, spirit, corporeality, and substance (Descola 1996; Pedersen 2001, 2007; Praet 2009; Viveiros de Castro 1998). However, far less contemporary ethnographic attention has been given to instances of shapeshifting that do not directly imply people or their shamanic technologies.

Notes for this chapter begin on page 53.

Through a focus on the metamorphosis of spirit entities, in this chapter I explore two Latin American possession cults—one in Cuba and the other in Brazil—that reveal cosmoses with varying degrees of open-endedness. In both religious traditions, people perceive spirits to be aware of themselves, of their possibilities and limitations as metaphysical entities, and of the dividends of their awareness for human experience. Recursivity here is thus deeply related to self-reflexivity or self-awareness: it is because the cosmos is aware of itself *as cosmos* (in its constitution) that it is able to describe, produce, and change itself, thereby transforming the world. In these two cases, I argue that we can observe this recursivity in the interplay between the spirits' expressions of their autonomy from living beings and through the spirits' own contingency as effective beings on human belief, representation, perception, and action. Spirits and persons appear as two sides of a single proverbial Möbius strip (cf. Handelman 1998: xxiv), each with its own horizons and scope for self-generation that are the result of having a meta-perspective (self-reflexivity).

In the Cuban-Creole practice of Espiritismo Cruzado (a mixture of European-derived spiritualist philosophies and Afro-Cuban religious ontologies), some spirits that are conceptualized as components of persons exhibit metamorphic properties. These spirits unfold themselves in manifold 'skins', which betray their multiplicity of (past) lives, the myriad aspects of these lives, and their cultural and cosmic influences. Mediums—or *espiritistas*, as they are known—think of these metamorphoses, called *desdoblamientos* (unfoldings), as the means by which spirits signal the need for their human hosts to undergo complementary changes and as certain consequences of those changes (e.g., material offerings or emotional developments). In what can be described as a world-making endeavor between spheres, spirits and persons enfold each other in the production of their respective selves or personhoods.

In Brazilian Umbanda, an early-twentieth-century mediumship cult with indigenous and African influences, some spirit entities go further, disentangling themselves from the ontological categories afforded to them by human actors and critically playing with their alternatives in a trickster-like fashion. Spirits transgress through a largely taken-for-granted process of 'evolution', which sees categories of spirits transforming into others over time, and, more subversively, by producing discourses that test the public and cultural stereotypes that often pertain to them. However, Umbanda's entities spin a very particular form of meta-anthropology by recognizing that these labels afford the success of their own manifestations on a human sphere, which they criticize as increasingly impoverished in its 'culture' of remembering names.

These two examples are arguably comparable because they take the 'relation' between cosmos (spirit, entity, virtualities) and the world (culture, minds, persons) as ontologically eventful. In Cuba, the 'world' at stake is the person and her or his 'parts', while in Brazil it is collective cultural consciousness and its representations. It is no coincidence that both of these religions are intrinsically self-transformative and innovative sets of practices. To put it simply, one of my points here is to show that this self-transformative nature derives in part from the Trickster open-endedness of their models of spirit and/or person. Yet although the figure of the Trickster may epitomize this open-endedness, what is ultimately at stake is the anthropological willingness to discern more complex alternatives to the relationship between cosmos and people.

There is no doubt that relationships exist between the various aspects of socio-political, socio-structural, and economic life and spirit or entity-laden cosmologies. The question is whether we can isolate 'trickster phenomena' from these broader contingencies and see what purchase this yields for understanding how cosmology behaves and impinges upon the human actors that regenerate it. Trickster phenomena may end up not being about tricksters at all, but about the boundaries of cosmological exchange and renewal. Yet this may require a step back, in the direction of the Trickster itself.

In his commentary on Paul Radin's treatise on Native American trickster figures, such as Coyote, Jung (1972: 200) notes that the "phantom of the trickster haunts the mythology of all ages." As an archetypal psychic structure of ancient origins, Jung says, the trickster represents the primitive, animalesque component of the psyche, "a faithful copy of an absolutely undifferentiated human consciousness" (ibid.), most prevalent in the present day among minds in cultures still immersed in darkness. While Jung underscores the creative potentialities of this chaotic subworld, most scholars recognize the Trickster as more than intra-psychic baggage from the lower echelons of social evolution. Combs and Holland (1996: 82) describe him as "the quintessential master of boundaries and transitions." Trickster is paradoxical, at once a clown and a creator, a gift giver and a thief, a disrupter of "convention, order, and preconception" (ibid.: 87) and an originator of institution, culture, and technology, "found symbolically wherever rigid notions of life exclude part of life's totality" (ibid.: 93). Tricksters the world over typically embody contradictory mixtures of attributes, one of which is innocence or naiveté—he is the "eternal child who cannot be significantly damaged," as Lewis Hyde (1998: 70) notes. It is not simply that the Trickster transgresses morality; he holds the world and all its possibilities (including moral ones) in abeyance, yielding novel avenues of truth and boundary making, loose from rigid dualisms or sets of opposite significations. The Trickster wields "mind-boggling falsity that calls the truth itself into question" (ibid.: 70) and "statements that double back to subvert their own contexts" (ibid.). Tricksters hold A and not-A true at once, playfully revealing the traps of rigidity where they exist, in culture, destiny, and psyche. As Rane Willerslev (2007) shows, it is not just the spirits who may embody the Trickster, but persons too. For the Siberian Yukaghir whom he writes about, hunters may transform themselves into various 'others' via forms of partial identification through mimesis. But as imitator, the hunter "must move in between identities, in that double negative field" that Willerslev (citing Richard Schechner) calls "not me, *not* not-me" (ibid.: 12).

In the rest of this chapter, I would like to hold the Trickster close at hand: in the first instance, because my materials from Cuba and Brazil point to considerations brought about by trickster-like aspects of these spirit-cultures that are invariably unexplored in contemporary accounts; in the second instance, because Tricksters tell us to go beyond appearances and resist certainty in our perceptions and accounts of them. One potentially fruitful way to do this, it seems, is to refuse to reduce these tricksterish characteristics to how we think others constitute their reality through belief or representation, or by means of responses to their socio-cultural environment. Rather, as Handelman (2004: 10) argues for ritual in general, "[e]mphasizing the existential 'withinness' of phenomena points to their irreducibility to the intentions and desires of their makers or shapers." This does not mean ignoring the human element of the equation. Handelman proposes that "[s]elf-organizing phenomenal forms have variable capacities to generate new aspects of themselves" (ibid.: 13) and that this necessarily implies a double movement, "curving inwards, torquing outwards, through form recognizing itself within itself, and on the basis of this self-integrity moving outwards, driving into broader cosmic and social worlds" (ibid.). As with rituals and rites, many accounts of spirit ontologies have focused on the relationship between manifestations of spirit possession or shamanism and their social, historical, and political contexts (see, e.g., Boddy 1989; Mageo 1996; Ong 1987; Stoller 1989). However, similar to what Kapferer (2004: 45) argues relative to rituals, some spirit entities gain their force precisely because they are not always reflective of larger realities, but present their own internal logic that articulates with their human counterparts. What remains to be determined is the manner in which they articulate and what their effects are, without, by asking this, reducing them to this articulation.

Enfolding Cosmology in Cuban Espiritismo

Ontological multiplicity is arguably a pervasive quality of the larger spiritual universe that is accessed, generated, and manipulated by Afro-Cuban religious experts. For example, in Cuba's foremost popular religious cult, Santería, which bears strong West African influences, most of the 20 or so venerated *oricha* gods, or *santos*, as they are known, have multiple avatars, called *caminos,* or paths, sometimes as many as 21 (Bolívar 1990; David Brown 2003). The *oricha* gods exist in and through their physical indexes. They manifest as the person whose body and destiny become entwined with the god's 'making' on a human plane and as the material vessels and paraphernalia 'made', which become known as the *santo.* Far more complex forms of plasticity are evident in Palo Monte, an umbrella term for magical practices associated with Bantu-speaking slaves in Cuba (Figarola 2006; Ochoa 2010), whose officiants deal directly with the realm of the 'tricky' dead. Paleros forge power through the construction of a cauldron-like container, called a Nganga, in which are placed all manner of substances, from sticks, metals, stones, gun powder, and animal parts to the bones of a human being whose spirit works with the expert in achieving his magical ends, be it healing or provoking mishap. Palo witchcraft is feared for its effectiveness, not just because it is premised on work with the 'materialized' and morally pliable dead, but because these entities achieve their ends by means of deceit and metamorphosis. Paleros and *espiritistas* see a fluid transit between their spheres of practice, but whereas Palo has the human expert as the ultimate orchestrator of the products of his craft, in Espiritismo the notion of a spirit's 'presentation' (*presentación*) cuts through an ontology of self that has both spirits and persons as each other's makers.

Espiritismo is practiced by individuals with the ability to see, hear, feel, or incorporate spirits of the dead. Unlike the cults mentioned above, popular forms of Espiritismo are characteristically informal, requiring no initiation rites or consecrations for officiation. They are practiced organically as the need arises in people's homes by individuals who have nurtured their sensitivities. While more formalized congregations of spiritists gather in Havana in a handful of centers dedicated to the philosophical and moral teachings of Allan Kardec, the founder of European Spiritism, the vast majority of active mediums require little in order to work, with the exception of a small altar on which water-filled vessels, candles, and spirit representations are usually placed. These serve as the cornerstone for spirit evocations during collective rites called 'spiritual masses' (*misas espirituales*), in which the dead are summoned in prayer and song to 'come down' (*bajan*). While Espiritismo honors its nineteenth-century Kardecist roots through concepts of spiritual evolution, metempsychosis, and karma, in a contemporary setting it is largely inseparable in its basic ontological assumptions, and by virtue of its quotidian function, from the Afro-Cuban ritual universe in which *espiritistas* circulate (see Palmié 2002: 288). Practitioners of Santería and Palo request the dead's permission and guidance before any rite is effectuated, and this is achieved through *misas espirituales* and consultations. The dead, people say, always 'come first' (*iku lobi ocha*). But underlying such imperatives is the idea that spirits do not simply appear to people or accompany them; rather, they 'structure' them. In this section, I aim to show that Cuban spirits manifest a logic of 'enfoldment', whereby they bring a 'withoutness'—a capacity to stand as other to persons— to bear on a 'withinness', their necessary implication in the constitution and ontogeny of selves. The concept of *desdoble* (unfolding) captures the important dynamic between the manifestation of often unknown 'virtualities' on the part of spirits, on the one hand, and the effects of (and on) human knowledge, action, and self-structure, on the other.

In Cuba, a particular category of spirits is believed to 'come with' the person, and people refer to these entities in possessive phraseology, for instance, as '*my* spirits'. In the widely diffused mediumship cult of Espiritismo Cruzado (Millet 1996), this collective is known as one's *cordón espiritual* (lit., spiritual cord), or simply one's *muertos*—that is, disincarnates of varied ethnic, cultural, intellectual, and religious backgrounds whose mission is to protect and guide. The close proximity of other categories of *muertos*, such as deceased family members or spirits sent by witchcraft, is regarded as undesirable, and great efforts are made to 'elevate' or dispatch them from the material and human anchorages at which they clutch. The entities of one's *cordón* are thus conscientiously cultivated since, paradoxically, they are both present and absent. Conceived to exist as potential presences (or qualities) starting at birth, these spirits must be worked on and strengthened into existence as effective beings through acknowledgment, communion, and exchange. From an initial state of 'dormancy' or 'passivity', *muertos* become forceful, creative influences in the material or social lives of their protectees, as well as in their deeper psychological and emotional attitudes. Not to 'develop' one's *muertos,* as people say, is tantamount to allowing one's potentialities to lie permanently in the shadows.

These influences are premised on what is generally understood as the processual, emergent, and circumstantial character of a person's relationship with his or her protectors. This translates into two main implications. First, it implies shifts in the intensity of a given spirit's presence at any one time, which includes the possibility of a substitution of one main spirit for another. "There are spirits that are there for a time with us, let us suppose, playing an important part in the journey we are undergoing, say, the spirit of a Gypsy," says Leonel, a middle-aged *santero* (Santería practitioner) and spirit medium, "and afterward, it's like they're gone. There is a particular affinity at that moment, and then it disappears ... and you may have information of a new entity, say, an African with whom you may start to work. It's like the Gypsy moves into a secondary plane, like I have no more need to work with what it symbolizes." Leonel has experienced these transitions several times in his religious career. More recently, his main African spirit has allowed an Arab astronomer entity to gain salience in his *cordón* in order to better guide his study and exercise of astrology. Second, the processual nature of a *cordón espiritual* results in transformations in the appearance of existing spirits. Spirit mediums implicitly refer to this mutability when they say that "the spirit is letting me see it" in ways that can vary substantially. Spirits may 'appear' to mediums' eyes in distinct guises, evoking specific points in the life whose appearance they now manifest, for example, younger or older versions of themselves.

"The spirit can change," said Olga, an experienced middle-aged medium with whom I worked extensively, "depending on the things that you are developing in your life at the moment. There can be a change in physiognomy, of aesthetics, a transformation, so that the spirit can help you with the phase you are going through." According to Eduardo, Olga's husband, material things, such as offerings of honey, fruit, flowers, rum, perfume, and even tools or weapons, which are placed at the foot of spirit representations, enable these changes by affording spirits certain powers of intervention. But the notion that these transformations are often the consequence of a person's growing internal landscape and imaginary is reinforced by the belief that people bring about these changes as a result of their mere transit or movement through the world. For example, Eduardo observed that one of my 'nun spirits', described by him as a Carmelite, was now manifesting an Orthodox Christian appearance, which he explained by the fact that I had traveled through Eastern Europe earlier that year.

One of the most common assumptions *espiritistas* articulate is that a critical condition of a spirit's potential for multiplicity is the person herself, but ahead of and often despite herself. Throughout my exposure to *espiritistas* and their domains of knowledge retrieval in the years following my doctoral fieldwork, I observed how descriptions of my spirits mutated, accompanying the flow not simply of my life developments as they occurred, but of their perceived gaps and underlying needs.[1] "Your spirits all look different this time," Olga remarked in 2009. "Your Gypsy doesn't come with castanets and cards anymore [as she had in 2006]. She's more like an Arab *gitana*." My Iberian Gypsy spirit now wore a transparent tunic over loose trousers, a set of necklaces, and a chain around her head with gold coins. Her skin was light and rosy this time, rather than the dark-olive complexion of before. "She reflects a certain joy, clarity," Olga continued, "and she's bringing you much light for all things love-related," which Olga regularly remarked I should be working on harder at that time. However, in 2011 my Gypsy spirit had again changed. "There was a transformation here once more," Olga said in my first *misa espiritual* of the fieldwork season. "Your Gypsy comes as a sort of emissary of Ochún [Santería's goddess of love and fertility], dressed in vibrant yellow and with a turban on her head. It's like she comes with a *paso de santo*," by which Olga meant that the Gypsy was now signaling an alliance with the forces of Santería, in which I would indeed receive some minor initiations this time. "She brings with her a clay pot in which are five small river stones, and she places them in front of you, cleansing you with the river water," Olga continued. In other words, this spirit was encouraging and reflecting my future involvement in Santería. To consolidate the positive changes that the Gypsy was willing to bring to me, the mediums said, I should dress her doll spirit representation in yellow, procure five small stones from the river to offer to her, and proceed with my initiations. Along with the Gypsy, some of my other spirits had undergone metamorphoses. For example, my much-described Middle Eastern–Jewish bureaucrat spirit now came as a nineteenth-century European intellectual, complete with dark suit, top hat, moustache, and sideburns. While in both versions the spirit carried a small suitcase and was a man of 'letters and papers', the more recent one seemed to relate directly to my then book-writing phase, according to Eduardo and Olga, thereby manifesting and empowering my literary drive.

While the question of which came first—the spirit or my writing activities—seems moot here, *espiritista* circles provide no shortage of examples showing how spirits propel, rather than simply follow, human endeavors. This is especially the case in a determination of ritual allegiances. Both in Santería and Palo Monte, an individual should shun initiation if he or she does not have a *muerto* who knows about such things. Moreover, very often it is this *muerto* who induces illness, alters sensory experiences and dreams, or simply appears to other mediums, requiring that initiatory steps be taken. There are interesting parallels here with Olga Ulturgasheva's analysis (this volume) of the Siberian concept of *djuluchen*—a spirit that travels ahead. For the Eveny youngsters she works with, a part of the person travels to the future (a forerunner) and the rest of her must catch up, as if the latter were a 'shadow reality' of a potential yet to be fulfilled.

However, in Espiritismo this picture is complicated by the idea that *muertos* are embroiled in individual moral development steps, called *evoluciones*, and that their appearances and requirements alter according to these 'evolutions', to which the living must also respond. While a protective *muerto*'s trajectory of moral ascension is generally gauged by its relationship to the person, there are instances of opacity in mediums' accounts of spirit transformations. Ivan, a Palero and *espiritista* in his fifies, says that he has seen one of his daughter's husband's spirits unfold into three distinct psychological phases or states, and that when one of these 'comes down' (*baja*), so do its characteristics, be they politeness or uncouthness. As Ivan explained: "It's like the spirit has a multiple personality disorder. In one of these personalities, the spirit has a beautiful voice, and he even sings for us. However, in the other phase he's sad, depressed, and cries all the time. It's very curious. How can we define this, say it's the same entity, if it comes in fragments?" Other, more radical shifts include those when the spirit betrays two or more discrepant 'skins' by unfolding into a different spirit altogether. For instance, it is not uncommon for the same entity to unfold into two or three distinct identities—a Gypsy who turns into a nun who turns into a native Indian—which mediums theorize as the past lives of a single spirit. Moral shifts are thought possible within this frame. One Palero I spoke to said that he had seen the spirit of a monk unfold into a Nganga *muerto*, although the mechanisms underlying this dramatic shift remained ineffable to him at the time, given the intuitive gap between these categories of entities.

An important part of this 'ineffability' derives from understanding that spirits do not simply manifest aspects of diverse and temporally distributed forms of personhood: through such ethnic, religious, or cultural transformations, they are able to embody and transmit cosmic forces or powers, known in Cuba as *corrientes*. These *corrientes* are usually linked to Santería's *oricha* gods and their respective life domains. Thus, the fact that mediums apprehended my Gypsy spirit as a version of Ochún, the love deity, would not prevent the same entity or another from appearing, for example, as old, crippled, and followed by dogs (the symbolism associated with the Cuban Yoruba deity of illness, Babalú-Ayé) if the message were explicitly about my own health. Most of the entities making their entry in *misas espirituales* or other spaces of mediumistic acknowledgment come 'crossed' (*cruzado*), that is, bearing signs that create connections to broader life circumstances and cycles, generally articulated through Santería's imaginary. *Oricha* gods, in turn, associate with Catholic saints, which encourages further articulations. Finally, spirits express an openended transformational logic through their implicit relation to all other entities who 'vibrate' in similar groupings or categories, called *comisiones*. Countless of these *comisiones* exist, from the medical to the African, giving rise to multiple and different types, each with its own domain of expertise. The spirits' seemingly limitless capacity for crossing thresholds of cosmic influence and alliance suggests that while spirit appearances are knowable through their relation to a person's life circumstances, including speculative future ones, selfhood is ultimately subject to the spirits' unknowable potential for dynamic transformation. Linked to this is the notion that no one can comprehend the full scope or composition of a *cordón espiritual*. *Desdobles* (unfoldings) of *corriente* or another identity further contribute to the ineffability of a person's selfhood, influencing reflexive interactions with the world, and are key to the transformational logic expressed in Espiritismo and further afield as well.[2]

In their ethnography of a Santiago-based Afro-Cuban religious practitioner, Garoutte and Wambaugh (2007: 140) argue that developing as a *religioso* (someone who has faith in or is initiated into Afro-Cuban religions) implies a type of "unwrapping of self," following the accumulation of layers of initiations and rites over time. However, the evidence from Espiritismo suggests that this 'self' does not pre-exist the spirits that are made visible and experiential through it. 'Making' spirits is a cosmogonic act that brings forth tangible entities via their materialization in bodies, things, and persons. *Espiritistas* use mimesis and representation to achieve these acts, which, far from theatrical, underscore the profound effects of performance, not just in the "creation of presence" (Schieffelin 1985: 708), but in the ongoing construction of understandings and scopes of self. The logic of this re-creative aesthetic is underpinned by the notion that material things have the power to consolidate the potential of a given spiritual constitution, such as when a doll that represents a Gypsy spirit helps brings forth the spirit. This alters conditions for the manifestation of further potentials: the strengthened presence of the spirit encourages the expression of some Gypsy-related tendency in the person. This mutuality, propelled by material engagement with spirits, is not dissimilar to what Kathleen Richardson (this volume) describes in the context of robotics, whereby robots and roboticists structure one another, affectively and otherwise, through forms of technological animism.

We are reminded here of Kapferer's (2005: 131) evocative argument that Singhalese exorcistic rites work precisely because there is no reality that is not at once illusory, "that is, constituted and sensible through the operation of the human perceptual faculties and rooted in the process of human symbolic construction." Aesthetic approaches are efficient because they reconstruct alternative realities, Kapferer suggests, thereby reorienting the victim to a legitimate, healthy perspective. This is often true for both healers and healed, as Edith Turner (this volume) suggests in relation to her experience of the aesthetics of healing an interlocutor. The cultivation of a sympathetic sensitivity in her fingers leads Turner to a reflexive healing consciousness that emerges in the act. A similar reflexive strategy of re-creating the cosmos obtains during rituals among *espiritista* mediums, who, for example, mimic the spirits' identities and characteristics through songs, material artifacts, and bodily postures that evoke the *muertos'* response and thus instantiate their proximity and presence. We could say that *espiritista* ritual evocations exemplify Carlo Severi's (2002: 27) cogent argument that a "reflexive stance ... is not always *exterior* to ... the performance" but "can become a constitutive part of ritual itself," situated within it as a condition for the narration and possession of emergent realities. This reflexivity is not engendered by the linguistic devices of the chanters; rather, it is a fundamental property of the spirit beings who choose to instantiate themselves through it, precisely because, in trickster fashion, they simultaneously do and do not identify with the mediums' miming of them during the ritual. The participative dimensions of human consciousness are thus as ontologically vital for the *muertos'* existence as they are for those who call on them. *Desdobles* are quintessential examples of "self-propelling difference" (Handelman 2004: 13) that reveal the spirit-person complex as unbounded in its potential to generate new knowledge structures and to self-organize and self-integrate in light of them.

If in Cuba spirits provoke an ontological dialogue with persons in order to achieve their production as components of those persons, which is predicated on the spirits' capacity for mutation and multiplicity, in Brazil spirits harness a fluid transit of identities that reveals the boundaries of human culture, memory, and representation. At stake in both cases, it seems, is not just the negotiation of states of transition and ontological ambiguity in a given cosmos, but the nature of its animation devices and their limitations.

Exus and the Universe of Names in Umbanda

Umbandist mediums can assert apparently contradictory notions. On the one hand, the spirits of the indigenous Indians (Caboclos), the Old Black slaves (Pretos Velhos), the children (Crianças), the entities known as the 'people of the street' (*o povo da rua*)—that is, lustful female Pombas Giras, Gypsies, sailors and cowboys, prostitutes and pimps, con men and hustlers—and other spirits who come under the cosmic grouping of the Yoruba deity Exu (aka Exus) are all widely considered to form the metaphysical cornerstones of Umbanda's cosmology. Organized in a military-like structure, implying lines and sub-lines, each led by superior spirits, this assortment of entities is constitutive of Umbanda's identity as prototypically 'Brazilian' amid an ecology of other seemingly more exclusivist religious traditions, such as Candomblé Keto or Kardecist Spiritism. On the other hand, this spiritual architecture betrays an indeterminacy captured well in statements such as the following one pronounced by the leader of Rio de Janeiro's Primado de Umbanda (one of the city's main Umbanda associations): "We all know that the Preto Velho (the Old Black slave) need not be either black or old, or even a slave." In a nod to this notion, a medium I sat with once during an Umbanda ceremony turned to me suddenly and observed that he saw, walking in through the door at that moment, "the spirit of a middle-aged white man, who gradually doubled over as he approached the altar and transformed into the bent, tired body of an old black slave."

The flagrant arbitrariness of identities in such examples was noticeable in the discourse of other-than-human entities. For instance, in an interview I conducted one evening with a charismatic Exu, the limitations of human-made categories emerged as a frank irritation to the spirit world. "Everyone nowadays wants an Exu Caveira. Nobody wants one of the less well-known ones, like Exu Magê. They've just forgotten him," he said indignantly, referring to a sub-category of Exu entities that come under more 'evolved' *falanges* (phalanxes).[3] According to this spirit, many an Exu has been constrained by Umbanda's dwindling repertoire of names and is forced to manifest under the better-known spirit categories. Yet this spirit was equally keen on disarming any preconception that Exu is always Exu. Indeed, as another Exu remarked in the same ritual session: "I am an Exu, but as I've told you, I come as Caboclo, Preto Velho, Criança. Not many are the spirits, but many are the forms."

Umbanda was looked on by early scholars of Afro-Brazilian religion as Brazil's first 'national' religion (Bastide 1971), a discourse perpetuated by contemporary practitioners. Under this light, its complex armies of entities were described as a stage for Brazil itself (Prandi 1991), or as a 'microcosm' for Brazilian society, whose genesis implied the co-opting of Candomblé's *orixá* gods and European Spiritism's notions of evolutionary stratification and morality. On this basis, Umbanda purportedly encompassed the manifold images of Brazilian society and its historical dramas, articulating stereotypical, often racialized narratives of its denizens while making room for novel social personas. As Diana Brown and Mario Bick (1987: 74) argue, understanding the complexities of modern Umbanda requires "an examination of Brazilian class formation and interaction, race and racial identities, national political institutions and ideologies, as well as national and international re-evaluations of the image of Africa and its people." Umbanda is certainly a fertile ground for an analysis guided by nation, class, and race-driven concerns. Its practitioners routinely evoke or disavow aspects of national consciousness to suit their positional and ideological interests, giving rise to discursive subcategories of Umbanda known widely as 'pure' or 'white' or 'orthodox Umbanda', on the one hand, and *macumba* (a term associated with sorcery by white elites) and *bruxeria* (witchcraft), on the other. However, my contention is that cosmology should not be regarded as just a refraction of wider, more tangible processes; it should be understood at least partly in its own terms as a producer of certain worlds. The point here is to acknowledge how Umbanda generates ontological possibilities that afford their own disentanglement from modes of social and racial determinism. My data on selected temples in Rio de Janeiro reveal the significance of local theorizations on a cosmology in permanent and reflexive relation to itself and to the practitioners who think and live through it. Nowhere is this more evident than among the spirits known as Exus.

The hundreds of entities known under the category of Exus in Umbanda reveal themselves in ritual settings as trickster types. While contemporary neo-Pentecostal movements look on Exus as refractions of the Devil, these spirits are better thought of as masters of possibilities. They are seduced by devoted mediums and believers into providing advice and effective paths for problem resolution, reserving merciless punishment for those on the receiving end of their wrath. As usurpers of normative ideals, such as moral stature, socially acceptable parameters of sexuality and desire, and ethical exchange, Exus—particularly Pombas Giras and other street-type spirits—threaten the fabric of archetypal Brazilian social roles maintained by the greater community (cf. Hayes 2011). But this transgressiveness is not only of a moral sort. Exus reveal a concern for the creative potential of ontological thresholds. As the quintessential form-givers of Umbanda's ontology, they disclose the mutability of spirits, who can always be other than what they appear, as well as the contingency of these appearances on their believers' languages of evocation and materialization.

Lalu and Midnight are Exus at Pai César's temple in an area of Rio called Jacarepaguá. When they descend in ritual ceremonies amid cackling laughter and song, their bodies are cloaked in long velvet capes with insignia specific to them, one of which is a pitchfork. They enjoy smoking cigars, guzzling bottles of whiskey offered by visitors or the house's 'children', and dancing to the beat of drums. But while they remain in the body of César, the temple's young founder and leader, Lalu and Midnight are prone to lengthy and public philosophical speeches in which key, widespread assumptions are deliberately inverted. These provocative monologues frequently take issue with the bad reputation of Exus in Brazilian society. On one occasion, Lalu said the following to the temple's gathering: "People think we're inferior spirits, that we need to evolve, and that this is why we come to work with the mediums. They're wrong! It's the opposite! The ones who most need light are the mediums! Why is it that we sometimes assume the form of the Devil? The cape, the skull, the fire? The form we take is this one because if you work down in the depths of the dark shadows dressed like an angel, you'll be eaten alive! … These are spirits who don't know forgiveness or mercy or charity, only destruction. That's where we work. So much so that people sometimes mistake us for that evil. People think we're the Devil, but we fight against him!" To fight evil, Lalu suggests, you must dress as—and even be—evil. This mimesis-as-effectiveness argument went to the core of the temple's subversion of Exu renditions and was presented as a necessary ethical recourse to ontological transformation. "There are a lot more Exus at your temples than you think," Midnight sarcastically declared to a group of Umbanda leaders from other filiations. "There are many Exus whom you think are Caboclos," he chuckled, targeting a common conception of the Caboclo as spiritually superior to Exu. In his explanations before the start of a ceremony that I attended, Pai César touched upon these points: "Many spirits have unfortunately used the name of Exu. They've spread meanness, promiscuity, mischief, and all that is negative. But the truth is that these belong only to us, not them."

Instances of metamorphosis are arguably central to Umbanda's founding narratives. In his ethnography of the Umbanda movement in São Paulo, Lísias Nogueira Negrão (1996) notes that while mythical stories regarding the biographies of *entidades* (spirit entities) are few, particularly when compared to those of Candomblé's *orixás,* he recorded a series of versions relating to the Caboclo that impart Umbanda's Kardecist teleological concerns with reincarnation. In one such account, the Caboclos are identified as former priests, who, on first contact with the Indians, slowly 'turned' into Caboclos, while nevertheless retaining their knowledge and wisdom. "They began to lose their clothes, lose their clothes, until one day they began to be similar to the Indians," says the Umbandist to Negrão (ibid.: 210).[4] For Negrão, these stories evoke a critique of scientific rationalism and its exclusive realms of knowledge, while expressing the ambiguous relationship with the Catholic Church that is formative of Umbanda's ideology (ibid.: 211). But the spirits at the genesis of Umbanda are infused not just with these transformational aspects, premised on the succession of lives and notions of evolution, but with forms of knowledge or being that transcend their mundane manifestations and display a sense of playfulness. For instance, Emerson Giumbelli (2010: 114) notes that Leal de Souza, one of Umbanda's first documenters and authors, used the phrase "high knowledge disguised as mediocrity" to characterize Umbanda's entities. According to Giumbelli, Souza proposed that the entities use African *cabildo* languages and those of Brazilian tribes between themselves, while using common language (albeit distorted) with people. This is strategic, Giumbelli suggests, and is meant to give the impression that they are somehow savage or inferior to people. Souza is quoted in Giumbelli in a passage that I translate from the Portuguese: "These space laborers [i.e., spirit entities] wish to be considered more backward, so that the individuals who are reputed to be superior, when obliged to seek recourse to these humble spirits, perceive and understand their own inferiority" (ibid.).

Elsewhere, in a chapter that traces the multiple lives of the Caboclo das Sete Encruzilhadas (considered to be the entity at the heart of Umbanda's creation), Giumbelli (2013: 188) further proposes that Leal de Souza posits the "inferiority" of Caboclos and Pretos Velhos as necessary. In Souza's reading, Giumbelli says, entities with greater affinity for their enemies could confer greater force and efficacy to their combat (ibid.). This is an interesting point that brings an indigenous perspective to bear on cosmological mimesis, masking, or even deceit in the pursuit of successful intervention, as Lalu's speech above indicates. It suggests that we should take a closer look at what an 'entity' is in Umbanda.

For Pai César, his medium wife Patricia, and members of their religious family, *entidades* of Umbanda's *falanges* are complex beings generally exempt from the vicissitudes of human reincarnation and material cycles. While joining the *falanges* of an Umbanda temple requires permission from superior forces, César believes that the 'vibrations' behind these entities are worldly: "They have them in China, India, and in other places under different names." Exu Midnight confirms this hypothesis: "Many of the spirits of Umbanda appear according to the spiritual forms [given by each religious tradition]. They may have never, however, stepped on earth. And, contrary to their human appearances, they may have never lived as human beings at all. There are even some that come from different galaxies to offer their services in the body of the medium. And they use names like Pena Verde, Pena Branca, Estrela Dourada, Arcoíris, Caboclo Tamandaré, Exu Marabô, and so forth. And there are others who are normal people. They are spirits of beings who were here before."

Midnight's observation on the nature of spiritual beings behind Umbanda's fixed sets of names underscores one major difference between Candomblé and Umbanda. While the former receives deities or gods—the forceful, majestic, but silent *orixás*—the latter is thought to incorporate personalized beings. Technically, in Umbanda, 'entity' refers neither to the spirit of a dead person nor to a divinity, such as an *orixá*, but lies somewhere in between. The 'entity' is the point at which differentiation is seen to occur. While referring to two well-known Preto Velho spirits, Rogério, an Umbanda medium, once told me: "There are many Pais Joaquims. Tias Marias are plentiful … This doesn't mean that the Tia Maria that is working on that medium over there is the same one that works right here in this temple. The name is similar, but it's just a label, created by the spirit or by the formalization of the work done in Umbanda proper." According to Rogério, an entity can subdivide infinitely because entities are not individual beings but 'vibrations' that agglutinate themselves to the medium's body during trances. Their essence, never contained, is multiple, fluid, and, importantly, born from the subjective. Luis Fernando, a temple leader in the neighborhood of Piedade, Rio, compares the relationship between an entity's cosmic 'vibration' and its local, personal instantiation to how an energy transformer is distributed to multiple outposts. "The Caboclo Sete Estrelas that comes on myself is not the same one that comes on that medium's head over there, irrespective of whether the entity's name is the same," Luis Fernando explains. "It is only *our* reference for it. We always need one, like you and I need names. I cannot just stand in front of him and say, 'Hey, you over there.'" Accordingly, when mediums begin to work with their *entidades*, the temple leader gradually hones this affinity into a functioning unity.

However, for other mediums, the exact nature and reverberation of larger entities remains enigmatic. Mãe Lenita, the ritual and spiritual assistant to a well-known Umbanda medium in Brazil, Jair de Ogum, says of his main entity in the Candomblé 'line', with whom both have worked for over 30 years: "Sometimes we ask him [Ogum Yara]: 'Who are you?' And he answers me: 'I am you. I am what you think I am.' He looks in my eyes, and he says 'I am what you think I am.' And he doesn't change his mind. If you think he's good, he is good. He says that he is a star, he is a sun, he is a moon, he is a pregnant woman, he is an old man. I am a tear, I am a child, I am a smile." These forms of ontological reflection—doubt, even—speak to what Katherine Swancutt and Mireille Mazard identify in the introduction to this book as an increasing tendency among native thinkers toward what they term 'hyper-reflexivity', resulting in ideas that are sometimes articulated or reinvented with the tools and concepts of anthropology itself. Building on this, I argue that Umbanda has wielded its modes of 'deep reflexivity' since its inception, enabled by concepts of a largely plastic, metamorphic cosmos that is responsive to its environment.

For instance, the concept of ineffability has been taken up by Mattijs van de Port (2005) in his analysis of Candomblé ceremonies in Bahia. He suggests that possession trance is often as "mysterious a phenomenon for the Candomblé community as it is for anthropologists" (ibid.: 152). In a world where authenticity is sought arduously, Candomblé possession is attractive precisely "because it seems to escape all attempts at signification," and its realities are beyond conventional knowledge, thus creating a locus for the "*really real*" (ibid.: 153). Van de Port thus views possession "first and foremost as the production of the ineffable in a symbolic universe in which meanings are adrift and truth regimes are in disarray" (ibid.). At first sight, Umbandists might also be understood as players in the production of ineffability. The notion that certain 'truths' are beyond a medium's grasp is so taken for granted among practitioners—even among intellectuals—that we might be tempted to see a process of 'authentication by mystification' occurring in Umbanda. But this would be simplistic. Umbandistas deal with a sense of knowledge that is ineffable—or better, infinite—and yet immanently ordinary and tangible. In other words, in Umbanda ineffability is not the opposite of common or conventional knowledge, but its node of access or origin. Possession is, then, not beyond the comprehension of practitioners, because in Umbanda trance is experienced more often as a conjunction of agencies than as an annihilation of consciousness. Practitioners demonstrate that incorporation is often a juggling act constituted through parallel awareness of the worlds born from both infinite potential—as 'vibration'—and instantiation, the epitome of which is name, identity, and form. This is, too, what Exus so poignantly reveal in their discourses.

Stefania Capone (2010: 61) argues that we should replace a rigid conceptualization of the Afro-Brazilian religious sphere with one that stresses a continuum, "where the potential combinations are constantly renegotiated" and orthodoxy is fabricated *a posteriori*. This is certainly true for a heterogeneous Umbanda. But Umbandists go further, as do their spirits, in suggesting that their religion's ontological structure may comprise a multitude of spiritual 'bodies' or 'personas' (in the Maussian sense), rather than pre-formed substances. Behind these personas resides something more complex, unpredictable, shapeshifting—and this may account for Umbanda's appeal, efficacy, and perceived dangers. The absence of knowledge, as Lars Højer (2009: 585) argues in his study of religious 'loss' in post-socialist Mongolia, is often more powerful than its presence: "the more unknown and residual the spirit powers, the stronger, the more compelling, and the more unpredictable they become."

Conclusion

The presence and persistence of inherently transgressive entities such as tricksters remind us that what is often at stake in otherwise stable cultural universes are features of the cosmos that exhibit unpredictable shifts of categories, forms, and functions, thus defying ontological absolutes. We should, therefore, place the idea that cosmological order is a precondition of religious experience under scrutiny. This can be done by paying closer attention to the transformational logics underscoring its specific mutations and fluidities and their clearly social consequences. It is not surprising that in Brazil scholars have sought to intertwine spirit identities with national themes of racism, domination, resistance, and suffering. But the spaces created for social change and critique through Brazilian trickster spirits should arguably be read as fragments of broader, often overlooked processes of ambiguity and shapeshifting in Afro-Brazilian religious ethos, which allow for pervasive forms of creativity and renewal in Umbanda's spirit pantheons. In Cuba, the Trickster appears not just in Santería as the deity Elegguá, who must be placated before work with any of the other *oricha* gods becomes possible. The Trickster also appears as Palo Monte's 'tricky dead' and, in a more subtle way, manifests itself in Espiritismo's concepts of the person, whose extensions, the *muertos*, appear alternately as self and not-self, furnishing modes of self-construction and understanding that transcend their forms.

In both contexts, these processes point to reflexive trickster components of religious experience and to cosmologies that recreate themselves and their actors through their apparent autonomy from these same human actors, thus challenging mediums in their structuration efforts. Spirits, in turn, present themselves as both in and out of spaces of description and experience, oscillating between domains of knowledge and ineffability. What I have been calling the trickster aspects of Espiritismo and Umbanda brings into consideration gray areas of classification, not only in the lives of those we study and the constitution of the spirit worlds they commune with or embody, but arguably also within the armament of our own research assumptions. Cultural categories, as Swancutt and Mazard point out in their introduction, are active participants and collaborators in the processes of world making experienced by our interlocutors. For both *espiritistas* and Umbandists, it is human culture in the broader sense that is at stake, at the individual and national level. Hyper-reflexivity is thus taken to the limit by Exus in Umbanda, for whom human categories are a mere 'garment' with which to effectively work. Human categories in Umbanda therefore transcend both anthropological and native categories. But Exus do more than represent 'trickster-dom': they point to the broader fluidity of a cosmos that seems to self-generate, unfolding and enfolding in directions not immediately envisaged by mediums. Due its potential for connections, refractions, and multiplications, the Umbanda cosmos is then much like Cuba's *cordón espiritual*.

My ethnography of Cuba and Brazil points to a concern with the fabric of appearances, categories, and their limits, including those of our ethnographic representations. Spirit cosmologies in these contexts reveal a plain world where nothing is missing, where everything is somehow in excess and in the process of 'becoming' itself, as Marcio Goldman (2007) maintains for Candomblé. But what is evident to me is that, in Espiritismo and Umbanda, this cosmogony occurs with the shifting complicity of a universe of entities that foregrounds both the ontologically participative nature and the limitations of human classification. In Espiritismo, the 'animate' is mutually constituted and constituting, but never still. In Umbanda, the spirits allow us to glimpse the mechanics of this animation as a cultural product, in which they perceive themselves to be enmeshed, even as they gain from it the distance and scope for metamorphosis.

Acknowledgments

I am grateful to my funding institution in Portugal, the Fundação para a Ciência e Tecnologia, for enabling the postdoctoral fieldwork on which the data used in the chapter were collected, as well as to my research center during this time, Centro em Rede de Investigação em Antropologia (CRIA). Special thanks go to my Cuban and Brazilian interlocutors and friends, especially Eduardo and Olga (Cuba) and César, Patricia, and Mãe Lenita (Brazil). Finally, I thank Anastasios Panagiotopoulos for reading an early version of this text, the anonymous reviewers for their helpful suggestions, and the editors of this book for their kind invitation to participate.

Diana Espírito Santo received her PhD in 2009 from University College London, writing on concepts of knowledge and personhood in Cuban spirit mediumship practices. Since then she has studied notions of cosmological change in the Afro-Brazilian religion of Umbanda in Brazil. Currently, she is an Assistant Professor in the Anthropology Programme at the Pontifical Catholic University of Chile. She has recently authored *Developing the Dead: Mediumship and Selfhood in Cuban Espiritismo* (2015) and has edited three books, including *The Social Life of Spirits* (2014, with Ruy Blanes).

Notes

1. In this sense, my relationships to my interlocutors—through my spirits—could be considered 'hyper-reflexive' (see the introduction to this book).
2. See, for instance, Mireille Mazard's account (this volume) of how 'soul attributes' and metamorphosis are intrinsic to Nusu persons and spirits in Southwest China.
3. Phalanxes, or *falanges*, are 'lines' of spirits operating under the command of a more evolved entity. For example, the phalanx of Pretos Velhos is headed by the West African-derived god Obaluaiê.
4. Unless otherwise indicated, all translations are my own.

References

Bastide, Roger. 1971. *As Religiões Africanas no Brasil*. Vol. 2. Trans. Eloisa Capellato and Olivia Krahenbuhl. São Paulo: Livraria Pioneira Editora.

Boddy, Janice. 1989. *Wombs and Alien Spirits: Women, Men, and the Zar Cult in Northern Sudan*. Madison: University of Wisconsin Press.

Bolívar, Natalia. 1990. *Los Orichas en Cuba*. Havana: Editorial Ciencias Sociales.

Brown, David H. 2003. *Santeria Enthroned: Art, Ritual, and Innovation in an Afro-Cuban Religion*. Chicago: University of Chicago Press.

Brown, Diana DeG., and Mario Bick. 1987. "Religion, Class, and Context: Continuities and Discontinuities in Brazilian Umbanda." *American Ethnologist* 14 (1): 73–93.

Capone, Stefania. 2010. *Searching for Africa in Brazil: Power and Tradition in Candomblé*. Trans. Lucy L. Grant. Durham, NC: Duke University Press.

Combs, Allan, and Mark Holland. 1996. *Synchronicity: Through the Eyes of Science, Myth, and the Trickster*. New York: Marlowe.

Descola, Philippe. 1996. *In the Society of Nature: A Native Ecology in Amazonia*. Trans. Nora Scott. Cambridge: Cambridge University Press.

Figarola, Joel J. 2006. *La Brujería Cubana: El Palo Monte*. Santiago de Cuba: Editorial Oriente.

Garoutte, Claire, and Anneke Wambaugh. 2007. *Crossing the Water: A Photographic Path to the Afro-Cuban Spirit World*. Durham, NC: Duke University Press.

Giumbelli, Emerson. 2010. "Presença na recusa: A Africa dos pioneiros Umbandistas." *Esboços* 17 (23): 107–117.

Giumbelli, Emerson. 2013. "Amerindian and Priest: An Entity in Brazilian Umbanda." In *The Social Life of Spirits*, ed. Ruy Blanes and Diana Espírito Santo, 179–197. Chicago: University of Chicago Press.

Goldman, Marcio. 2007. "How to Learn in an Afro-Brazilian Spirit Possession Religion: Ontology and Multiplicity in Candomblé." In *Learning Religion: Anthropological Approaches*, ed. David Berliner and Ramon Sarró, 103–120. New York: Berghahn Books.

Handelman, Don. 1998. *Models and Mirrors: Towards an Anthropology of Public Events.* New York: Berghahn Books.

Handelman, Don. 2004. "Introduction: Why Ritual in Its Own Right? How So?" *Social Analysis* 48 (2): 1–32.

Hayes, Kelly E. 2011. *Holy Harlots: Femininity, Sexuality, and Black Magic in Brazil.* Berkeley: University of California Press.

Højer, Lars. 2009. "Absent Powers: Magic and Loss in Post-socialist Mongolia." *Journal of the Royal Anthropological Institute* 15 (3): 575–591.

Hyde, Lewis. 1998. *Trickster Makes this World: Mischief, Myth, and Art.* New York: Farrar, Straus and Giroux.

Jung, C. G. 1972. "On the Psychology of the Trickster Figure." Trans. R. F. C. Hull. In Paul Radin, *The Trickster: A Study in American Indian Mythology*, 195–211. New York: Schocken Books.

Kapferer, Bruce. 2004. "Ritual Dynamics and Virtual Practice: Beyond Representation and Meaning." *Social Analysis* 48 (2): 35–54.

Kapferer, Bruce. 2005. "Sorcery and the Beautiful: A Discourse on the Aesthetics of Ritual." In *Aesthetics in Performance: Formations of Symbolic Construction and Experience*, ed. Angela Hobart and Bruce Kapferer, 129–160. New York: Berghahn Books.

Mageo, Jeanette M. 1996. "Spirit Girls and Marines: Possession and Ethnopsychiatry as Historical Discourse in Samoa." *American Ethnologist* 23 (1): 61–82.

Millet, José. 1996. *El Espiritismo: Variantes Cubanas.* Santiago de Cuba: Editorial Oriente.

Negrão, Lísias Nogueira. 1996. *Entre a Cruz e a Encruzilhada: Formação do Campo Umbandista em São Paulo.* São Paulo: Editora da Universidade de São Paulo.

Ochoa, Todd R. 2010. *Society of the Dead: Quita Manaquita and Palo Praise in Cuba.* Berkeley: University of California Press.

Ong, Aihwa. 1987. *Spirits of Resistance and Capitalist Discipline: Factory Women in Malaysia.* New York: State University of New York Press.

Palmié, Stephan. 2002. *Wizards and Scientists: Explorations in Afro-Cuban Modernity and Tradition.* Durham, NC: Duke University Press.

Pedersen, Morten Axel. 2001. "Totemism, Animism and North Asian Indigenous Ontologies." *Journal of the Royal Anthropological Institute* 7 (3): 411–427.

Pedersen, Morten Axel. 2007. "Talismans of Thought: Shamanist Ontologies and Extended Cognition in Northern Mongolia." In *Thinking through Things: Theorising Artefacts Ethnographically*, ed. Amiria Henare, Martin Holbraad, and Sari Wastell, 141–166. London: Routledge.

Praet, Istvan. 2009. "Shamanism and Ritual in South America: An Inquiry into Amerindian Shape-Shifting." *Journal of the Royal Anthropological Institute* 15 (4): 737–754.

Prandi, Reginaldo. 1991. *Os Candomblés de São Paulo: A Velha Magia na Cidade Nova.* São Paulo: Huicitec.

Schieffelin, Edward L. 1985. "Performance and the Cultural Construction of Reality." *American Ethnologist* 12 (4): 707–724.

Severi, Carlo. 2002. "Memory, Reflexivity and Belief: Reflections on the Ritual Use of Language." *Social Anthropology* 10 (1): 23–40.

Stoller, Paul. 1989. *Fusion of the Worlds: An Ethnography of Possession among the Songhay of Niger.* Chicago: University of Chicago Press.

van de Port, Mattijs. 2005. "Circling around the *Really Real*: Spirit Possession Ceremonies and the Search for Authenticity in Bahian Candomblé." *Ethos* 33 (2): 149–179.

Viveiros de Castro, Eduardo. 1998. "Cosmological Deixis and Amerindian Perspectivism." *Journal of the Royal Anthropological Institute* 4 (3): 469–488.

Willerslev, Rane. 2007. *Soul Hunters: Hunting, Animism, and Personhood among the Siberian Yukaghirs.* Berkeley: University of California Press.

Chapter 3

SPIRIT OF THE FUTURE
Movement, Kinetic Distribution, and Personhood among Siberian Eveny

Olga Ulturgasheva

In this chapter, I consider the notions of time, space, and destiny that are interwoven in the constitution of human and animal personhood among Siberian Eveny reindeer herders and hunters. I pay particular attention to the ways in which personhood precipitates a future event through the medium of a narrative about one's own future. Specifically, I explore how the framework of 'becoming' and the transformability of personhood can assist us in understanding the ways that the future is perceived and construed in animist ontologies. I focus on the Eveny concept of *djuluchen*—translated as 'a spirit that travels ahead' or 'forerunner'—among a nomadic group of Eveny reindeer herders and hunters in northeastern Siberia (Ulturgasheva 2012: 43–55, 154–172; see also Ulturgasheva 2014; Ulturgasheva et al. 2015). The concept of *djuluchen* productively illuminates the human potential to foreshadow one's future by sending one's own partible component ahead of oneself into the future along the envisioned life trajectory.

Notes for this chapter begin on page 71.

Djuluchen is an inherent component of human and animal personhood, whose literal translation reads 'a shadow that falls or runs ahead of a person'. It is a nomadic concept signifying the partible component of human personhood (referred to by some locals as one's 'traveling spirit'), which departs ahead of its owner and arrives at the destination prior to the owner's actual appearance. *Djuluchen* stays on hold until the owner arrives later on and 'catches up' with the *djuluchen* part of his or her personhood. 'Catching up' is thus understood as an act whereby the owner reassembles with her or his partible, that is, *djuluchen*.

Djuluchen and its detachable, partible, and kinetic nature may recall the way that Émile Durkheim ([1912] 2001: 48) characterized the human soul and particularly its capacity to leave the body momentarily in the event of temporary loss of consciousness, for example, during fainting fits, apoplexy, catalepsy, ecstasy, or dreams. However, the difference lies in the fact that *djuluchen* travels to or moves into the future destination while its owner is fully conscious, and it is the act of his or her conscious planning or narration of the future trajectory that makes it leave for the destination. Durkheim's discussion of the concept of the human soul is quite relevant for accounting for this difference as he posited that the soul is "a double of a human body which reproduces all its tangible features that serve as its external envelope. At the same time it is distinct in several ways; it is more mobile, since it covers vast distances in an instant. It is more malleable, more plastic, for to leave the body it must pass through the body openings, in particular the nose and mouth. So it is imagined as made of matter in some way, but a finer, more ethereal matter than any that we know empirically. This double is the soul" (ibid.: 49).

Contrary to ethereal characterizations of the soul, the ethnography that I shall present will show that Eveny do not locate *djuluchen* within the domain of ethereal 'soul' (in Eveny *hanjyan*). Rather, they view it as an incorporeal double of the body that is released from the body at the moment when the future event of a person's arrival at a particular destination is conceived. Nor does *djuluchen* fit the Durkheimian duality of spirit and soul, because, according to Durkheim ([1912] 2001: 50), "the soul is attached to a body which it leaves only at rare moments … By contrast, although the spirit generally resides in a particular thing, it can distance itself at will, and man transforms into a spirit only at death when body and soul separate." Hence, the soul acquires the mobility of the spirit only after the body's death. But in Durkheim's analysis, the soul is defined by its attachment to the body, whereas the spirit is defined by its detachment and separation from the body. What, then, distinguishes *djuluchen* from both soul and spirit is that although it is able to extend and depart for the future destination, it remains simultaneously attached, albeit loosely, to the body. *Djuluchen* can thus be characterized as an incorporeal avatar of a body that is distributed along the spatial trajectory toward the point of a person's arrival, while moving the person irreversibly toward his or her destiny and future 'self'.

In drawing from the ethnographic data on *djuluchen*, I argue that the moment of a person's planning, narrating, or reflecting on forthcoming events should not be viewed as a mere act of contemplation on future possibilities. It may also be understood as a form of 'kinetic distribution' and, borrowing from Deleuze (2004: 116–120), as an 'actualization in progress'. This idea can be taken further, since the Eveny person's planning of forthcoming events, which entails envisioning and thereby influencing how her or his own biography will unfold in the future, bears within it the 'hyper-reflexive' potential for charting one's own life course (see Swancutt and Mazard in the introduction to this book).

By deploying Deleuzian vocabulary, which I consider most helpful in capturing the ontological ramifications of *djuluchen*, I aim to illustrate how the realization of the planned action can be animated by the principle of kinetic distribution of personhood. The Deleuzian notion of 'becoming' will be instrumental for considering the actualization of personhood within the framework of partibility, implicated by a subject's capacity for predicting and fulfilling the future event through the act of visualization (Deleuze 1986, 2004). The account will illustrate how the relationship between a subject's intention and a future event reported from the point of view of the future uncovers an ontological connection between prediction and fulfillment.

The Eveny, or Lamuts, are one of the Tungus-speaking groups in the north of Russia. A majority of Eveny live in northern Siberia and have a double economy, combining reindeer herding and hunting. Whereas in pre-Soviet times Eveny nomadic clans and their families moved along their traditional hunting routes and through vast territories of reindeer pastures, in the early 1930s the new regime launched a coercive process of sedentarization as part of the Soviet project of modernization in the Russian Far North. This included constructing villages and placing Eveny children in boarding schools (Kerttula 2000; Rethmann 2001; Slezkine 1994; Vitebsky 2005). The post-Soviet era of the 1990s brought socio-economic collapse, withdrawal of state support, poverty, and desolation. Despite earlier and later social upheavals, the Eveny economy continues to rely mostly on the subsistence activities of reindeer herding and hunting. These economic activities, which involve human movement alongside herds of reindeer, contribute to and still play a crucial role in Eveny cosmology, rituals, oral traditions, and perceptions of human and animal personhood. The small group of Eveny reindeer herders and hunters discussed here is based in the settlement of Topolinoye in the Verkhoyansk mountains in the Sakha Republic (Yakutia).

In 2003–2004, I conducted 12 months of fieldwork studying young Evenys' ideas of their own futures in Topolinoye, a village with a population of 700. The starting point for my research was the local discourse of 'futurelessness' throughout this region (Vitebsky 2002). The term *vymiraiushiy narod* (a people who are dying out) has become a rhetorical tool used on the political level since the 1990s by representatives of the intelligentsia from northern indigenous minorities. I wished to explore how far this claim had become an integral part of young people's identity, what social resources they were drawing on, and what strategies they might be devising for dealing with this situation. For this purpose, I asked children and adolescents to narrate their future autobiographies. I was not aiming at a literal forecasting or any sort of diagnostics of the participants' life trajectories. My inquiry was intended to elicit young Evenys' representations of their everyday lives through the medium of the story about one's own future life. I was observing how their narratives about imagined futures might reflect their perceptions of themselves and their family histories, as well as how those narratives could unfold the connection between the young people's imagined futures and the community's present and its past. All of this was done in order to look at the ways Eveny children and adolescents reflected on the social and economic instability that has emerged since the collapse of the Soviet Union in the early 1990s and what impact this situation had exerted on their plans for the future.

I returned for a follow-up study six years later. During my first visit in 2003, I was not aware that the participants' stories of their future lives that were shared with me, particularly by my key interlocutors, were part of a much broader process that was beyond simply their perceptions of themselves as products of the recent drastic social changes. When I revisited the research area in 2009–2010, the most surprising thing for me was that those stories about future lives that I had harvested at that earlier time had actually been fulfilled. This made me realize that my adolescent informants were narrating their future lives as if they knew what would happen to them—that they envisioned themselves in the future as if they had already become the persons they were talking about. Figuratively speaking, they were narrating the past disguised as their future. That is to say, the sequence in which young Eveny narrated their own future lives and their fulfillment six years later is directed backwards, contradicting the usual order of memory production in which the knowledge or memory of an event is generated only after the event has happened.

Since I was the one who had devised such an inquiry, I also played a certain role in shaping the children's and adolescents' futures. But I was not to know that I had done so until six years later. Only then did I realize that my research questions inverted the order of things, with the events unfolding as if in a reversed mirror image. In other words, the standard narratological sequence, in which it is the experience (event) that comes first and the later oral or written report of the lived experience (narrative) that follows, moved backward: the future event was narrated in the first instance, and the actual experience happened afterward (cf. Shuman 1986).

If, right after my fieldwork in 2003–2004, I naively perceived adolescents' future autobiographies as only products of their imaginations and individual representations of their social world, six years later I realized that, at the time of their narrations to me, my informants were foreshadowing nearly everything that would happen to them during the next half-dozen years. It was the unpredictability of the adolescents' predictions that puzzled me as a researcher. The act of Eveny adolescents envisioning events in their future and how their actual lives unfolded over the following six years invoked a specific connection between prediction and fulfillment. Processually, I had invited my main informants to narrate their futures at the stage when they were just about to step into their adult lives, and they went on to turn that narrated future into the present.

The Evenys' envisioned autobiographies accidentally marked the shadow reality of *djuluchen* and allowed me to track young narrators' future movements through it. Those narrated futures turned out to be neither youth's random fantasies nor accurate and realistic calculations. Rather, they captured the Eveny phenomenon of the *djuluchen* whereby 'the spirit travels ahead' through its own foreshadowing force, which is discharged from the moment of its narration (as a future instantiation of personhood) toward the moment of its actualization, when the person catches up with this forward-traveling spirit in the future. The framework of *djuluchen*, then, affords a unique and penetrating lens for observing how narrative gives shape to subsequent lived events and transforms the act of narrating the future into a phenomenon of social and cosmological status.

The inverted sequence questions the analytical perception of the narrative as secondary or complementary to some primary reality from which it is alienated (Barthes 1984; Kristeva 1980). The latter dynamic suggests that the narrative has the capacity to set the event horizon that a young narrator cannot escape, as she or he will be drawn into the event horizon, actualizing what has been envisaged and narrated in the story. That is to say, the Eveny future-oriented narrative—which unleashes the narrator's *djuluchen* or traveling spirit—may work as a constitutive element and mediator of the narrator's personhood, thereby fulfilling and actualizing events in the future, as envisioned in a young person's 'future autobiography'.

The unexpected fulfillment of the adolescents' narratives about their future lives would not have been revealed without my long-term engagement in the destinies of my key informants, which has allowed me to uncover more nuanced perceptions of their personhoods. The ethnographic data suggest that the very moments of envisioning served as a catalytic force for the enactment of future life scenarios. Furthermore, these emerged as specific projections of the Eveny notions of destiny and destination, both of which are central features of nomadic ontologies and are ingrained in the concept of *djuluchen*.

Foreshadowing the Future

In order to illustrate this, I shall start with the story of an adolescent Eveny girl, Vera, who was 17 years old when she narrated her future autobiography. Vera comes from a single-parent family and is the eldest of her mother's six daughters. In her narrated vision of the future, Vera expressed her sincere desire to leave her native community for the city. She dreamed about graduating from school, leaving the village, and moving into the city where she would acquire higher education, marry a man from outside of her native community, have one child, send remittances back home, and live with her own family in the city. While explaining her motives for moving out, Vera reflected on the socioeconomic situation in the village, with its high rate of youth unemployment, a general sense of social desolation, poverty, and the breakdown of the local infrastructure. Her plan to leave the village emerged as the most prominent future life trajectory in her narrative, which was spatially oriented toward the city. Six years passed, and I learned that Vera had finished school in 2004 and left for the city the same year. She completed a course in one of the technical schools there and works as a shop assistant on the outskirts of Yakutsk city. She married a man from a different Siberian region, and they have one child. She has never returned to her native community since she left and seems to be happy staying where she is now. As it has emerged, the imagined life she was narrating when she was an adolescent girl turned into her life in the present. It seemed as if she knew what would happen to her during the next six years.

Another adolescent was a 17-year-old Eveny boy, Kirill. He is an orphan whose parents worked in one of the local brigades of reindeer herders. His father died many years ago in a violent fight, and a few years later his mother was found frozen to death not far from the village during an extremely cold winter. After his parents' deaths, Kirill spent most of his childhood in the forest with his uncle and aunt. When he was in the village, he stayed with his aunt, who took care of him. But during school holidays, he usually left for the forest.

When I interviewed him in 2003, he envisioned himself finishing school and leaving for the city to gain a university degree. While speaking about his own future life, he emphasized his willingness to come back to his native community. He spoke of compulsory army service, his possible failure to get further into higher education, and his eventual return to the village. He concluded his story by stating that their herd of reindeer and the forest might pull him back, putting this most eloquently by using the Russian word *magnitiat'* (to magnetize). Kirill introduced this word when talking about his reindeer, telling me that reindeer possess a beauty that has the capacity to magnetize him. In his vision of the future, the magnetism of the reindeer was the dynamic force that would drive his eventual return. The trajectory of his movement would thus culminate in his return to the point of his departure, that is, a reindeer camp.

When I revisited the community in August 2010, I learned that after graduating from school in 2004, Kirill did in fact go to the city to study at a technical college. However, he could not finish his studies as he was obliged to do military service. Having served two years in the Russian army, he came back to his native community and joined his uncle's reindeer herding brigade. It seems his *djuluchen* followed the same cosmological trajectory that he had envisioned six years earlier. The reindeer had indeed drawn him magnetically back to the forest where he now lives and works, taking care of his family's reindeer herd.

A third future autobiography that struck me with its predictive nature belongs to a forest girl, Tonya, who spent most of her childhood next to reindeer in the forest. While speaking about her future, alongside her ambitious aspiration to gain a university degree, she dreamed about returning to her family camp to help her parents take care of her younger siblings and their family reindeer herd. Tonya envisioned herself returning as a veterinary doctor in order to provide medical treatment for reindeer. After school graduation, she had indeed entered a veterinary course in the city, studied there for several years, and returned in the capacity of a veterinary nurse. As in the future that she envisioned in 2003, she is now helping her younger siblings, is employed as a vet in the local reindeer herding *obshina*—a post-Soviet alternative to the Soviet state farm (see Fondahl 1998; Sirina 1999)—and spends most of her time close to reindeer in the forest. As in Kirill's case, it was reindeer that pulled Tonya back to her family camp.

The magnetizing power of Kirill's and Tonya's reindeer is a highly important point: it should be viewed as the opening to their future, the moment of the *djuluchen*'s activation. In this sense, the reindeers' magnetism amplified the kinetic force of the *djuluchen*, anchoring the young people's future movements and events.

Discussing the cinematic image, Deleuze (1986: 20–41) suggests considering human perception not as the reception of a singular representation—the image captured by a camera—but as a 'becoming'. In this sense, becoming is a duration between two differences: 'now' and 'then'. It is an interval within which an entity or particle extends to become a discrete element of an assemblage. In other words, it is an image envisioned in the future that can be understood as an interval of becoming that orients a particular future. Drawing from this proposition, I view Kirill's and Tonya's acts of formulating a wish and envisioning their return to the village as an event of becoming that emerged from emotional interaction with their future destinations associated with reindeer. As I shall describe later, non-humans (wolves and reindeer) can also project forerunners, and the Deleuzian notion of becoming helps to illuminate this phenomenon as well.

The six-year span between my informant's future autobiographical narration and my return to witness their current lives shifted my understanding of this material in a profound way, as over those years the future life scenarios narrated at my request gradually moved into the stage of fulfillment. In the current situation of social despair, poverty, the collapse of local infrastructure, and isolation as a result of the dismantling of transport systems, one would have thought that everything imagined and dreamed by Eveny young people could easily have gone wrong. In this light, it might be argued that the fulfilled fantasies are simply an outcome of the limited choices that narrowed the Eveny adolescents' visions of the future and that it was their very realistic assessments of possible future events that proved accurate. But I would not reduce the relationship between prediction and fulfillment down to the calculative character of the adolescents' expectations of the future, which would make the causal link between the two unjustifiably linear and too straightforward. Rather, I would suggest that the Eveny adolescents' visions of the future struck an extraordinary balance between agency and constraint, that their wishes for the future respected the limitations of the situation yet belonged to the realm of imagination. Although their imagined futures were conceived and worked within a local repertoire of restraints and possibilities, the fulfillment of those futures should not be viewed as automatic or guaranteed.

Tonya and her mother Polina were the first to make a connection to the concept of *djuluchen*. It occurred when Tonya and I were discussing her story in the presence of her mother at their family place in the village. When Tonya saw my sheer surprise at her fulfilled future autobiography, she responded in Eveny: "Bi tachimur *djulittiv*." In literal translation, this would be: "It seems I sent *djuluchen* that time." Her mum nodded, adding: "Adjit, Olga, nongan *djulittin*"

(Yes, indeed, Olga, she sent her *djuluchen* that time). Here I should note that the verb *djulukhendei* and the noun *djuluchen* are both derivatives of the adverb *djulekhki*, which in literal translation means 'forward', 'toward the front', or 'ahead in time and space'. Figuratively speaking, Tonya sent a part of her personhood into the future, ahead of herself, along an imagined life trajectory. After this conversation with Tonya, I had separate conversations with Kirill and Vera. I asked them whether they also *djulititten* (sent their *djuluchen*s). In response, both of them repeated what Tonya had articulated before: "Bi tardadukun *djulettitiv*" (That time I sent *djuluchen*).

Within the shamanic ontological framework, the adolescents' envisaged futures can be understood as certain speech events during which the Eveny person asks spirits to send luck and to assist in vital activities such as hunting or herding. For example, while feeding the first portion of food to the Master of the Spirits or a spirit of a locality, or when sprinkling vodka on the fire as an offering, the Eveny person discreetly utters his or her wish in order to make it come true. By speaking aloud a wish for luck or safety during a trip, the Eveny person makes himself or herself heard by the spirits, and so, in this sense, the pronouncement of this wish is directed both inward and outward. Following the Durkheimian notion of 'sacred speech', which, according to Durkheim ([1912] 2001: 226; italics added), is "another *powerful* way of entering into relations with persons or things," I suggest that these adolescents' relations with their future destinations had already been created in the act of contemplating and verbalizing their plans for the future. In this act, they exhaled breath—*djuluchendei*—and, so to speak, released their *djuluchen*s, which moved the narrated prediction toward its fulfillment.

In his discussion of prayers among Siberian groups, Shirokogoroff ([1935] 1999) posits that prayers and addresses are heard and understood by spirits since they share the same language as human beings. It therefore does not matter to these spirits which language—Tungus, Russian, or Manchu—is used in a prayer. For example, the Tungus spirit *buga*, which is believed to be common to all peoples, "can understand all human beings whichever language they would use in praying" (ibid.: 204). If people are in need of spirits' favor or are menaced by spirits, there is no other way to satisfy them except through prayers and sacrifices, for these spirits cannot be avoided.

Verbalized pronouncements are for the benefit of the self and all members of a social domain. As John Austin (1962: 9–10) puts it in his discussion of acts of uttering and awe-inspiring performatives, what is uttered outward "is a visible sign of … an inward and spiritual act: from which it is but a short step to go on to believe or to assume without realizing that for many purposes the outward utterance is a description … of the occurrence of the inward performance … It is not merely a matter of uttering words! It is an inward and spiritual act!" By contrast, young Evenys' acts of pronouncing their wishes for the future were not only inward, spiritual acts. They also appeared to be outwardly directed illocutionary acts that triggered the movement of their *djuluchen*s. In a sense, these pronouncements activated my informants' personal traveling spirits or *djuluchen*s.

In this respect, I suggest that the Eveny adolescents' speech acts corresponded more to the genre of prayer than to autobiography per se. Figuratively speaking, in a prayer one is plugging one's own wish into the pipelines of the cosmos in order to have the wish make its own way to a moment of fulfillment. Precisely because it is an autobiography of the future, the prayer cannot be simply a narrative account. It has to be the pronouncement of a wish. Hence, instead of viewing the fulfillment of their future autobiographies as a calculation or mere coincidence, I would rather see it as a result of Vera's, Kirill's, and Tonya's pronouncement of prayers in which the forward-looking nature of narration and the act of envisioning events are closely intertwined with the Eveny concept of *djuluchen*. Their narratives from six years earlier had left, so to speak, an imprint (in Eveny *udj*) on the pathway of the destinies to which they were drawn and which they had to follow. The act of speaking aloud their anticipation for the future and, more specifically, of articulating their intention to move toward their future destinations triggered a dormant component of their personhoods and moved the future event to its fulfillment.

Since the adolescents whom I interviewed in 2003–2004 were about to embark on their life journey, their acts of narration can be viewed as sending *djuluchen*s ahead of themselves into the future. That is to say, by fulfilling their future autobiographies, my young Eveny informants had 'caught up' with their *djuluchen*s six years later. Moreover, it is my conversations with young Eveny about their future lives that made them produce the exhaled breath of *djulukhendei* that ultimately set in motion not only their *djuluchen*, but also my *djuluchen*, which made me return to the village for more fieldwork, learn that the children's dreams had come true, and feed that exhaled breath of *djulukhendei* into my contribution to this book on hyper-reflexive relations. In other words, the production of the future narratives served as the 'reflexive feedback loop' (Swancutt and Mazard, this volume) that, to a significant extent, informs this account of Eveny conceptualization of destiny and personhood (see Ulturgasheva 2012).[1]

Djuluchen and the Partibility of Personhood in Eveny Ontology

The issue of divisibility, detachability, and partibility of human persons has been a focus of anthropological research for several decades, most notably for Marilyn Strathern (1988, 1999). In Strathern's view of Melanesian personhood, people live through moments of partibility, whereby they are 'transacted' (e.g., in marriage exchanges between two or more parties) much as gifts are exchanged, so that the exchange, movement, and to some degree even the 'liquidation' of gifts or people make them 'equivalents'. The act of separating—or detaching—people from an existing set of relations creates a distinct, but not complete, temporary identity that Strathern (1988: 185) dubs the "partible person." She writes: "The general enchainment of relations means that persons are multiply constituted. There is no presumption of an innate unity: such an identity is only created to special, transient effect" (ibid.: 165). Hence, in the

Melanesian contexts that Strathern speaks of, a singular person is composed of many different partible elements—their 'roles' as daughters, sisters, wives, or mothers, each of which entails a specific constellation of obligations to yet other kin. Moreover, Strathern argues that Melanesian people continually shift between these different, partible aspects of themselves, each of which is composed of and maintained by numerous relationships to yet other people. The upshot is that the so-called partible person is always in the process of being incorporated into something, as well as adjusting to something as he or she navigates through a wide range of different relationships throughout his or her life course (see also Strathern 2004). Strathern's notion of the partible person, then, offers us highly useful analytical leverage for the Eveny phenomenon of *djuluchen*. Namely, it draws our attention to the poignant moments and different degrees in which Eveny use their narratives and traveling spirits to foreshadow their destinies and compose their future experiences of personhood.

The concept of *djuluchen* also emphasizes the partibility of Eveny personhood, which, however, manifests in an ethnographically specific way. If the Melanesian concept of divisible personhood points to the person as a multiple product of others (clan or kin) who may become temporarily 'partible' from those same clan or kinsmen through acts of gift-giving, then *djuluchen* offers a conceptually different treatment of partible capacity. This is because *djuluchen* is not understood in relation to the extraction of 'parts' of a person, which are analogous to 'gifts'. Instead, it is understood as an inherently unstable component of a person that can become separated from that individual and is even perceived of as a 'shadow' of that person. Thus, *djuluchen* is not 'fully individuated' in Strathern's sense of the partible person, who may in certain contexts stand in for the total person. Instead, *djuluchen* always remains at least loosely attached to the person, even as it can be extended or advanced to a person's destination on an extremely elastic scale.[2] This also goes in parallel with Mireille Mazard's (this volume) study of the Nusu in Southwest China, who, at certain critical moments in life (e.g., emotional crisis) experience their human souls emerging and acting as semi-independent agents, such as a doppelgänger (*yān-hla*) or an envious soul (*yisu*). There are thus some important ethnographic confluences between Eveny personhood and Nusu selfhood, both of which are partible in an elastic (but not fully individuated) sense, while containing latent and multiple aspects of the self that come into being at critical moments when a person is compelled to formulate an intention.

It is important to note that *djuluchen* should be viewed as embedded in the reindeer herding practices of movement in which envisaging one's destination and visualizing or even narrating one's arrival at the end of one's travel amount to near actualization of the envisioned event, as in seasonal migration patterns of reindeer herds. What I find remarkable is that at the point of a person's destination, prior to that person's arrival, people hear and see the arriving person's *djuluchen*. The *djuluchen* is seen as a shadow that imitates the body image of the arriving person and even reproduces the movements and sounds of the person as he or she walks around the camp and unpacks. So without even knowing that a person is traveling toward them, people may recognize that a specific, known person will arrive in their camp sometime soon. The *djuluchen* traveling spirit awaits his or her owner, who reunites with the *djuluchen* upon 'actual' arrival.

Furthermore, I suggest that the partibility of *djuluchen* might be interpreted as the act of spatial extension of one's personhood, as the shadow does not completely separate itself from the person but falls ahead of the person, creating some sort of shadow imprint for the person's future movement trajectory. What implicates or forms this shadow is not so much the movement itself as a person's *intention* to move. The latter perception comes from the practice of people's traveling together with their reindeer across the vast landscape of Siberian boreal forest and tundra. First, herders plan their movement toward a new encampment and then prepare for a trip. They pack all their belongings, fix broken sledges, tie down their luggage (including tents and movable ovens) to the sledges, and arrange a reindeer caravan. After the preparations are complete, the caravan of people and reindeer starts moving. The caravan follows the leading transport reindeer, which is tied to a sledge and sets the path for the rest of the caravan. It is followed by other reindeer, and only then come herders who are driving sledges.

The leading reindeer (in Eveny *baeretchik*) is believed to be the strongest reindeer and to have its own *djuluchen*, so it is the first to send its *djuluchen* forward. As I mentioned above, *djuluchen* derives from the adverb *djulekhki* ('front' or 'forward'), whereas *baeretchik* is a mispronounced word for *peredny/perednik* ('frontal' or 'at the front'). Since *baeretchik* derives from the Russian noun *pered* (front), *djuluchen* and *baeretchik* convey the same meaning—forerunner, a spirit or animal that travels ahead. There is a striking resonance between the *djuluchen* who foreshadow the future and the Cuban *cordón espiritual* (spiritual cord), which encompasses spirit entities believed to protect those who practice the mediumship cult of Espiritismo Cruzado (see Espírito Santo, this volume). Just like the Eveny *djuluchen*, the spiritual cord accompanies the practitioners, acts on their behalf, guides and foreshadows their future, and even serves as an animation device that reveals the potential of human personhood "to generate new knowledge structures and to self-organize and self-integrate in light of them" (Espírito Santo, this volume).

Moreover, it is not only humans and reindeer that have *djuluchens*. Other animals such as wolves are believed to project *djuluchen*. A powerful wolf can project its traveling spirit from a dozen to even several hundred miles ahead of itself. One local Eveny hunter had a rare chance to observe this during a cold winter night when he had to cross a river. He presented the following account:

> It was the full moon. Everything was covered with luminous white snow, and the river ice was glowing like a clean and glittery mirror. When I stopped my caravan to take a short break, I suddenly noticed a wolf, which appeared out of nowhere. It was rapidly moving toward my caravan of reindeer and sledges. The wolf was just about to reach me when I suddenly realized that there was something strange and wrong about it. I noticed that the wolf was not leaving its footprints in deep snow. At a certain point the wolf also seemed not really to be moving forward but

was running on the spot as if it was stuck in some broken machine that repeated itself—like a broken record over and over again. All the wolf's movements were clearly visible as it moved against the shimmering mirror of the frozen river. The wolf was so perfectly perceptible at this moment that anyone could have taken it as a shot from a movie, strangely stuck in the middle of the frozen river. The ghostly wolf suddenly disappeared in the mist, leaving me speechless. But six days after I had seen that wolf on the frozen river, a pack of wolves attacked my small herd of reindeer and tore half of the herd apart. It was a leading wolf's *djuluchen* that had already caught up with my caravan, and I was not quick enough to realize that the pack of wolves would be reaching my reindeer pretty soon.

This hunter's account of a wolf's *djuluchen* shows that it was the wolf's intention to reach a herd of reindeer that served as an expressive point, determining the trajectory and destination of the wolf's movement. His eloquent testimony demonstrates that it was the emotive power of the wolf's intention that projected itself toward the moment of its spatio-temporal realization. The hunter's initial encounter with the ghostly image of the wolf should not be taken simply as a cause, and what happened six days later should not be seen as an effect. I suggest that we should see both events as aspects of one continuum, within which the interior partible element of a wolf's personhood found its expression through the exteriority of *djuluchen*.

Hence, the hunter's description of his perception of a wolf's *djuluchen* represents lucidly the Deleuzian notion of becoming. While discussing the notion of the event, Deleuze (2004: 8) comes up with the suggestion that "[t]he event is coextensive with becoming." I find this particularly relevant for our understanding of the event of the hunter seeing the wolf—which we then learn becomes co-extensive with the wolves' attack that took place six days later. Within this framework of becoming, the leading wolf released its incorporeal double (*djuluchen*) in order to catch up with it six days later. A partible aspect of the wolf extended itself to become an element in the assemblage that was the future wolf.

Conceptually, the wolf's *djuluchen* originates from the same rubric of animal doubles as the concept of a guardian reindeer, or *khaevek*, which has been understood as a non-human component of a human personhood (see Ulturgasheva 2012: 109–130; Vitebsky 2005; Willerslev and Ulturgasheva 2012: 51–58). The Eveny distinguish between wild reindeer (*buyun*) and domesticated reindeer (*oron*). One type of reindeer belonging to the *oron* category is termed *khavek*, which means 'double soul', and it serves to guard a human being, in particular a young child, from attacks of malicious spirits (Ulturgasheva 2012: 43–45). The *khavek* may stand in for the child, taking her or his place when malevolent spirits launch their vicious attack on the child. The *khavek* is the first to receive this attack by disguising the child's human identity in the eyes of the spirits, which may take it for a reindeer. Here, an animal double—that is, a guardian reindeer—serves to stand in for its human double in order to neutralize or minimize the risk of harm. It is the ability of a reindeer to receive the attack instead of its human counterpart that should be understood as one expression of animist personhood's capacity to split, double, and depart.

In contrast to a guardian reindeer, *djuluchen*'s capacity to split and depart has its limits, as it is also associated with the danger of its residue, *khedoke*, which may remain permanently awaiting its owner.[3] The term *khedoke* refers to a traveling spirit that was never caught up with and remained ahead, in the future destination. This suggests that there is always a possibility that *djuluchen* can be stranded in the future due to a person's accidental death, illness, or sudden misfortune. In this situation, *djuluchen* transforms into a ghostly trace of a person, or *khedoke*, a traveling spirit that still remains on hold waiting for its owner's arrival. Therefore, any locality associated with *khedoke* is, by definition, haunted as it is a site of a former *djuluchen* that a deceased owner had sent but never caught up with while he or she was alive.

As the cases of the three adolescents, the wolf, and guardian reindeer have indicated, the Eveny conceptualization of animal and human doubles points at animist personhood's propensity to extend into the future and the past through the process of splitting, doubling, and departing. However, the concept of *khedoke*, that is, *djuluchen* that remain 'on hold', also suggests that personhood's potential for splitting and departing has its limitations as it may lead to cosmologically permanent incompleteness.

Kinetic Distribution

If in Vera's case it was the image of herself and her future family that produced an effect of *djuluchen*, in Kirill's and Tonya's case it was the image of future reindeer that got invested with the transformative power of becoming. In other words, the magnetizing power of Kirill's and Tonya's reindeer served as the moment of their *djuluchens'* activation. As Kirill put it, it was the powerful magnetism of his reindeer that made him extend his *djuluchen* to its future destination where it was reunited with the reindeer, his animal double. In this sense, we can view two adolescents' acts of envisioning their own return and the pronouncement of their wishes as an event of sequential double-reassembling with partible components whereby the owner sequentially reassembles— first with *djuluchen* and then with a guardian reindeer (*khaevek*). This act of double-reassembling (or the event of becoming) emerges from and is propelled by the adolescents' emotional interaction with their future destination, associated with the reindeer.

In his discussion of Malangan art objects—specifically, the notion of distributed personhood—Alfred Gell (1998) suggests that the internalized memory image or 'simulacrum' of the ancestors who are depicted in Malangan art gives those same art objects the agency to be redeployed and reproduced in the future. Each part of the ancestral body charged by its agentive capacity becomes a socially distributed memory image, that is, a material object, which retains its potency and efficacy as long as it remains socially relevant (ibid.: 227–228). In the case of *djuluchen*, we observe a similar type of transaction in which a human or an animal distributes a memory image (simulacrum) that carries with it the intention to move toward a certain destination. Note, however, that in Gell's case it is a material object (in the present moment) and the body of a deceased ancestor (from the past) that are transacted in order to reproduce and perpetuate the agentive capacity of the deceased. By contrast, the Eveny *djuluchen* unleashes a future memory image of *djuluchen* and the present agentive capacity of a subject that are kinetically linked at the moment when the movement toward the future destination is being conceived. So the principle of *djuluchen*'s distribution between future and present points at the capacity of human and animal personhood to transmit kinetically (through movement) rather than statically (in place). It is the intention to move that propels the distribution of *djuluchen* and, by extension, Eveny personhood.

The present moment of *djuluchen* should be understood as a shadow moment between a person's departing and arriving, since *djuluchen* is always in between departure and arrival. In other words, *djuluchen* contains a temporal and spatial point from which the memory of the future unfolds over the Eveny person's (or animal's) life trajectory.[4] As we can see from the story about the wolf, the hunter was informed about the pending attack by the wolf's *djuluchen*. This suggests that the information or knowledge about the future event was transmitted by *djuluchen*, which serves as an envelope or a vehicle of the memory about the future. In the cases of Vera, Kirill, Tonya, and the hunter, we have seen how the Eveny *djuluchen* traveling spirit opens up a kind of 'time travel', whereby an entity's traveling spirit simultaneously stretches into the past and the future, through the narrated (and potentially infinite) expansion of the present.

We can see that the adolescents' future life stories, which were fulfilled six years later, present us with a unique mode of futurity, as they cannot be easily placed within the well-established distinction between intuition and intellect and, respectively, pre-reflective and reflective consciousness (cf. Grosz 1999: 21; Young 1987: 11–12). Here, the narrative, which is often viewed as reflexive, fixed, typified, and representational in most anthropological literature, turns out to be a product of ongoing and unreflective presence in the world (Barber 2007; Goffman 1969; Gullestad 1996).

I suggest defining the predictive, foretelling, and transformative force of the future autobiography as 'kinetic distribution'. By sending the *djuluchen* ahead on the path that the person plans to take, it places the subject's intentions in the present and puts the future of the event into contact. This dynamic makes a subject's intention to move and the subsequent event resonate by means of volitional, intuitive force. That is to say, it was a wolf's and an adolescent's intentions that projected to 'actualization in progress'. It is thus the volitional power of *djuluchen* that offers us a glimpse into the ways personhood operates in shamanic and animist ontologies or, more specifically, in a wider Eveny shamanistic cultural complex (Brightman et al. 2012; Shirokogoroff [1935] 1999; Vitebsky 1995, 2005).

In most ethnographic literature on shamanic societies throughout Siberia and Inner Asia, it is virtuoso shamans, powerful game players, and other elite practitioners who come closest to mastering their spiritual transportations for the purpose of divination and to transmit their souls to other realms at will

(Eliade 1964; Swancutt 2007; Vitebsky 1995: 70–71). However, the *djuluchen* provides us with evidence that lay people inherently possess a capacity to fore-shadow events in the future by having part of one's personhood travel ahead of oneself. In a sense, it operates on the level of inchoate potential, which is several degrees or stages away from shamanic or other specialist skills. Here, *djuluchen* should be understood as a foreshadowing agency that is literally opened and accessible to any ordinary person, including children and adolescents.

Conclusion

This account of *djuluchen* has illustrated the capacity of a subject, that is, the Eveny person or animal, to predict a future event by communicating the intention to move and to arrive at a particular destination in a certain period of time through the medium of a narrative about one's own future (as in the case of the adolescents) or by means of a ghostly image (as in the case of the wolf). In the accounts of Vera, Kirill, and Tonya, it was a six-year span between the pronouncement of their wishes for the future and the fulfillment of those wishes, and it was an interval of six days between the moment the hunter saw the image of the running wolf and the point when the wolf reached his rein-deer herd. During the interval between prediction and fulfillment, *djuluchen* becomes an extension of the internal and external, the body and its shadow, the soul and its envelope as it kinetically distributes itself into the future destination or moment of fulfillment. *Djuluchen* can thus be sent on a rapid or slow journey, remaining 'on the move' for shorter or longer intervals of time.

Djuluchen instantiates what Tim Ingold (2006: 14) defines as "the animic world … in perpetual flux." But the foreshadowing force of *djuluchen* takes this argument a step further, offering ethnography that shows more precisely how Ingold's 'perpetual flux' can be set in motion. It emphasizes that personhood is always in some process of unfolding, splitting, doubling, and departing. By and large, the Eveny *djuluchen* (as both a concept and a phenomenon) is an outcome of having envisioned one's destination while focusing on movement toward it. Calling to mind—and pronouncing—the distant vision of one's desti-nation forms a relationship between the Eveny person or animal who envisions movement toward that destination and the actual destination itself as a point of arrival. It is thus movement—or more precisely human and animal move-ment—that provides the foundation for the very concept of *djuluchen*.

Finally, *djuluchen* points at the capacity of a human or an animal to form this relationship, not only when reaching the destination, but also when mov-ing toward the destination is only an intention. *Djuluchen* starts moving toward an Eveny person's destination long before that person makes any such observ-able move. The individual's intention is projected ahead of his or her actions and can be picked up by the target of this intention. As we have seen in the hunter's account of a wolf, at a certain point, *djuluchen* turns into the wolf's traveling spirit, which spatially and temporally distributes itself ahead of the wolf. The process of 'catching up' between *djuluchen* and the Eveny person or animal may take time to reach its fulfillment. But Eveny believe that once the *djuluchen* is set in motion, reassembling with its owner is inescapable and even 'already actualized'. It is the image of the future event that simulates the emotional power of *djuluchen* and transforms its potential for foreshadowing the future into an 'actual' destiny.

Acknowledgments

This chapter has benefited greatly from comments of the editors of this book, Katherine Swancutt and Mireille Mazard. I thank them for inviting me to contribute and for their helpful suggestions. I am especially grateful to the Arctic Social Sciences Program of the National Science Foundation (ARC-1207894 and ARC-0755348) without whose support this research would not have been possible.

Olga Ulturgasheva is a Lecturer in the Department of Social Anthropology, University of Manchester. Since 2006 she has been engaged in a number of international projects exploring human and non-human personhood, movement patterns, and youth resilience in Siberia, the American Arctic, and Amazonia. She is the author of *Narrating the Future in Siberia: Childhood, Adolescence and Autobiography among the Eveny* (2012), a co-editor of *Animism in Rainforest and Tundra: Personhood, Animals, Plants and Things in Contemporary Amazonia and Siberia* (2012), and an editor of the Berghahn Books series Studies in the Circumpolar North. She is a Principal Investigator for an international, collaborative project that focuses on adaptation strategies and resilience patterns among Alaskan Yup'ik and Siberian Eveny. This four-year comparative research project offers new insights on the human capacity to navigate through the latest dynamics associated with climate change and environmental transformations in the Siberian and Alaskan Arctic.

Notes

1. In this book, see Katherine Swancutt and Mireille Mazard on the lens of hyper-reflexivity, and Vanessa Grotti and Marc Brightman on collaboration and indigenous autobiographies.
2. See Diana Espírito Santo on plasticity and cosmology in this book.
3. See also my discussion of the Eveny concept of 'trace' in Ulturgasheva (2012: 131–153).
4. In this book, see also Espírito Santo on the Cuban notion of 'enfoldment'.

References

Austin, J. L. 1962. *How to Do Things with Words*. Oxford: Clarendon Press.
Barber, Karin. 2007. *The Anthropology of Texts, Persons and Publics: Oral and Written Culture in Africa and Beyond*. Cambridge: Cambridge University Press.
Barthes, Roland. 1984. *Image, Music, Text*. Trans. Stephen Heath. London: Flamingo.
Brightman, Marc, Vanessa Elisa Grotti, and Olga Ulturgasheva. 2012. *Animism in Rainforest and Tundra: Personhood, Animals, Plants and Things in Contemporary Amazonia and Siberia*. New York: Berghahn Books.
Deleuze, Gilles. 1986. *Cinema 1: The Movement-Image*. Trans. Hugh Tomlinson and Barbara Habberjam. Minneapolis: University of Minnesota Press.
Deleuze, Gilles. 2004. *The Logic of Sense*. Trans. Mark Lester. New York: Columbia University Press.
Durkheim, Émile. (1912) 2001. *The Elementary Forms of Religious Life*. Trans. Carol Cosman. Oxford: Oxford University Press.
Eliade, Mircea. 1964. *Shamanism: Archaic Techniques of Ecstasy*. New York: Pantheon.
Fondahl, Gail A. 1998. *Gaining Ground? Evenkis, Land, and Reform in Southeastern Siberia*. Boston: Allyn & Bacon.
Gell, Alfred. 1998. *Art and Agency: An Anthropological Theory*. Oxford: Clarendon Press.
Goffman, Erving. 1969. *The Presentation of Self in Everyday Life*. London: Allen Lane.
Grosz, Elizabeth. 1999. "Thinking the New: Of Futures Yet Unthought." In *Becomings: Explorations in Time, Memory, and Futures*, ed. Elizabeth Grosz, 15–28. Ithaca, NY: Cornell University Press.
Gullestad, Marianne, ed. 1996. *Imagined Childhoods: Self and Society in Autobiographical Accounts*. Oslo: Scandinavian University Press.
Ingold, Tim. 2006. "Rethinking the Animate, Re-animating Thought." *Ethnos* 71 (1): 9–20.
Kerttula, Anna M. 2000. *Antler on the Sea: The Yup'ik and Chukchi of the Russian Far East*. Ithaca, NY: Cornell University Press.
Kristeva, Julia. 1980. *Desire in Language: A Semiotic Approach to Literature and Art*. Ed. Leon S. Roudiez; trans. Thomas Gora, Alice Jardine, and Leon S. Roudiez. Oxford: Blackwell.
Rethmann, Petra. 2001. *Tundra Passages: History and Gender in the Russian Far East*. Philadelphia: Pennsylvania State University Press.
Shirokogoroff, Sergei M. (1935) 1999. *Psychomental Complex of the Tungus*. Berlin: Shletzer.
Shuman, Amy. 1986. *Storytelling Rights: The Uses of Oral and Written Texts by Urban Adolescents*. Cambridge: Cambridge University Press.
Sirina, A. 1999. "Rodovyye obschiny malochislennykh narodov severa v Respublike Sakha (Yakutiya): Shag k samoopredeleniyu?" [Clan Collectives among Minority Peoples of the North in the Sakha Republic (Yakutia): A Step toward Self-Government?] Working Paper No. 126. Moscow: Issledovaniya po prikladnoy i neotlozhnoy etnologii, Institut Etnologii i Antropologii, Rossiyskaya Akademiya Nauk.
Slezkine, Yuri. 1994. *Arctic Mirrors: Russia and the Small Peoples of the North*. Ithaca, NY: Cornell University Press.
Strathern, Marilyn. 1988. *The Gender of the Gift: Problems with Women and Problems with Society in Melanesia*. Berkeley: University of California Press.
Strathern, Marilyn. 1999. *Property, Substance and Effect: Anthropological Essays on Persons and Things*. London: Athlone Press.
Strathern, Marilyn. 2004. *Partial Connections*. Walnut Creek, CA: AltaMira Press.

Swancutt, Katherine. 2007. "The Ontological Spiral: Virtuosity and Transparency in Mongolian Games." *Inner Asia* 9 (2): 237–259.

Ulturgasheva, Olga. 2012. *Narrating the Future in Siberia: Childhood, Adolescence and Autobiography among Young Eveny.* New York: Berghahn Books.

Ulturgasheva, Olga. 2014. "Attaining *Khinem*: Challenges, Coping Strategies and Resilience among Eveny Adolescents in Northeastern Siberia." *Transcultural Psychiatry* 51 (5): 632–650.

Ulturgasheva, Olga, Stacy Rasmus, and Phyllis Morrow. 2015. "Collapsing the Distance: Indigenous Youth Engagement in a Circumpolar Study of Youth Resilience." *Arctic Anthropology* 52 (1): 60–70.

Vitebsky, Piers. 1995. *The Shaman: Voyages of the Soul from the Arctic to the Amazon.* London: Duncan Baird.

Vitebsky, Piers. 2002. "Withdrawing from the Land: Social and Spiritual Crisis in the Indigenous Russian Arctic." In *Postsocialism: Ideals, Ideologies and Practices in Eurasia,* ed. C. M. Hann, 180–195. London: Routledge.

Vitebsky, Piers. 2005. *Reindeer People: Living with Animals and Spirits in Siberia.* London: HarperCollins.

Willerslev, Rane, and Olga Ulturgasheva. 2012. "Revisiting the Animism versus Totemism Debate: Fabricating Persons among the Eveny and Chukchi of North-eastern Siberia." In Brightman et al. 2012, 48–68.

Young, Katharine G. 1987. *Taleworlds and Storyrealms: The Phenomenology of Narrative.* Dordrecht: Martinus Nijhoff.

Chapter 4

THE ART OF CAPTURE
Hidden Jokes and the Reinvention of Animistic
Ontologies in Southwest China

Katherine Swancutt

Anthropologists have typically viewed animism as a cosmology in which every being has a soul or 'vital essence'. While animism has undergone many theoretical metamorphoses since anthropology's early days, radically outstripping Edward B. Tylor's ([1871] 1920) original uses of the term, it would likely surprise many anthropologists to learn that animism is being reinvented across the People's Republic of China (PRC). Animism in China is referred to as 'nature worship' (Ch. *ziran chongbai* 自然崇拜) or the notion that 'every being has a soul' (Ch. *wanwu youling* 万物有灵), and it is currently being propounded as a cosmological-cum-ecological ethos capable of mobilizing widespread environmentalist sensibilities. The official Chinese take on animism underpins new ecological policies that offload environmental management onto ethnic

Notes for this chapter begin on page 90.

minorities, who are dubbed the 'animistic custodians' of local landscapes. This eco-friendly animistic view is the counterpart to a neo-Confucian environmentalist movement that is intended to galvanize China's ethnic majority, the Han, to undertake "a radical transformation of hearts and minds" (Chang 2011: 262) through everyday acts of self-cultivation, ensuring the planet's vitality for future generations. Like other foreign-sourced concepts, including Marxian-Morganian views on social evolution, animism in China has become a tool for social engineering, capable of transforming formerly taboo phenomena, such as shamanic rites, into a new means of production. However, today's production is oriented toward reforesting lands that the state ordered to be leveled a generation ago. Animistic peoples in China are responding equally resourcefully, caricaturing themselves as the age-old forestry managers who inspired the new ecological jargon in the first place.

Drawing on my fieldwork among the Nuosu of Southwest China, my aim in this chapter is to show how the 'art of capture' underpins the native reinvention of animistic ontologies that shadow our fieldwork efforts at uncovering ethnography, even as interlocutors return our gaze through their interpretations of animism as a founding concept in our discipline. I argue that animistic ideas take on lives of their own. Fieldwork or academic writing may transform them into lynchpins to several co-existing ontologies with differing definitions of animism, or into what Scott (2007) aptly terms a 'poly-ontology'.

One important finding in my Nuosu ethnography is that different views on animism can take root in the knowledge and practices of animistic peoples who have acquired a supple command of anthropological concepts. In this chapter, I examine Nuosu anthropology, ethno-history, and different Nuosu ethno-theologies. I suggest that their reinvention of animistic ideas parallels the animistic transformations of material objects and sacrificial animals used to lure spirits, ghosts, and human souls into their ritual purview (Swancutt 2015: 136–138). On another level, my case studies suggest that the concept of animism commands an extraordinary influence on anthropological thought, possessing the agency—much like that of spirits among our fieldwork friends—to impinge on our own thinking.

I have carried out fieldwork since 2007 among Nuosu, who are a Tibeto-Burman group officially classed with numerous neighboring ethnic groups under the Chinese ethnonym Yi. The Nuosu I know inhabit a temperate, forested mountain region colloquially referred to as the Lesser Cool Mountains (Xiao Liangshan) of Ninglang County in Yunnan Province, which borders the Greater Cool Mountains (Da Liangshan) of Sichuan Province, from which their forebears migrated 120–150 years ago. Yunnan is famous in Southwest China for having the densest population of minority groups in the country and for being a 'hotbed' of minority politics, where groups have lobbied for greater autonomy for generations and, more recently, for state benefits as well. Across wider China, the Nuosu are notorious for their recent history of slaveholding and ranked lineages, which are upheld by an essentialist theory of "blood superiority" (Pan Jiao 1997: 109). Today's Nuosu say that when their ancestors first entered Ninglang, they either drove out the resident populations they encountered or incorporated them as slave labor, which remains a source of ethnic pride. They further point out that, traditionally, any Nuosu of noble, commoner, or slave extraction could own slaves; thus, prestige and wealth were routinely displayed through slave retinues. Ann Maxwell Hill (2001: 1037–1038) has shown that Nuosu slavery boomed for roughly 50 years (1906–1956) when China outlawed the production of opium in Han-held areas, effectively opening the market to minorities like the Nuosu, who traded opium (grown by slaves) to Han merchants for silver and rifles. Moreover, in the early years of the PRC, Chinese ethnologists sensationalized the Nuosu as living exemplars of a slave society, eagerly fitting them into the Marxian-Morganian model of social evolution then in vogue in the Chinese Communist Party (CCP) and academic circles (ibid.: 1033–1035). Nuosu slaveholding practices were therefore targeted during the 'democratic reforms' (Ch. *minzhu gaige* 民主改革) undertaken across China's southwest in 1956–1957 to incorporate ethnic others within the body politic of the PRC. However, the Nuosu defended their ideals of blood superiority with guerrilla warfare, battling the People's Liberation Army across their highlands until—as they commonly attest—the Han seized their shotguns. Thus, while swidden agriculture and pastoralism are nowadays the most visible pursuits in the Nuosu countryside, the themes of warfare, slavery, luring, and capture remain palpable in their animistic imagery.

Nearly every Nuosu rite entails an exorcism that expels ghosts from the home by shotgun, dynamite, fireworks, burning, scalding, priestly or shamanic chanting, or some other ritualistic means. Nuosu 'priests' (Nuo. *bimo* ꀘꂾ), whom I refer to as 'text-reading shamans', recite formulaic litanies that they occasionally trace back to a 4,000-year history of exorcising ghosts, calling back lost souls, and removing illnesses. There is a parallel Nuosu tradition of shamans (Nuo. *sunyit* ꌠꑊ) who do not read texts but carry out the same ritual tasks accompanied by spontaneous recitations. Both kinds of practitioners often direct ritualistic warfare against a specific class of ghosts commonly called *shubi*, which is also referred to by some Nuosu ethnologists as *shuo bbot* (ꎭꀧ). *Shubi* are comprised of former slaves captured from other ethnic groups, especially the Han. As I have described elsewhere (Swancutt 2012b: 67–68), *shubi* appear at night as phosphorescence (Nuo. *bbit dut* ꀜꄏ) on mountaintops, flashing like live flames as they race to disband and reaggregate. They often form into bands of ghosts (Nuo. *nyit cy* ꑊꊰ) that include the higher-ranked Nuosu dead who never gained entrance to the ancestral afterlife located in Shypmu Ngehxat (Nuo. ꎹꃅꉢꉙ)—conceptualized as a kind of afterlife world kingdom not far from Zyzypuvy (Nuo. ꍂꍂꁧꃅ, or present-day Zhaotong)—since they were expelled from the lineage or failed to produce male descendants for it. While reparatory rites can be held to incorporate these higher-ranked *nyit cy*, they are rare and difficult to conduct.

Each of these various ghosts are 'non-ancestors', doomed to wander mountaintops seeking food and, in the case of *shubi*, searching for roads to reunite them with the families they lost when captured as slaves. Some *shubi* benignly haunt their former masters' homes, where they continue to carry out agricultural tasks for them. If treated well, they may remain as good help, although Nuosu are wary that *shubi* might one day insidiously inflict illnesses on them.

Most of the haunting, though, is ascribed to the hunger, lack of clothing, and insufficient shelter that ghosts suffer when barred entrance from the afterlife, where they could have eaten the 'spirits' of dead livestock and crops. Out of starvation and spite, wandering ghosts thus enter the homes of living Nuosu, where they inflict illnesses and capture people's souls. To combat them, Nuosu hold exorcisms in which they offer portions of sacrificial animals to the ghosts and produce attractive effigies of their 'homes' or 'jails'—presented as alternative 'shelters'—before expelling them from the household.

Exorcisms are central to the Nuosu art of capture that permeates their animistic thought and practice. So too is yet another cornerstone of their art of capture, that is, the Nuosu notion that the human soul takes the form of a tiny 'soul-spider' (Nuo. *yyr* 粜), which resides on the outer surface of the human body and is usually visible only during soul-calling ceremonies (Swancutt 2012a, 2012b, 2012c). Ghosts are chiefly responsible for causing soul loss by capturing the person's soul-spider, often hiding it under a stone. When this happens, Nuosu ritually retrieve the lost soul by placing a white thread—which is meant to resemble a real spider's thread—across the threshold and calling to it from within the home. They lure the soul-spider back with promises of warmth and food. Eventually the soul-spider comes visibly into focus and climbs the white thread, whereupon the person handling the thread rolls it up and deposits it with the soul-spider in a winnowing basket or lacquer box, shutting the lid over it in an act of capture. When the next good astrological day arrives, the lid is removed to allow the soul-spider to return to its owner. Tellingly, the art of capture evidenced in the ritual retrieval of the soul-spider presupposes an asymmetric power relation that is more transparent to the captor than the would-be captive, which as I show below, is a recurrent theme in Nuosu efforts to manage relations between people and their souls, the living and the dead, anthropologists and informants, or even native scholars and foreign anthropologists.

On another level, the art of capture cuts across the essentialist views on Nuosu lineage rankings, since a Nuosu person may obtain a prestigious 'seat' (Ch. *weizhi* 位置) in society by taking up a specialist occupation, such as priest, clan leader, mediator, craftsperson, or warrior, or by virtue of having accumulated wealth without setbacks. Through any of these occupations, Nuosu may attract 'followers', who (like the slave retinues of recent history) increase their fame, popularity, and accomplishments (Swancutt 2012b). Besides establishing a reputation as a vocational expert, Nuosu may 'capture' followers by claiming to hold 'hidden knowledge'—such as rare priestly litanies or lineage secrets—which they may sometimes use as the platform for a 'hidden joke', as I describe here. Nuosu deploy their art of capture in a variety of settings, ranging from soul retrieval and village exorcisms to interactions with Chinese social workers who propound an eco-friendly 'animistic' discourse and behavior. In so doing, Nuosu reflexively harness the animism of anthropology, the animistic ideas in their rituals and cosmology, and the 'ideology of animism' that pervades China's new environmentalist discourse.

Building this chapter on a trio of case studies, I now bring you into dialogue with the Nuosu ethnologist Mitsu, followed by rural Nuosu living in the village where I carried out fieldwork in late 2011 and the Nuosu anthropologist Tuosat, who was born and raised in that same village.[1] Although ethnology and anthropology are closely related disciplines, I differentiate Mitsu's and Tuosat's occupations according to their academic training and the different types of research they conduct. Mitsu and Tuosat have collaborated on publications about Nuosu religion, and Tuosat is aware that he returns the anthropological gaze when talking about his own culture. Tuosat is, furthermore, the relative of two villagers who appear in this chapter: Katba, who raised Tuosat like a father, and Datlamuo, Tuosat's nephew. My case studies reveal how 'hyper-reflexivity' emerges between academics and villagers who traverse each other's respective ontological domains. With its unique viewpoint on Nuosu animistic life, my ethnography demonstrates how Nuosu use hidden jokes and the art of capture to influence other Nuosu, their Chinese colleagues, and even Euro-American anthropologists.

Ethno-history and Classic Animism: The Soul as Shadow

My trip to Ninglang in September 2011 began with a series of banquets, one of which was held by members of an ethnological institute based in the county seat. Among the people attending was Mitsu, an expert on Nuosu religion who was in his fifties and whom I had briefly met during my first visit to the area in 2007. The banquet progressed quickly, and I soon realized that the academics were testing my understanding of Nuosu culture with questions about arcane notions and practices that are largely unknown to present-day villagers. Accepting that there would be differences between our research paths, I directed my thoughts toward traveling to my fieldwork village. To my surprise, though, once we had left the company of his colleagues, Mitsu asked me with eager and genuine interest what I was *really* working on. I started off by saying that, some years earlier, my original focus was the Nuosu soul (Ch. *linghun* 灵魂), which takes the form of a soul-spider. Visibly excited, he told me that he, too, had worked extensively on the soul. On the spot, he invited me to his home for a discussion and visit with his wife and children, which I accepted. This was no serendipitous meeting. Given the importance of the soul in animistic religions, it makes sense that Mitsu and I would both have taken an interest in it. What Mitsu did not anticipate, however, was that my thoughts on the soul-spider—which reflect common knowledge in the Nuosu countryside—only partially overlapped with his understanding as an ethno-historian based in the county seat. Over the following two months, I kept in close contact with Mitsu whenever I made short visits to the county. During each of our visits, he viewed me as a 'foreign anthropologist' and acted as a 'mentoring informant' toward me.

At first, Mitsu was keen to tell me that Nuosu villagers, including Fijy, the institute's then-consultant priest who was my village host in 2007, had "messy," "confused," or "chaotic" (Ch. *luan* 乱) ideas about complex notions like the soul. Mitsu stressed that villagers often distort or acquire only partial understandings of classical notions about Nuosu life. Contrasting his understanding to that of the villagers, Mitsu said that he had read many ancient Nuosu texts, which only the most elite *bimo* priests understand deeply. By studying these texts in combination, Mitsu felt that he had acquired a thorough understanding of the esoteric and hidden elements in Nuosu religion, which trumped the villagers' knowledge. He did not mind that I focused on the soul-spider, but advised me to clarify that the Nuosu soul takes this form only when it is lost or being ritualistically retrieved. However, in the course of our conversation, Mitsu's wife mentioned that the Premi ethnic group have a similar idea, namely, that real spiders are the transmuted forms of lost human souls. I added that a Naxi man had told me a few days earlier in Kunming that they, too, consider lost souls to take the form of spiders, while in the 1980s the Chinese anthropologist He Shutao (2000) made a similar finding among another shamanic group, now largely Christianized, called the Nusu (see also Mazard 2011, this volume). Mitsu's wife and I agreed that human souls and spiders are considered synonymous, or even equivalent, by many ethnic groups in Southwest China. Still, Mitsu maintained that it did not matter if rural Nuosu nowadays envision the soul in the form of a soul-spider. What he stressed was that the Nuosu soul originally was conceived of as a 'shadow'.

When I asked him why, Mitsu replied that the symmetry of Nuosu ancient and modern characters for the soul-spider depict a shadow or, more precisely, the casting of a reflection. We debated the shapes of these characters, which, four years earlier, Fijy and his fellow villagers had told me resembled a spider (Swancutt 2012a). I wondered whether Mitsu's studies were informed by classic anthropology texts on the soul and shadow, as they had filtered into Chinese ethnology. Inwardly, I also reflected that my views on the soul-spider were as much influenced by my fieldwork experiences as they were by my training, including my reading of anthropological and ethnological texts. But Mitsu raced ahead with his explanations, and I soon found that he had gathered his ideas from the study of ancient and medieval links between Nuosu animistic religion and Daoism. Historically, Daoism has equated souls and shadows, populated the landscape with nature spirits, and propounded the view that people can obtain saint-like immortality after death. Revealingly, the Daoist's discipline of daily self-refining physical exercises makes the person capable of either radiating light that conceals his or her shadow (Ch. *ying* 影), which is equated with the soul (Ch. *hun* 魂), or of hiding the person within that same shadow-soul, so that he or she disappears from sight (Robinet 1993: 165–166). Still, since most present-day Nuosu are unfamiliar with Daoist texts, they emphasize the spidery appearance of souls, the rites held to capture them, and their personal efforts to attract fame and followers.

Shortly afterward, I traveled to the village that is home to the Nuosu anthropologist Tuosat. After my discussions with Mitsu, I felt that I should confirm whether the soul-spider is indeed the accepted understanding about the soul, as I had learned during my earlier fieldwork. I relaxed when Tuosat's fellow villagers agreed that the soul-spider was indeed the common view. Many of them added that it is ideally white in color, like a freshly hatched spider, since this suggests it has not been absent from its owner for long. Significantly, the local shaman, who can see ghosts and had not heard of Mitsu's research, scoffed at the idea that human souls and shadows have anything in common. He felt that only ghosts—and not human souls—can be perceived in an outline form that resembles a shadow. But a fortnight later, Katba, a relative and 'interlocutor' of Mitsu, told me that souls and shadows are traditionally linked together in Nuosu understanding. He did not know why this was the case, but believed that the link between them is a 'folkloric saying' (Ch. *chuanshuo* 传说). Over a glass of strong Chinese grain liquor (Ch. *baijiu* 白酒), Katba, a retired schoolteacher, jovially revealed that he had raised the anthropologist Tuosat like a father and had taught him everything he knew. He added that he had helped Tuosat and Mitsu write a book on the soul during a week they spent together in Kunming.

On my next visit to the county center, I asked Mitsu whether Katba had helped him write a book on the soul. For several minutes, I received a genuinely puzzled expression, followed by startled statements that Katba had done none of the co-authoring. Mitsu even queried Datlamuo, the 25-year-old nephew of Tuosat who was present at the time, whether Katba had been drinking when he claimed authorship to his work. But then Mitsu's face suddenly lit up in recognition of a hidden joke, and he burst out laughing at the idea that Katba might have, in a roundabout way, tried to compete with his expertise. He confirmed respectfully that Katba did inform his study, but also proudly declared Katba had done none of the writing for the volume, which appeared under the name of Mitsu's former research team leader in Kunming (Asu Daling 2008). It transpired instead that Mitsu's Daoist-inspired links between the soul and shadow informed Katba's understanding. Katba took these views to the village where they gained no further popularity, since he had not challenged anyone with them—apart from telling me in a single joking conversation that he was the true fount of information for Mitsu and Tuosat's work. Moreover, Mitsu added that while Tuosat had joined the academic discussions in Kunming, the publication was devoted to discussing Nuosu religion in ethno-historical rather than anthropological terms.

It would be too simple to write off Mitsu's views as purely ethno-historical or as a skewed source of information about present-day Nuosu notions. Like the villagers, Mitsu cut to the chase when discussing animism. He confirmed that there is no Nuosu-language equivalent for the term 'animism', which he preferred to gloss in Chinese as *ziran chongbai*, or 'nature worship', as distinct from the officially sanctioned 'religions' (*zongjiao* 宗教) of China—one of which is Daoism. Nuosu, he corroborated, have no term for the animistic cosmologies familiar to anthropology or for the eco-friendly ideology of animism propounded by the Chinese state. This is because Nuosu typically consider their religious knowledge to be part of the general know-how they acquire when growing up in the countryside. Yet Mitsu anticipated, through his Daoist-inspired outlook, that Nuosu cosmology contains a vast ontological diversity and is populated by more spirits than the villagers seemed to recognize.[2] Enthusiastically, Mitsu related that Nuosu villagers believe there are nature spirits in every portion of the landscape. He added that once locals had told me the names of the spirits for every turn in the road, fork in the river, bend in the hillside, mountain passage, and so on, I could produce an 'animistic map' of their village. However, all the villagers I met, including Katba, held that just their large mountain had a nature spirit, which was simply named after the mountain. Only closer to the end of my stay, when Tuosat passed through the village and spoke to me 'anthropologically', did I receive vague confirmation that nature spirits inhabit every portion of the landscape. Yet even Tuosat, who seems to have acquired this understanding from Mitsu, could not name or fully imagine what those spirits would be.

Revealingly, when I met with Mitsu in the county seat just before concluding my research trip, I observed him returning the anthropological gaze. He had taken increasing interest in my findings over the course of my fieldwork in Ninglang, drawing impressive links between his historical work and the present-day rites I had observed. Meanwhile, I had tried taking on board his ethno-historical outlook, actively working to bridge our views through a kind of hyper-reflexivity and to gather hidden knowledge from him. During a moment when we were lost in thought, I asked Mitsu about the soul-spider again to see whether he might also consider the art of capture a lynchpin to Nuosu sociality. Each of the five village exorcisms I had observed during the previous two months concluded with rites to recapture lost soul-spiders. I invoked resonances between these rites, Nuosu slavery, warfare, and even the practice of capturing pheasants to be domesticated for their eggs. Expanding on this theme, I noted that the Nuosu hunter sometimes travels to the forest wearing a round cape woven from hemp and a conical hat like those worn by the Han for agricultural labor, while carrying a domesticated pheasant in a large oval basket commonly used in agricultural work. Hiding under his cape and hat, the hunter squats down behind the basket, which resembles the scrub where wild pheasants live, and waits for his domesticated pheasant to cry out. Attracted to these calls, a wild pheasant approaches the basket, at which point the hunter carefully lifts up one edge of the basket, allowing it to enter, and then lowers the basket to the ground to capture it. This pheasant-capturing technique, I commented, parallels the ritual technique for recapturing lost soul-spiders.

Mitsu quietly agreed that Nuosu people and even ghosts do have a penchant for 'luring' or 'attracting' (Ch. *yinyou* 引诱) others. He offered a parallel example that he heard adults invoke when growing up in his home village. His elders said that gremlin-like ghosts (Nuo. *syp lup* ꑭꋊ) would put bright red berries inside these large agricultural baskets, using the attractive color to lure children. Once a child got close enough, the ghost would lift up the edge of the basket and capture the child's soul inside it, using the same ambush tactics of the pheasant hunter. According to Mitsu, this strategy is a variation on the wider Nuosu theme of ghostly capture, whereby ghosts lure away or forcibly capture the souls of people walking through forests and trap them beneath stones on the ground. When these souls are recovered in rituals, they take the form of soul-spiders, often yellowed from dirt and the delayed return to their owners. While I was feverishly writing this down, Datlamuo, who had arrived and joined our conversation, added that Nuosu ritually capture ghosts in wooden barrels traditionally used for storing water—and reminded me that we had witnessed this very tactic a few weeks earlier during a village exorcism.

Their observations were significant. Mitsu—influenced by my talk about the villagers' views (which perhaps had begun to appear to him as a form of hidden knowledge)—eventually concluded that luring and capture might be key tropes in Nuosu sociality. Furthermore, Datlamuo revealed that Nuosu view the art of capture as a strategy entailing several co-existing levels of awareness. The three of us discussed how, if a ghost captures a person's soul, Nuosu retaliate with rites that capture the ghost and force it to release the soul before they expel the ghost from the home and recapture the soul themselves. I recalled how Datlamuo had told me many times, during the village exorcisms we attended, that Nuosu priests or shamans make effigies of ghosts function strictly as representations (Nuo. *sat* 𖼄) of them, so as to lure ghosts into the ritual purview where they can be ambushed. However, this savvy tactic of reducing effigies to representations is a form of hidden knowledge that Nuosu persons use to prevent ghosts from 'animating' the effigies and launching a counter-ambush through them. We now turn to the ritualized warfare of exorcism, which lies at the heart of Nuosu villagers' views on animism.

Animism in the Village

When carrying out fieldwork in Tuosat's village, I quickly learned that the villagers did not have a Nuosu-language equivalent for the word 'animism', nor did they conceive of their religious life as a bounded whole. They focused instead on their rites, most of which entail exorcisms to expel ghosts, illnesses, and misfortunes from the home. Thus, when I experimented anthropologically by asking what their forms of animism could be, many villagers offered local views on the spirits, ghosts, and rituals. As one of them explained: "We venerate our mountain spirit, ancestors, guardian spirits [Nuo. *jjyp lup* 𖼄𖼄], and other spirits in the landscape. But we also have ghosts that come and cause illness. When this happens, we invite the priest or shaman, who holds a ritual to kick them out of our house and retrieve our souls." Villagers often added that they live within an ongoing cycle of exorcisms because they cannot kill ghosts, which simply wander to another home after they have been exorcised. Each Nuosu household, then, tends to hold an exorcism every three to five years and accepts the inevitable burden of it. Nuosu view ghosts as persistent, wily, and crafty at evading exorcism. Since ghosts hide in remote parts of the home and obstruct the priest's or shaman's efforts at expelling them, villagers use the art of capture to lure ghosts into the ritual space of the exorcism.

Both priests and shamans use the art of capture expertly to exorcise ghosts. Having prepared food offerings through animal sacrifice, as well as effigies of the ghosts and the 'homes' or 'jails' to which they will be ritually lured, the priest or shaman summons the ghosts into the space of the exorcism. Their summoning takes the form of chanted 'speech bullets' (Nuo. *ddop ma* 𖼄𖼄), a form of ritual weaponry that draws the ghosts out of hiding and weakens them (Swancutt 2015: 136–138, 149–150, 152–155). Nuosu persons therefore use effigies for the hidden purpose of capturing ghosts, while ghosts use invisibility for the purpose of eluding capture. Shamans, who can see ghosts, watch the offerings and effigies attentively. Every Nuosu ritual specialist is assisted by at least one male layperson, and shamans tell these assistants when the ghosts have entered the ritual purview and can be captured and expelled from the home. Priests, who cannot see ghosts, use a juvenile cockerel as their proxy: suspended by the legs, upside down, over the effigies and offerings, it will shake, flap its wings, and cluck at the approach of a ghost. This is the cue that the ghosts can be captured and expelled from the home. As soon as ghosts settle into the space of the exorcism, Nuosu ambush them. Datlamuo explained that people and ghosts battle for mastery of the household and its resources during exorcisms, which are ritualized warfare. We attended several exorcisms together, including two in late October 2011 that were central to my case study: a local family exorcised ghosts that had to be exorcised again from a neighbor's home just a few days later.

I had been living in Tuosat's village for about a month when I learned the story behind these exorcisms, which started with the tragic death of a healthy five-year-old boy. The oldest of three sons, the boy was playing at home one afternoon when, feeling lonely, he placed two mobile phone calls to his father, who was working on a construction job about a 20-minute drive from the village. His father suspected that these calls might be bad omens, since they were out of character for his son. In both calls, the boy pleaded: "Dad, I'm all alone and really want to see you. But you're too far away, and I just won't be able to reach you." Shortly after putting down the phone for the second time, the boy's father saw many magpies overhead, circling and chattering loudly on the wing, which Nuosu take to be an omen that either bad or good news will arrive soon. Getting increasingly nervous that something had gone awry, the boy's father suddenly heard his phone ring again. This time family members told him to come home immediately because his son was on the brink of death. Minutes before, the boy had suddenly raced toward a ladder made from heavy logs, which are often balanced at an angle inside of Nuosu homes to access grain lofts. Climbing up in play, the boy's weight was just enough to unbalance the ladder. When he came toppling down, one of the logs struck his forehead at full force. The father drove home at top speed but arrived too late—his son had died.

As he was too young to have produced male descendants and thus been eligible for a proper funeral and send-off to the ancestral afterlife, the child was quickly cremated in the hope that he would become a guardian spirit for the home, rather than a wandering ghost. Preparations were also made for an exorcism. In the lead-up to the rites, villagers circulated the story of the tragedy, commenting that the boy had never complained about being lonely before and highlighting the prophetic phone calls, which indicated that the child would die soon at the hands of ghosts. Villagers speculated that ghosts had made the boy speak with an ominous maturity beyond his years and had ensured that he would meet a swift death before his father's return. But the haunting was also traced to the fact that this was the second son to have died in the household within a short stretch of time. Two years earlier, the couple's second-born child had died of a sudden fever. Yet the parents, who were in their early thirties, had not held an exorcism at the time because of the enormous expense (about 10,000 yuan or £1,000) entailed in procuring the animals necessary for slaughter. However, given the violence of this new tragedy and the loss of two sons, the family finally felt compelled to carry out the exorcism. The parents hoped that the rites would protect their third and only remaining son from a similar fate. The couple's situation was especially dire because if they lost their last son and failed to produce more surviving sons for the lineage, they, too, would likely be barred from entering the ancestral afterlife—at least until a special reparatory rite could be successfully held to reverse the situation.

A priest arrived on 26 October to hold a six-partite exorcism, which entailed the near-continuous chanting of esoteric texts for 48 hours to capture and expel four ghosts from the home. Datlamuo and I attended these rites, which identified two ghosts as Nuosu men who had failed to bear any sons, one of whom had been a priest and was tricky to exorcise. The third ghost was a Nuosu man who had shamed the lineage, and the fourth was a gremlin-like ghost that took the form of a horse ridden by the third ghost. Each of these ghosts was barred entrance to the ancestral afterlife and jealously wanted to inflict their fates on the young couple. I will highlight just a few techniques that the priest and others attending the rite considered especially potent in their art of capture.

To weaken the ghosts, the priest first held the common, yet elaborate, rite called *sit ke bur* (ꉢꀊꆈ) in Nuosu, which literally means a 'sacrifice to send back harmful speech', and is held to return spoken words that cause harm to those who sent them. During the pinnacle of this rite, the priest slaughtered a cock and lifted its windpipe out of the body, blowing air into it while holding the bird's neck extended skyward. He thereby produced three slow, haunting cockcrows from the dead cockerel's vocal chords to be heard by Ngetit Guxnzy, the chief sky god of Shypmu Ngehxat, in an appeal for the god to weaken the ghosts by returning their harmful words and bad influences to them. Next, to further disable the ghosts, two militantly inspired rites were held, lasting nearly until dawn. One rite entailed creating an effigy of the jailhouse and luring the ghosts to it for capture. Having chanted numerous speech bullets that commanded the ghosts to the jailhouse, the priest prepared to eject them from the home. He heated an iron plowshare in the open hearth pit until it glowed red and asked a male assistant to spit mouthfuls of water against it. This steam would sear the ghosts with scalding water and produce thick clouds of steam, helping the priest to rout the confused and injured ghosts, using another round of speech bullets, toward the open doorway at the household's threshold. Other assistants carried bowls filled with hot coals from the hearth in order to burn the ghosts and marshal them closer toward the threshold. Blinded by the smoke, steam, and pain, the ghosts could not tell when or from where the next attack would come. Relentlessly, the priest cued two other assistants, who had already tied two sticks of dynamite to a thin bamboo rod, to set them alight and suspend the rod across the threshold. With a dramatic explosion, the dynamite propelled the ghosts across the threshold and into the outdoor courtyard. Not yet done, the priest instructed the household members to burn down the effigy of the ghosts' jailhouse and sweep its cinders outdoors.³ On the following day, three more rites were held: to flush out any ghosts still hiding in the home, to incapacitate them, and to ensure that they would release the householders' souls. These rites also lured the ghosts into the ritual purview with offerings and effigies, only to capture and then battle them out of the home. The rites culminated on 27 October by retrieving the souls of the couple and their surviving son.

Just a few days later, however, some neighbors were troubled by a bad omen: a small bird flew into their home. Talk again circulated in the village about the boy's death and the magpies his father saw portending that tragedy. Convinced that the small bird's arrival signaled that the exorcised ghosts had entered their home, these neighbors held their own exorcism on 1 November, which I attended and which lasted for 10 hours. No hard feelings were directed at anyone in the village about the need to hold the fresh exorcism, as it was understood that ghosts could not be prevented from visiting other homes after being expelled. Instead, these neighbors held a successful triptych of exorcisms, starting with *sit ke bur* and its requisite cockcrowing to enfeeble the ghosts by returning their harmful words and bad influences to them. The priest offered the ghosts sacrificial meat and attractive effigies that resembled them, chanted speech bullets to rout them into the ritual space, and had a young boy in the home perform a militant 'drumming'—by using a bamboo rod to strike an empty lacquer box placed afloat in a bucket of water—to intimidate the ghosts into surrendering. This rite also ended by retrieving the souls of the household members.

As the villagers explained to me later, these two rites did a beautiful job of revealing how Nuosu experience animism, that is, as ritual warfare built on a reflexive battle of the wits. In both cases, the priests and their assistants lured the ghosts into the ritual purview with attractive offerings and effigies, before flushing the ghosts out of hiding and exorcising them from the home. Still, the villagers felt that 'animism'—as a non-native and anthropological concept—would be best conveyed to me by Tuosat, since he had grown up with them in the village but later had become both a great lineage mediator and an anthropologist living in Kunming. They told me repeatedly that they were awaiting Tuosat's arrival in the village so that they could watch the two of us researching animism together.

Hyper-reflexivity in Action: Nuosu and Foreign Anthropologists

Tuosat arrived in the village a few days later, on 4 November, for a brief visit with his relatives. It was through discussions with him that I learned how Nuosu harness the art of capture to manage the eco-friendly ideology of animism propounded in today's China. Tuosat's arrival was dramatic. On the last stretch of his drive between Ninglang County and the village, he managed to have a car accident that left a large dent in the back of his brand-new truck. A tractor driver in front of him had been driving at what Tuosat considered to be an intolerably slow pace for 4 kilometers, before he had the chance to overtake it. Having passed the tractor, Tuosat decided to teach its driver a lesson. He stopped his truck in the middle of the road and got outside, intending to lecture the tractor driver about his poor manners. But since the tractor driver was hard of hearing and slow-witted, he did not stop but barreled his vehicle into the rear of Tuosat's truck. To save face, Tuosat simply delivered his lecture and drove off, satisfied that he had shamed the tractor driver for failing to offer him any financial compensation whatsoever. This account was repeated many times during the day by Tuosat's relatives, all of them important men in the village. They considered that Tuosat's concern for morality rather than cash clearly showed he had masterfully used his skills as a renowned mediator. So when I arrived at the home of his uncle, where Tuosat and I exchanged anthropological thoughts in a mixture of English, Chinese, and Nuosu at the request of the villagers, our discussion revolved around the animistic elements of this car crash, which showcased Tuosat's ability to dexterously navigate hidden jokes and religious knowledge.

Holding court among his important relatives, Tuosat started off with a joke, jovially announcing that the pig just slaughtered according to the Nuosu custom of celebrating a guest's arrival with fresh meat could be considered a needed "sacrifice" to his injured truck. In the Nuosu view, Tuosat continued, cars and other objects have souls like people, or rather, they "contain" souls. Laughing, he took this esoteric interpretation further, telling me that since his car had recently crashed, it needed "to see blood," which made the pig slaughter "doubly necessary." I surmised that Tuosat was only partly joking and asked if the car could have lost its soul due to the crash, requiring it to be retrieved. Tuosat replied, "No," explaining that car souls are not lost as easily as the Nuosu person's soul-spider. But, he said, fortunately every car is involved in only about one to five crashes over its lifetime. This big crash was good because it meant that probably his new car would suffer no further accidents. He seemed genuinely pleased with the crash. Seeing that he had captured my full attention, Tuosat smiled broadly and said: "So you see? This is animism. We Nuosu think everything has a soul." Giving a big belly laugh, he told me that Nuosu love to be happy and smile and that joking is a main feature of their culture. Jokes are not necessarily intended to undermine what people say but instead may lead to personal interpretations—or even reinventions—of their common sayings and hidden knowledge.

By way of further explanation, Tuosat instructed me to follow him outdoors to the small field adjacent to his host's home, which had been planted with small fir trees. "Do you know what these trees are for?" he asked rhetorically. "They are for reforesting that hillside over there, where all the trees were cut down by government order two to three decades ago. Now they're paying people to reforest the hills, and we're doing it—one yuan per tree. So these small trees will bring our hosts one million yuan in a year's time. That's £100,000. Not bad, yes? The government has introduced policies for environmental responsibility, and we can make money by helping them implement those policies." He explained that nowadays Chinese reforestation representatives occasionally visit the village, exhorting local Nuosu to reclaim their 'ancient' animistic practices of protecting trees, neglected in the recent decades of official land clearances and the wood-trafficking racket. I realized that Tuo-sat was gradually revealing the larger implications of his hidden joke about animism, namely, that Nuosu were profiting from eco-friendly policies built on neo-Confucian inspired ideals of animistic forest management.

Just then, I recalled how, only a generation ago, the Nuosu responded to the demands of the Han market by boosting their poppy growing for opium sales. I reminded Tuosat of this and asked if the new reforestation efforts truly arose from government efforts to promote animism. He replied: "Yes, they want to reintroduce trees, so they use the ideology of animism. Of course, this ideology is different from the local animistic ideas found in our own rites and sacrifices. But when joining their reforestation projects, we talk in terms of animism as an ideology because this brings money to the village." Tuosat mused that after being exposed to official views on animism, some villagers, especially the younger generations, have begun to assimilate them, interlacing Chinese ideas with Nuosu ones—or at least juxtaposing them in the joking terms that lead to personalized adaptations of Nuosu knowledge. Tuosat added that the government always wants to implement environmental policies in the cheapest possible way, sourcing trees at low cost and having villagers do all the work of caring for their lands. Yet, he said, Nuosu welcome opportunities to contribute to governmental efforts by planting fields of trees—with unexpected diligence—in order to bring prosperity to the village. Amused that they can profit from these sales, some Nuosu seek to capture further profits from (now illicit) wood-trafficking at night, which perpetuates the market for reforestation work. Ironies like these abound across China, and, as Hans Steinmüller (2011) notes, they are commonly invoked among 'insiders' to the community when speaking about sensitive matters. Drawing on Michael Herzfeld (2005), Stein-müller (2011: 227) suggests that, for those who can detect it, irony "point[s] towards a space of intimate local self-knowledge," producing a "community of complicity." Nuosu often assume that their local knowledge is not fully per-ceived across the cultural gulfs that divide them from outsiders—at least not until their hidden jokes have enabled them to succeed in the art of capture.

Tuosat took me on a brief walk to point out more hillsides that would benefit from the reforestation policies. He proudly stated that Nuosu are a very clever people, contrasting them to the Tibetans, who make a high-profile fuss about independence and attract many Chinese to their area. In contrast, he said, Nuosu keep a distance from the Chinese, patiently awaiting the introduction of benefit schemes that might enter—or be lured to—their areas. Suddenly, he said: "Look, you see? There are no Chinese flags flying in the village here. It's just the Nuosu livelihood all around. We ensure that we have everything we need, keeping our lives happy and filled with jokes and laughter in the Nuosu way, and that's good enough." Pausing a few moments, he wistfully added: "The only other thing we need is to raise the standard of living without turning the countryside into the city. So I'm helping the villagers with projects like growing the trees." I realized that Tuosat was indirectly sharing with me, in the Nuosu style of revealing hidden knowledge or a hidden joke, that their art of capture underpins more than everyday competition between Nuosu or the ritualized warfare of village exorcisms. More fundamentally, the art of capture enables Nuosu to engage, quite often on their own terms, with the peoples, politics, and economics of China and beyond. Just as this observation was formulating in my mind, Tuosat gave it further clarity and force by musing aloud: "Maybe this is the difference between us. You miss the people when you leave and think about them a lot, writing about animism and famous anthropologists. But I should do more, since this is my home village. I should help them recognize opportunities, such as understanding how animism brings money to the village."

We picked up this discussion a week later when we met in the provincial capital of Kunming. Tuosat spoke as a rather inspired native anthropologist, fully aware that I planned to write a piece on animistic ideas that would feature his viewpoint. Starting with his own understanding of animism, Tuosat reiterated that Nuosu do not follow the ideology of animism propounded by the CCP. Yet, in everyday life, they believe that everything has a soul and should be feared and respected, since people are just one part of the world. Summing this up anthropologically, Tuosat concluded that animism is neither a philosophy nor an ideology for Nuosu, but social life itself. He even felt that his Nuosu animistic upbringing informed his anthropological writing and personality. Continuing, Tuosat said that, nowadays, the irony is that animism is practiced by the whole of China to protect the environment, even though many people have lost or never had animistic ideas of their own. Up until 20–30 years ago, he explained, Nuosu had notions about tree protection built into their animistic ideas, but the government sent Chinese workers to their area to lead the way in cutting down trees. Then in 1998, the policies shifted again, and no one was allowed to cut trees along the Jinsha River. Since then, the CCP has superimposed views about 'protective animism' onto the Nuosu. However, Nuosu do not find it easy to recover animistic ideas that were undercut by the government. Reminiscing about practices learned in his youth, Tuosat (about 40 years old at the time of our meeting) noted that Nuosu who fell trees from the mountain still cover the freshly denuded stumps with soil in order to avoid angering the mountain spirit by flagrantly revealing their logging. In the past, when building a new wooden home, they also carried out a practice of divining which side of a tree to cut first before worshipping and felling it. Tuosat critiqued the inconsistency of the CCP for officially denying spirits and gods through Marxist materialism while at the same time propounding environmental protection through the ideology of animism.

I asked Tuosat if he felt that, by shifting the definition of 'animism as a practice' to 'animism as an ideology', the CCP had given the term 'animism' a life of its own that impinges on Nuosu people much like spirits, ghosts, or souls do. After all, once animism was transformed into political rhetoric, it mobilized new (even if ironic) animistic practices, encouraging the locals in Tuosat's home village to undertake fir tree cultivation in order to bring government funds their way. In both reforestation work and ritualized warfare, I noted, Nuosu approach animism as a reflexive battle of wits, using hidden knowledge or jokes to lure others into close enough range to accomplish the art of capture. Tuosat laughingly agreed that I could take this view and reminded me that

Nuosu would patiently keep awaiting remunerative opportunities in reforestation, capturing what resources they could from the new animism.

Concluding Thoughts on the Life of Animistic Ideas

Returning to the themes introduced at the beginning of this chapter, I suggest that the Nuosu art of capture offers a fresh platform for parsing the substance of animistic thought and practice. Classic studies of animism have focused on the process of life, highlighting the notion that the soul outlives physical death. There is an additional layer of complexity when studying the life of animistic ideas among peoples like the Nuosu, who have been exposed to our disciplinary concepts through anthropological friends and Chinese state ideology. Nuosu animistic ideas unfold reflexively through hidden knowledge and jokes, such as Katba's declaration that he was the true source of information for Mitsu's book on the Daoist-inspired elements of Nuosu religion. Yet hidden knowledge also inspires native scholars like Mitsu to rethink their ethno-historical assumptions; it inspires villagers to battle with ghosts for their captured souls; it even inspires native anthropologists like Tuosat to sarcastically harness the state's ideology of animism in hopes of increasing their village's revenue. At another level, academics like Tuosat not only hold that animistic ideas impinge on their anthropological writing and personalities; they also put this observation rather reflexively into practice. What the Nuosu art of capture brings to anthropology, then, is a new heuristic tool for revealing how certain people might use hidden jokes or knowledge to unleash personalized reinventions of their cosmologies, ways of life, and engagements with the anthropological world.

Acknowledgments

Earlier versions of this chapter were presented at departmental research seminars in social anthropology at the London School of Economics, the School of Oriental and African Studies, and the University of Kent, as well as at the Magic Circle seminar under Piers Vitebsky at the Scott Polar Research Institute, University of Cambridge. My fieldwork among the Nuosu, on which this chapter is based, was funded by an AHRC-ESRC Large Research Grant (AH/H0016147/1) and an earlier ESRC Large Research Grant (RES-000-23-1408) at the University of Oxford, as well as the Frederick Williamson Memorial Fund at the University of Cambridge. I extend thanks to my Nuosu friends and colleagues, the two anonymous reviewers, and my co-editor of this book, Mireille Mazard, who generously shared many valuable insights with me.

Katherine Swancutt is a Senior Lecturer in the Anthropology of Religion in the Department of Theology and Religious Studies, King's College London. She is the author of *Fortune and the Cursed: The Sliding Scale of Time in Mongolian Divination* (2012). Her main area of interest is Inner Asia, and she has conducted fieldwork among Buryat Mongols, Deed Mongols, and, more recently, the Nuosu of Southwest China. A major theme running through her work has been the rise of innovative religious practices, especially among animistic or shamanic groups. Currently, she is taking her work in several related directions that reveal the links between imagination and ethno-theology in China, from the study of fame and the production of ethnographic dreams to the internationalization of indigenous peoples through native and foreign scholarship.

Notes

1. All persons in this chapter have been given pseudonyms.
2. See the chapters by Espírito Santo, Grotti and Brightman, and Ulturgasheva in this book for resonant discussions about how autobiographical narratives—like academic works produced by native ethno-historians—are built on and become part of a person's powerful extended selfhood.
3. This inhospitable sweeping parallels the faux pas Nuosu sometimes make when sweeping their homes too soon after a relative has departed on a journey, which makes the traveler lose his or her soul.

References

Asu Daling. 2008. *Poyi Qiangu Yijing: Jianlun Yi Han Wenhua de Tong Yuanxing* [A Translation Laying Bare the Book of Changes throughout the Ages: The Dual Theory of Shared Origins Underpinning Yi and Han Culture]. Kunming: Yunnan minzu chubanshe.

Chang, Peter T. C. 2011. "China's Environmental Crisis: Practical Insights from Chinese Religiosity." *Worldviews: Global Religions, Culture, and Ecology* 15 (3): 247–267.

He Shutao. 2000. "Zhizhu shi Ren de Linghun Huashen." [Spiders Are Transformations of Human Souls] In *Zhongguo Ge Minzu Yuanshi Zongjiao Ziliao Jicheng: Naxizu, Qiangzu, Dulongzu Juan, Lisuzu, Nuzujuan* [Collected Materials on Primitive Religions of All Chinese Nationalities: Naxi, Qiang, Dulong, Lisu, and Nu Nationality Chapters], ed. He Zhiwu, Qian Anduan, and Cai Jiaqi, 845. Beijing: Zhongguo shehui kexue chubanshe.

Herzfeld, Michael. 2005. *Cultural Intimacy: Social Poetics in the Nation-State.* New York: Routledge.

Hill, Ann M. 2001. "Captives, Kin, and Slaves in Xiao Liangshan." *Journal of Asian Studies* 60 (4): 1033–1049.

Mazard, Mireille. 2011. "Powerful Speech: Remembering the Long Cultural Revolution in Yunnan." *Inner Asia* 13: 157–178.

Pan Jiao. 1997. "The Maintenance of the LoLo Caste Idea in Socialist China." *Inner Asia* 2 (1): 108–127.

Robinet, Isabelle. 1993. *Taoist Meditation: The Mao-shan Tradition of Great Purity.* Trans. Julian F. Pas and Norman J. Girardot. New York: State University of New York Press.

Scott, Michael W. 2007. *The Severed Snake: Matrilineages, Making Place, and a Melanesian Christianity in Southwest Solomon Islands.* Durham, NC: Carolina Academic Press.

Steinmüller, Hans. 2011. "The Reflective Peephole Method: Ruralism and Awkwardness in the Ethnography of Rural China." *Australian Journal of Anthropology* 22 (2): 220–235.

Swancutt, Katherine. 2012a. "The Captive Guest: Spider Webs of Hospitality among the Nuosu of Southwest China." *Journal of the Royal Anthropological Institute* 18 (S1): S103–S116.

Swancutt, Katherine. 2012b. "Fame, Fate-Fortune, and Tokens of Value among the Nuosu of Southwest China." *Social Analysis* 56 (2): 56–72.

Swancutt, Katherine. 2012c. "Masked Predation, Hierarchy and the Scaling of Extractive Relations in Inner Asia and Beyond." In *Animism in Rainforest and Tundra: Personhood, Animals, Plants and Things in Contemporary Amazonia and Siberia,* ed. Marc Brightman, Vanessa E. Grotti, and Olga Ulturgasheva, 175–194. New York: Berghahn Books.

Swancutt, Katherine. 2015. "Imaginations at War: The Ephemeral of the Fullness of Life in Southwest China." In *Objects and Imagination: Perspectives on Materialization and Meaning,* ed. Øivind Fuglerud and Leon Wainwright, 133–159. New York: Berghahn Books.

Tylor, Edward B. (1871) 1920. *Primitive Culture: Researches into the Development of Mythology, Philosophy, Religion, Language, Art and Custom.* Vols. 1 and 2. London: John Murray.

Chapter 5

NARRATIVES OF THE INVISIBLE
Autobiography, Kinship, and Alterity in Native Amazonia

Vanessa Elisa Grotti and Marc Brightman

> Before I was born, Sirirumai knew that I would be a shaman. 'He will be a sha-
> man,' he said about me to others. 'He is destined to be a shaman, for there are
> spirits all around him and within him.' He said that before I was born. (Wetaru
> and Koelewijn 2003: 338)

Native Amazonian societies live and engage with a world in which what is
visible is never given, where things and people change form and where appearances are deceiving. Apprehending the invisible—that is, relating to persons
who cannot be seen by all—is the skill given to shamans. Shamans have 'sight',
the capacity to see what others cannot, and this powerful ability allows them to
interact with spirits and develop bonds of commensality with invisible others.
This ambiguous commensality places them in a constant oscillation between
spheres of intimacy that are both visible and invisible (Chaumeil 1983; Rivière
1994, 1995). The spirit world, a place of power and transformation, is rarely

described by native interlocutors in a detached, objective way, but rather in terms of experiences and events.[1] Personal accounts of experiences with the invisible have been studied widely with regard to the shamanic initiation and quest, a genre also familiar to students of shamanic societies outside Amazonia (Chaumeil 1983; Eliade 1964; Harner 1973). In native Amazonia, a genre of ritual autobiography exists that combines mythic narratives and stories of personal experience in performances of dreams and visions, and the analysis of such oral texts, together with studies of native Amazonian mythology, has already given rise to an important body of work (e.g., Basso 1995; Basso and Senft 2009; Course 2009; Déléage 2007; Oakdale 2005, 2009).

Instead of focusing on the formal qualities of personal accounts of the spirit world by analyzing either ritual performance or the genre of shamanic quests, we shall consider life histories as autobiographical accounts, to explore what they reveal about the relationship between history (and indigenous historicity) and the spirit world (cf. Hendricks 1993). In our analysis, we suggest that this is characterized by a form of 'double reflexivity', by which we mean a reflexivity that is both internal to the self and constituted through relationships between interlocutors. Such a concept has a particular poignancy in the context of native Amazonian personhood, which is understood to be malleable and relationally constituted. This notion of 'double reflexivity' is not identical to the concept of 'hyper-reflexivity' introduced by the editors of this book. The former is grounded in more pervasive aspects of native Amazonian thought and practice, whereas the latter appears as a more global phenomenon with a particular relationship to anthropological discourse. In an Amazonian context, hyper-reflexivity can be seen as a particular form of enactment of double reflexivity, although it may be difficult, even impossible, to identify where one ends and the other begins. However, to reduce our argument to this point would not do justice to the richness of the autobiographical material we discuss. We therefore deliberately seek to leave our chapter partially open-ended, giving scope for the material to speak for itself. In doing so, we attempt to put the ethnographic object on the same footing as the anthropologist's gaze, in keeping with the aims of this volume as a whole.

The life histories presented in this chapter were collected among the Trio people in the Surinamese village of Tëpu, in which a number of Wayana and most of the surviving nomadic hunter-gatherer Akuriyo also live today. Like the other main Trio and Wayana villages, Tëpu is an old mission station founded by North American missionaries from the West Indies Mission and the Unevangelized Fields Mission in the second half of the 1960s on the upper reaches of the Tapanahoni River in the district of Sipaliwini, in southern Suriname. Since 2003, we have both worked among these three Central Carib groups, mainly focusing on the Trio. The Trio and Wayana are swidden horticulturalists who, prior to contact and sedentarization,[2] lived in smaller, semi-nomadic cognatic groups of about 30 people, which usually settled alongside creeks and maintained a powerful ontological engagement with the forest and the river.[3] Since the 1960s, they have lived alongside each other in sedentary villages across the triple border that separates Suriname, French Guiana, and Brazil. While their kinship-making process through the quotidian conventions of nurture of kin and commensality with affines remains characterized by a strong ideal of endogamy and uxorilo-cality (Rivière 1969, 1984), and despite their distinct historical backgrounds, Trio and Wayana alike have developed in their individual and collective dis-courses a new emphasis on a historical shift that they respectively describe as 'pacification' and 'opening up' (Grotti 2009, 2013; cf. Chapuis and Rivière 2003). In these discourses, the Trio and Wayana emphasize the novelty of their paci-fied, post-contact bodily and communal states, marked by population aggrega-tion in village formations numbering between 100 and 300 people (and up to 1,000 for the Trio village of Kwamalasamutu in southwestern Suriname), situ-ated along large rivers. They contrast this with their past state, characterized by life in the shelter of the forest in small groups in a state of heightened predatory and transformational capacities. As Gabriel,[4] the Wayana son-in-law of our Trio host, once told us: "Before, people did not have many kin, they lived in little vil-lages, they did not go to the places of other people, they looked after their young daughters, they did not live like in this village here [Tëpu], they lived near the forest, just inside the forest. Then, they saw them [spirits] all the time, because we [the Wayana] could still transform into different beings—this was just before we transformed into real people [true Wayana]."

For the Trio and Wayana, contemporary life is characterized by a shift in the management of alterity, whereby other people—for example, distant affines, other Amerindians, and other types of people such as Maroons (*mekoro*)[5] and urban people (*pananakiri*, or *palasisi* in Wayana)—have become the privi-leged location of alterity, previously held by the forest and its spirits (Grotti 2013).[6] Native descriptions and interpretations of historical change are there-fore inseparable from the question of how people relate to the dead and to the spirit world, not to mention the 'new' world 'opened up' by the 'pacification' of sedentary living.[7] The past actions of kin and the interventions of spirits are also perceived as central elements in the formation of a person, and, as we shall see, they are at center stage in the accounts of individuals' biographies, their *iwehtoponpë* (lit., 'former way of being'). But first we will briefly discuss the forms and uses of biography in Amazonian ethnology.

Biographies: Mediated Lives or Dialogical Histories?

In contrast to lowland South America, indigenous autobiography is a highly developed form in North America, but this must be understood in its histori-cal context. Citing Brumble's (1988) study of Native American autobiography, Sáez (2007: 14) writes: "[T]he collection of indigenous autobiographies was a significant part of a civilizing process, a resource for educators, indigenists, and missionaries to obtain 'individual souls' to fit the psychological requirements of the West."[8] While they clearly engage with the Western individualist tradi-tion, native autobiographies do not simply emerge from it, nor are they simply mediated by outsiders. To say this would be to suggest that beneath the process of mediation (i.e., soliciting, transcribing, organizing, and publishing native testimonies) lies an 'authentic' version of the text that the reader glimpses as if through a glass darkly. We would suggest that any kind of text that is produced collaboratively bears the signs of the relationship out of which it grew, even to its core. We argue further that this has a special significance and resonance for the native peoples of Amazonia, for whom the growth and health of the person and the reproduction of society depend upon both predatory and nurturing relationships with alterity. The specific features of native Amazonian person-hood (Grotti and Brightman 2012; Miller 2007), composed of multiple relations with alterity, suggest an answer to Sáez's (2007: 15) question: "[W]hat is an indigenous narrator talking about when he talks about himself?" We shall argue that the answer to this question is that he or she is talking about others, yet in ways that inescapably reflect his or her own (often 'original') social perspective.

The emerging genre of native Amazonian autobiography characteristically situates its subject as an Amerindian in relation to non-Amerindians (Sáez 2007). Indeed, biographical texts are most often produced through a dialogue between an Amerindian and a non-Amerindian, whether the latter be an eth-nographer, a missionary, or some different kind of other (see Biocca [1969] 1996;[9] Cognat [1967] 1987, 1977;[10] Kopenawa and Albert 2012; Rubenstein 2002). This reflects the native perception of the genre as a white or non-Amerindian mode of expression, which frequently finds its way into the texts themselves, and of the production of the text itself as a way of relating to the non-Amerindian other.[11] This observation illustrates an important way in which the 'ethnographically astute' informant is produced. In fact, such autobi-ographical texts, despite being ostensibly about their authors and their cultures (Carneiro da Cunha 2009), can simultaneously be regarded as commentaries on the white, urban cultures for whom (or at least in whose formal tradition) they were written (see, e.g., Kopenawa and Albert 2010). When we read native texts that have been solicited and mediated by outsiders, a double reflexivity occurs as we see our own culture reflected back at us. This is perhaps the most common and the oldest form of indigenous testimony. The claims to authentic-ity made by early European travelers to the New World are based not only on having 'been there', but also on testimonies recorded by the authors. Ralegh's ([1596] 1997: 181) interview with "one old *Topiawari*, with whom I much desired to have farther conference" provides the source of strategic informa-tion for a prospective invasion of Guiana. But in such accounts, even those that seem most faithful to events (e.g., de Léry [1578] 2008; Staden [1557] 2008), the native voice is hidden behind that of the European narrator.

In Amazonia, and particularly in the past decade or so, anthropologists have paid attention to traditional ritual autobiographies and to the self-affirming nar-ratives of indigenous leaders. The autobiographies of leaders discussed by Sáez (2007) represent the use of a genre that focuses on the self to affirm the col-lectivity. Leaders embody the group, and, as 'magnified persons' (Fausto 2012), they submit a non-native genre to the logic of their role. But a form of indig-enous biography that has received scarcely any attention strikes us as having particular importance, especially in the context of emerging indigenous spiritu-alities through conversion to Christianity. Protestant evangelical missionaries have a particular interest in testimonies that is based on a long tradition.[12] With discernible roots in the biblical parable and, perhaps more directly, in Pauline conversion testimony, the (auto)biography plays a central role in missionary practice. Dowdy's (1963) *Christ's Witchdoctor*, a sensational account of the conversion of a Waiwai shaman in neighboring Guyana, is a clear example. The author explains that he chose to tell the story of the conversion of the Waiwai "through the experiences of their chief. He and their testimonies to the grace of God are living witness to the dedication and skill of those who brought the news about God to the jungles of British Guiana" (ibid.: ix). This book, a bestseller in evangelical Christian circles, was clearly intended for the home community of the church and donors to the missionary endeavor.

Here we will discuss a very different example of missionary autobiography, which highlights the important role that missionaries have played in introducing literacy, in the form of the Bible, as a source of knowledge and power, and as a practice through the teaching of reading and writing. *Tëmeta Inponopïhpë Panpira* (Tëmeta's Testament) (Wetaru and Koelewijn 2003) appears at first sight to be another evangelical parable—the story of a shaman who gave up his powers to embrace Christianity. In this case, however, the voice is that of the shaman Tëmeta himself, transcribed from a long series of interviews with the former missionary schoolteacher Cees Koelewijn. Tëmeta was not a cosmopolitan leader familiar with world cities and international conferences, like those discussed by Sáez (2007), yet he was known throughout the region as an exceptionally powerful shaman. The production of Tëmeta's 'testament' emerged from a long and affectionate relationship between him and Koelewijn and from their shared interest in spirituality. Koelewijn is an actively practicing Dutch Protestant, but despite his friendly relationship with the American missionaries who are active in Suriname, he does not share their belief in the necessity of radically transforming indigenous culture, of 'wiping the slate clean' to start anew. Instead, his long experience among the Trio, and especially his friendship with Tëmeta, nurtured in him a great affection for Trio culture, which he saw as containing glimmers of revelation, expressed in certain Trio myths. Koelewijn's mastery of the Trio language and his fascination with the invisible world of spirits and shamanism equipped him, perhaps uniquely, to mediate between these two worlds and, indeed, between these two autobiographical genres, the missionary and the anthropological.

Tëmeta's autobiography was published in a dual Trio and Dutch-language edition in 2003, a few years after Tëmeta's death. Its intended readership is not a home community of churchgoers and mission donors; instead, it is primarily conceived as a gift to the Trio themselves. Koelewijn played an important role in introducing literacy to the generation of young Trio who attended his school in the 1970s. He organized a party in Tëpu to formally present the book to the village, whose leader (*kapitein*) is one of Tëmeta's sons, and to open the small library that Koelewijn had built to house a collection of books related to the Trio, including his own transcriptions and translations of Trio myths (Koelewijn 1984; Koelewijn and Rivière 1987). In this case, the motivation for producing and, indeed, giving the book to the Trio people appears complex. Partly, it may be to encourage others to give up the 'old ways' of shamanism and embrace Christianity as Tëmeta did. However, Koelewijn writes in the Dutch version of the foreword that the book is a *studiebook* of information on Trio culture, and it is in fact a rich, complex testimony. Far from portraying the 'old ways' as uniquely evil and reprehensible, it offers them from a human perspective in all their beauty and tragedy.

Mapping the Past: Dead Relatives and Abandoned Villages

It is worth underlining that Tëmeta's autobiography is an exceptional text. Among Trio people, its author (who was crippled by polio) had an extraordinary ability as a storyteller. His knowledge of the spirit world was unmatched, and his family history was unique, as we shall see. Compared to other cases across Amazonia, Tëmeta's account stands out for its aesthetic and emotional qualities, even alongside those of other astute, politically self-aware subjects, who tend (like him) to be leaders or shamans. Everyday experience is sometimes left out of the accounts of such individuals, as Oakdale (2009) discovered when she solicited a life history from a powerful shaman. When he finally agreed to her requests, "[r]ather than the comprehensive life history I had been expecting, [the shaman Prepori] narrated an account only of how he had developed his shamanic skills" (ibid.: 164). We did not find quite such a marked contrast between ordinary and powerful informants among the Trio. It is possible that this difference arose in part from the intimate circumstances of the documentation of the shaman's story. Be this as it may, even the story of Tëmeta's initiation is unique in many ways.

We collected life histories from charismatic, respected senior figures accustomed to speaking to an audience and from more modest individuals without any pretensions to privileged experience. In each case, we asked our interlocutor to tell us his story,[13] to speak to us about his past, his *iwehtoponpë*, or 'former way of being'. Like Tëmeta's testimony, the former shamans who told us their stories gave us more than an account of their shamanic initiations, and all of our interlocutors gave us personal accounts without any features of ritual performance. Boaz, our host grandfather in Tëpu, related the following: "Today, Vanessa is here in Tëpu. She has come here. I have also come here from my own village. I was little in Pono Eku, which was a very large village; there were many of us there ... Now I live in Suriname, in the white people's village [*pananakiri ipata*]." Here Boaz illustrates a tendency shared with all of the people whose life stories we collected. They describe one or, more often, several places in which they spent their childhood and youth and mention their close kin with whom they lived in those places. Most narratives read almost like lists of people and places. By way of example, here is an extract from Tim's story:

> We were there before, at Pokorowa. I was at Tëpumïn Eneto, and I was in that village. I was small there, and my father was there, he had married my mother. My father went to Paruma, he had lived in Paruma. So there, in Pokorowa, my

father married my mother. So they had children, me and my brothers. I was born in Tëpumïn Eneto. But my grandfather did not want my mother to marry my father, because he was not kind to other people. But Tamarema was very kind, he was the father of my uncles. Tamarema was also the father of my mother. My mother was there in Tëpumin Eneto, there were Kuramenaru and Jukëre-ton, their father was kind and happy … Then, we left the village of Pokorowa because somebody died there, it was my aunt who died. Then we went to the new village of Oto Entu. I was there because my father had made a new village. Then my father died in Tïpokïnen Kentë … Two people died in our old village of Oto Entu. Then we went to the other village of Susare Eku … then my uncle died, my mother's brother. Then we went a bit further down, to Siririkane, near Surare Eku, we used to say that the Siririkane was a water spirit … then we left because we no longer had a leader. That's why we split, we separated. First we were with our relatives in Kuwatapenman. Sïkrai died in Kuwatapenman, he lived in Tïnkaipoeinkato …

The story continues with several more deaths and migrations, until the Americans appear and preach the gospel, and Tim and his family come to settle in Tëpu:

I still wanted to go back to my place. But we had come from Paru and we wanted to stay here in Tëpu … We have lived here since 1962.[14] But I do not know how long it had been since we were in Paruma, I do not know because then I could not read and count the calendar. Here in Tëpu, I learned to read the years of the calendar … so now there are calendars. Today we are in the month of May, we also know the days, because there are calendars, and we also know how to read the years. Now we remember everything.

The places and people of the speaker's youth represent a finished past that lacks continuity with the present. When Tim and others come to mention Tëpu, 'the white people's village', they appear to evoke another, more recent era—the present—and another time, one measured with clocks and calendars (Brightman 2012). In doing so, Trio narrators emphasize a rupture with a past that is associated with an isolated life in the forest and regular migrations through a landscape made of places created and abandoned to the spirits at the death of their founder (cf. Robbins 2007; Vilaça and Wright 2009). The present is a life of increased physical interaction with former enemies and distant affines alike, in permanent villages that have survived the death of their foreign, missionary founders. Rather than being abandoned, houses remain occupied by widows and grandchildren following the death of one of their occupants, and bodies of the dead are buried in a cemetery.

Most Trio people evoke the spirit world directly only when they mention the deaths of their kin, as this extract from Julius's story illustrates: "There. That's how it was. So I didn't have any more sisters. My father died because of *ëremi* [spirit curses]. My sister died because of curses. My uncle died because of curses, that's all. The Trio were terrible poisoners. They used to take the earth you walked on. They took the seeds of sweet peas, that's the fruit … they also scraped the paint from the skin, or they would cut our hair while we slept.

That's what the Trio used to do, they were terrible poisoners." These narratives focus on dead relatives and abandoned villages—people and places that return to alterity. They evoke encounters and events centered on social life in the village: initiation, growing as taught by parents, marriages and children, migrations between settlements, and death from witchcraft. Conversion comes as a point marked by the arrival of white people who, in the Trio's words, start to teach and 'grow' (*arimika*) them. Trio narrators struggle to reproduce concepts introduced through the conversion process. They often return to the missionary idea of spirits being 'bad', but they seem frustrated that neither spirits nor Jesus can be seen. Jesus, they are told, is a spirit (*omore*) who lives in the sky.

This emphasis on historical rupture is present in both Trio and Wayana discourse. Among the Trio, the state of 'pacification' (*sasame wehto*) becomes entangled with the arrival of the missionaries in Suriname, an event that did not occur among the Wayana who live in French Guiana and instead underwent a 'secular' process of sedentarization. The missionaries' intense interest and scrutiny of the invisible world, considered as the satanic source of the evils of indigenous Amazonian societies, is reflected in Trio life narratives, which all dwell on the missionaries' repeated questions and discourses on all matters mystical—a feature that, to our knowledge, is not found in French Guianan Wayana narratives. Conversion, 'trying God' (i.e., praying), and listening to missionaries' ideas are reproduced in most Trio life stories, and these elements take a dramatic turn in narratives of shamanic conversion, as in Tëmeta's case. Conversion was visually (and dramatically) represented in the action taken by shamans like Tëmeta when they destroyed their shamanic rattles containing their spirit familiars.[15]

Thus, with an ironic twist of circumstances, indigenous life histories that were 'informed' by missionary literary practices tend to spontaneously dedicate greater space to the invisible world, as opposed to those practices informed by a secular process. In this context, the life narratives of Trio shamans become rich narratives of encounters and travels to the invisible world, as if to provide a dramatic contrast to the conversion to Christianity whose description they anticipate.

Alterity Within: Encounters and Sociability in the Invisible

Even when they speak of their kin in the past, the Trio evoke another world—the world of the dead. But if ordinary accounts of the making of a life describe relatives in far-off times and places, kinship is further twisted and inverted in the case of the shaman, and alterity is explicit, a counterpoint to the image of incest. Tëmeta was haunted by the idea that he was the product of an incestuous relationship between his brother and his mother: "So that's how it was when I was small. That's why I'm here now. I had no father, and the others, well ... My brother said that he did have a father. 'Apatu is my father,' he said, 'the father of Poje. I'm your father,' he told me ... So, as a child I lived with the man who saved me, with Sirirumai. He brought me up. I lived with him and my mother then lived with him too as his wife. I remember the time when my family didn't love me. Neither my sister nor my brother loved me. So I went to live with others and to grow up with them" (Wetaru and Koelewijn 2003: 340). Because of the alleged incestuous relationship between his mother and brother, Tëmeta became estranged from his kin. His adoptive father, Sirirumai, was a shaman. It was from this point on that Tëmeta began to discover that his kin were spirits: "Sirirumai was a *pïjai* [a shaman]. Sirirumai had said that I was also the son of an *irïpï* [spirit]. 'Whose [from whom] is he anyway?' he had asked. 'He is definitely the son of an *irïpï*. Maybe he is indeed a Trio, but I always see an atmosphere of spirits around him.' That's what Sirirumai had said to others before he died" (ibid.: 341).

Kinship is at the heart of the relationship between the shaman and his familiar spirits. Both shamans and spirits have *ikopija*, or spirit helpers. Shamans keep material manifestations of their spirit helpers, *kuri*, in their rattles, and they feed them with tobacco smoke and address them as their children. Yet it is clear from Tëmeta's account that it is the spirits who solicit *him* (Wetaru and Koelewijn 2003: 341):

> One day the spirit began to make me into a shaman. I did not begin to be a shaman by myself. I made no effort of my own. I was quiet, I held still. I did not know what it meant to be a shaman. That's how it usually happens, we do not know exactly how it is when we are shamans. Who can know that he is a shaman as a child? That's how it also was with me, I did not know. It was exactly as though I were lifted up. How shall I say … dizzy, yes, I felt dizzy. I fell on the ground and then a spirit came to me. Maybe the spirit threw me on the ground in order to have a good look at me. Seeing a spirit makes you dizzy. That's how it was with me. It made me dizzy so that it could look … Then I really saw him, then maybe the spirit was with[in] me … What do spirits actually do with you? A spirit that dwells within us possesses something. "You are like our stuff, our material," said the spirit to me, "that's why we come into you and then we help you." That's how it was. The spirit then came into me. I became its possession. It happened quite naturally. It overcame me. I did nothing to become a shaman.

It is striking that here, as he becomes a shaman, Tëmeta is called, initiated, and 'possessed' by the spirit. The spirit is his master. This inverts the more common notion that the spirit familiars of a mature shaman are his possessions, his pets, his children (Chaumeil 1983; Fausto 1999; Miller 2007).

As we mention above, Trio shamans referred to their spirit familiars as their children, and when they converted to Christianity, they agreed to destroy the rattles in which these familiars were contained. Peter Rivière, who carried out field research among the Trio in the early 1960s, witnessed some of these events and even played a role by agreeing to take some rattles with him to England when he finally left the field. The three Trio shaman's rattles that Rivière took were considered as good as destroyed. Rivière donated them to the Pitt Rivers Museum in Oxford, and in his written comments on these objects,[16] he includes a quotation from Tëmeta's autobiography, which describes the pain Tëmeta felt at having to destroy his child:

At this point my rattle became distasteful to me, I did not want it, I looked on it as if it were a toy. God did this to me. Then I no longer had trust in it, I did not believe in it. I said to the missionary [Morgan Jones], "Perhaps it is rubbish." I said, "What shall I do with it, where will I put my rattle? Shall I just pour out its contents, shall I just throw them away?" However I did not want to throw them away myself. I proposed to Morgan that he should destroy them if he wanted to. He answered, "You had better destroy them." "I do not want to do that because they are like children to me. So you may do it if you like, just destroy it" I said. "Who in the world destroys something that is like a child to him. Maybe some-one else can destroy my child. So I want you to do it," I said to him. "Yes, that is all right," he said and then he poured them out and threw them into the river. (Wetaru and Koelewijn 2003: 357; trans. P. Rivière)

What these two passages show is that spirits may be both masters and pets/children of humans at different times: Tëmeta is solicited by spirits as a child, but later becomes their master. The theme of mastery has become a significant one in Amazonian ethnology, as the importance of ownership and nurture as structuring principles in native Amazonian relations in the areas of politics, cosmology, ecology, and kinship is becoming increasingly clear (Brightman et al. 2016; Fausto 2012). Bonilla (2005, 2007, 2016) has shown that the position of prey, pet, or client may be actively sought and desired, and that submission can be part of a 'parasitic' strategy of life. Tëmeta's case further illustrates that the relationship between master and pet can also be inverted during different stages of life.

Souls and Spirits

We can now turn to the nature of the invisible world, populated by souls and spirits. The most commonly mentioned type of Trio soul, *omore*, is the 'image soul' or 'eye soul', which is also equated with the 'shadow'. There are other kinds of soul, less consistently mentioned by the Trio, that live in other parts of the body. These aspects of soul or soul matter seem to reside where there is a pulse, such as in the wrists and neck, below the knees, and in the heart. This is why the Trio adorn these parts of the body with bead ornaments. They are especially placed on children since their souls are not yet considered to be firmly attached to their bodies, making them more vulnerable to spirit attack.

Along with body and soul, there is a further constituent element of the person for the Trio—a person's name, or *eka*, which has been interpreted as performing the role of binding the body and soul together (Rivière 1999). The name persists after death, although it is not uttered for a period until the body and soul are fully separated and the corporeal elements of the individual person have been forgotten. At this point, the name of a deceased person, often a grandparent, can be given to a baby. Names seem to be elements or emanations of the self, and the living cannot share names. Moreover, each individual has several names, at least one of which is never uttered. The others are 'public' names that have less powerful associations with the soul.

Souls are not the only invisible entities in the Trio's universe. There are also spirits, *wïrïpë* or *irïpï*. In terms of the distinction between bodies and souls, spirits seem to be invisible bodies—only shamans can see them, and they see them as persons with bodies of human or animal form.[17] Here Tëmeta is describing his experience as he was being turned into a shaman: "Then the real spirit changed me. It wanted to make my body the same as that of its own. I saw all kinds of figures. They looked like people [*wïtoto*], like Maroons, like animals ... I saw the transformations of animals, I saw the metamorphosis of anteaters. So I saw all that, animals and spirits that changed into people" (Wetaru and Koelewijn 2003: 342–343). Spirits are not only or always invisible to all but shamans, however. Levi, a former shaman who became a prominent church pastor, told us about some of the animals, especially birds, that are, at least in some cases, spirits: "Our grandfather told us ... 'the eagle, it's a spirit [*wïrïpë*]'. The eagle had a costume, it's a spirit. The eagle is like the costume of a spirit." Certain bird-spirits are also helpers or advisers in specific situations or are associated with specific animals. Certain animals—snakes, jaguars, eagles, rats—must not be touched or eaten because they are spirits.

Shamans and spirits are characterized by their ability to metamorphose by putting on the 'clothes' of other beings. This happened to Tëmeta even before he was born when a spirit came to inhabit his body. His mother thought her unborn baby was dying because when she went into the water to bathe, she could no longer feel it move. The water is also the spirit realm, and a shaman told her, "He is not dead. He is just keeping still. It is as if he is unconscious because there is an *irïpï* in him. The spirits have made him still. He will later be a shaman" (Wetaru and Koelewijn 2003: 341). As a child, Tëmeta grew ill with polio, and he thought that he was being attacked by spirits. But his shaman uncle and adoptive father told him that it was 'other people' who were sending spirits against him. As we have seen, he had said that Tëmeta had had spirits all around him, since his birth, and that these spirits wanted to help him. At this point, as he was struggling with his polio, Tëmeta came to know the spirits and to become a shaman. His uncle gave him a medicinal bath, and suddenly he was able to see clearly: "After the bath everything was clear to me, just as the shaman had predicted. The spirit came near me and spoke with me, he told me about everything, he was my kin [*jimoitïmeken*] ... If I went on a journey, in the air or on the ground, I had a solid path, my path was good. I learned how a spirit travels, I learned how spirits are ... I could see the spirits, and where they were and also what they did, which spirits were false and dangerous and which went hunting for victims" (ibid.: 344). At this point, Tëmeta is able to put on the 'clothes' of the spirits: "I was in him, I was in the *wïrïpë*, I wore his clothes [*ipotao*]. That's how we call it: we wear their clothes. That's what I did. So the *irïpï* made me like itself: self-assured and invincible" (ibid.: 345). So there are clear relations of kinship and even evocations of the life-course between shamans and their spirits. Tëmeta was the son of a spirit; when he became a shaman, he became the kin of the spirits that had been around him from birth. And he soon came to have his own spirit children, whom he nurtured and fed.[18]

The relationship between souls (*omore*) and spirits (*wïrïpë*) suggests that spirits are very much like bodies. The person is a combination of body and soul, sealed with a name, but the shaman is able to transform his bodily envelope into that of another species, and even into that of a spirit, without completely losing his original social perspective. However, Levi told us that the missionaries challenged these beliefs by preaching that the soul does not die. If a person has 'tried Jesus', then his soul goes to the sky (*kapu*); if he is sinful (*wïrïpëme*), or does not try Jesus, then it goes to the great fire, that is, *seitan*, or hell. Another informant, our host grandfather Boaz, told us that those who died before the arrival of the missionaries also went to *seitan*, but the difference between this description of hell and the traditional notion of *omorenpë pata*, the place of the dead souls, is not clear. This place traditionally had no moral accent, whereas hell clearly does. The missionaries have done their best to equate the two, but their success seems to be only partial. As Mazard also shows in this book, following the introduction of Christianity, the imposition of dualisms such as body and soul and the equation of spirits with evil and hell meet a peculiar sort of resistance on the part of animist cosmology, which diffuses and refracts such novelties rather than meeting them headlong.

Conclusion

Personal histories necessarily evoke the dead, and this does not come easily to Trio people. Like other Amazonians, they try hard to forget their dead kin (Taylor 1993), whose physical and spiritual disintegration is such that they are no longer human and their names and other souls are no longer one with their bodies (Vilaça 2000; cf. Mazard, this volume). As among the Javari in Taylor's (1993) account, it may be that forgetting is—or was—necessary to free Trio names and souls so that they might again circulate among the living and become attached to new, living bodies. The decision of the Trio to 'open up', to agree to live in white people's villages alongside affines, and to embrace Christianity signified the possibility of engaging with alterity without fear of reprisals. New names now circulate, as names from the city, from popular media, and from the Netherlands are given to children. This helps to explain why Trio people now have many kin and children and, like other Amazonian peoples, have undergone a rapid population growth in recent decades.

This proliferation of names, an illustration of a wider proliferation of relations with alterity, may well be related to the intense indigenous Christian activity that manifests itself most clearly in large 'Bible conferences' organized each year by Amerindians in different locations across the Guiana region. This can be read as one example of the tendency (transposed to Christianity) for shamanic activity to intensify in situations of contact, as several authors have noted (e.g., Butt 1960; Carneiro da Cunha 1998). This intensification has a corollary in life histories: missionary interest in the spirit world encourages former shamans to give precise descriptions of that world in their accounts. The shaman describes his relationships with invisible spirit others, producing a text in the medium of the white other as he speaks about the past, his former self, and his relations with dead kin. He is simultaneously here and elsewhere, a shaman and a pastor, white and Amerindian. Double (or even hyper-) reflexivity are in this way a source of shamanic power. As Carneiro da Cunha (1998) points out, the shaman is able to hold simultaneously several points of view and to translate harmoniously between them. We are reminded of the art of the storyteller, who is able to enchant his listeners and make them enter another world. Autobiographical storytelling emerges among the Trio as part of their 'becoming white' (Kelly 2005) and 'becoming Christian', but the form and content of these stories are also part of a structural relationship with alterity that transcends the rupture of conversion. (Auto)biography shows how people can turn from pets into masters and how they engage with the dead. It shows how Amerindians can become white, if only to remain more conscious of themselves (cf. Sahlins 2005), and it enables converted Christians to talk about their relationships with forest spirits.

No biography comes into existence without a reader, and even autobiography is produced through relationships with others. Animist or perspectivist ontologies may hold more clues for the interpretation of the infinite 'mirroring' of difference that may occur in such instances (Viveiros de Castro 2011). In the case of native Amazonians, life writing constitutes a relationship with alterity of the kind that is necessary for the processual production of the person. Beyond this, and more generally, the (auto)biographical text itself reflects on its subject (author), his or her interlocutor, and their respective social origins and cultural contexts (the differences between which may of course be blurred). In short, it is an artifact of a kind of double reflection that continues to reverberate with every reader.

Acknowledgments

We are grateful to the editors for their invitation to contribute to this book. Some of the initial ideas on which this chapter is based were presented in a short paper, "Relatives and the Invisible: Kinship, Spirits and the Dead in an Amazonian Society," at a workshop entitled "Ghosts and Apparitions in the Field," convened by Olga Ulturgasheva and Shane McCorristine at the Scott Polar Research Institute, University of Cambridge, on 27 May 2011. We carried out our research thanks to funding from the ESRC, the Gates Cambridge Trust, Trinity College Cambridge, the British Academy, and the Wellcome Trust. Last but not least, we would like to thank our Trio and Wayana hosts for taking good care of us and sharing the stories of their lives.

Vanessa Elisa Grotti is a part-time Professor at the Robert Schuman Centre for Advanced Studies, where she is leading research funded by an ERC Starting Grant entitled "Intimate Encounters in EU Borderlands: Migrant Maternity, Sovereignty and the Politics of Care on Europe's Peripheries" (ERC-2014-STG, 2015–2020). A social and medical anthropologist, she is interested in the study of kinship, personhood, and reproduction, especially in contexts of social change and crisis. Her publications include *Animism in Rainforest and Tundra* (2012, with Marc Brightman and Olga Ulturgasheva), *Ownership and Nurture: Studies in Native Amazonian Property Relations* (2016, with Carlos Fausto and Marc Brightman), and a forthcoming monograph, *Living with the Enemy: First Contacts and the Making of Christian Bodies in Amazonia.*

Marc Brightman is a Lecturer in Social Anthropology and co-director of CAOS, the Centre for the Anthropology of Sustainability, at University College, London. His research interests range from native Amazonian leadership to global political ecology and forest governance. His publications include *Animism in Rainforest and Tundra* (2012, with Vanessa Grotti and Olga Ulturgasheva), *Ownership and Nurture: Studies in Native Amazonian Property Relations* (2016, with Carlos Fausto and Vanessa Grotti), and *The Imbalance of Power: Leadership, Masculinity and Wealth in Amazonia* (2016).

Notes

1. On the theme of transformation, see also the chapters in this book by Diana Espírito Santo and Mireille Mazard.
2. We use the term 'sedentarization' to refer to the transition from a nomadic or semi-nomadic life in the forest to the establishment of long-term villages that survive the death of the founder or its elders. Although the Trio, the Wayana, and hunter-gatherer people proper, such as the Akuriyo, remain mobile and travel through the forest and, in the case of the Trio and Wayana, to distant places such as the city and Maroon villages, they now live alongside their dead, who are buried in a cemetery on the outskirts of the village. Sedentarization in this sense means a new relational pattern with the spirit world and the dead. We also aim to remain close to the Trio's description of their present village life and their own bodies as being different from the past and marked by stabilization.
3. The Akuriyo are a hunter-gatherer group who became captive slaves of the Trio following missionary contact expeditions in the 1960s and 1970s (Grotti and Brightman 2010).
4. The names of our main informants are pseudonyms.
5. All words in italics are Trio unless stated otherwise.
6. The management of alterity is a classic theme in Amazonian ethnology (Fausto 1999). For further discussion of the ways in which Trio people 'manage' alterity, see Brightman (2011), Grotti (2013), and Grotti and Brightman (2010, 2012).
7. To the Trio, humanity emerges in the mythic past through separation from the spirit world and the loss of certain capacities. This transformational story of the origin

of humanity exists alongside the Christian creation story, which Trio people accept as having been told to them by the 'Americans' (missionaries). This may seem paradoxical, even contradictory, unless one considers that each of these cosmologies has its own distinctive spatial and temporal dimensions. Christian stories are associated with a separate, distant past and with faraway places. The space-time of the spirit world, however, is at once distant and ever-present.

8. Unless otherwise indicated, all translations of cited texts are our own.

9. As described by Biocca ([1969] 1996), the case of Helena Valero raises intriguing questions about the relationship between native and outsider in the production of biography in relation to the question of the 'ethnographically astute' informant. A white girl captured as a child by Yanomami people, Helena met Biocca by chance during his expedition in Yanomami territory, and he took the opportunity to record her life history. She was able to communicate a white person's perspective on her experiences because of her background, but having 'become' Yanomami, she chose to remain among them. This case challenges the notion of an 'authentic' native account.

10. Known as Antecume in Wayana, André Cognat ([1967] 1987, 1977) raises another interesting parallel with Helena Valero (see above). Cognat was born in metropolitan France and was adopted into a Wayana household as a young man when traveling in southern French Guiana. He has been living among the Wayana since the early 1960s and is now a village leader and elder.

11. In contrast to some other native Amazonian peoples, the Trio do not have a traditional genre of ritual autobiography.

12. On other dimensions of the widespread influence of this tradition, see Robbins (2004) on confessional narratives and Keane's (1997) discussion of language and agency in a context of Dutch missionization.

13. Women were more reluctant to allow us to record their life stories. One woman, Boaz's sister, did agree. Her story remains typical in emphasizing former places and kin, as discussed below.

14. This date is no doubt a mistake as Tëpu was not founded until a few years later.

15. The relational nature of conversion processes is a feature common to Trio and other native Amazonian experiences and transformations of Christianity. These are discussed at length by Grotti (2009) for the Trio. For comparable cases across the region and a general discussion, see Vilaça and Wright (2009).

16. See Pitt Rivers Musuem, "1964.8.29 .1B: Shaman's Rattle." Online Database for Objects in the Collections of the Pitt Rivers Museum, University of Oxford, http://objects.prm.ox.ac.uk/pages/PRMUID23040.html.

17. On spirits as bodies and the non-dualism of spirits and bodies, cf. Mazard (this volume), Miller (2007), and Vilaça (2005). On the necessity of the relationship with alterity for the production of the person, cf. Espírito Santo (this volume). On the converse case of unfolding the elements of the dividual and projecting partible aspects of the self into the future, see Olga Ulturgasheva (this volume).

18. Also note that, as in Espírito Santo's chapter (this volume), the spirits act, by turns, as masters, guides, and helpers, occupying multiple shifting roles.

References

Basso, Ellen B. 1995. *The Last Cannibals: A South American Oral History*. Austin: University of Texas Press.
Basso, Ellen B., and Gunter Senft. 2009. "Introduction." In Senft and Basso 2009.
Biocca, Ettore. (1969) 1996. *Yanoáma: The Story of Helena Valero, a Girl Kidnapped by Amazonian Indians*. Trans. Dennis Rhodes, 1–20. New York: Kodansha.
Bonilla, Oiara. 2005. "O bom patrão e o inimigo voraz: Predação e comércio na cosmologia Paumari." *Mana* 11 (1): 41–66.
Bonilla, Oiara. 2007. "Des proies si désirables: Soumission et prédation pour les Paumari d'Amazonie brésilienne." PhD diss., École des Hautes Études en Sciences Sociales, Paris.
Bonilla, Oiara. 2016. "Parasitism and Subjection: Modes of Paumari Predation." In Brightman et al. 2016.
Brightman, Marc. 2011 "Archetypal Agents of Affinity: 'Sacred' Musical Instruments in the Guianas?" In *Burst of Breath: Indigenous Ritual Wind Instruments in Lowland South America*, ed. Jonathan D. Hill and Jean-Pierre Chaumeil, 201–218. Lincoln: University of Nebraska Press.
Brightman, Marc. 2012. "Maps and Clocks in Amazonia: The Things of Conversion and Conservation." *Journal of the Royal Anthropological Institute* 18 (3): 554–571.
Brightman, Marc, Carlos Fausto, and Vanessa Grotti, eds. 2016. *Ownership and Nurture: Studies in Native Amazonian Property Relations*. New York: Berghahn Books.
Brightman, Marc, Vanessa E. Grotti, and Olga Ulturgasheva, ed. 2012. *Animism in Rainforest and Tundra: Personhood, Animals, Plants and Things in Contemporary Amazonia and Siberia*. New York: Berghahn Books.
Brumble, H. David, III. 1988. *American Indian Autobiography*. Berkeley: University of California Press.
Butt, Audrey. 1960. "The Birth of a Religion." *Journal of the Royal Anthropological Institute* 90 (1): 66–106.
Carneiro da Cunha, Manuela. 1998. "Pontos de vista sobre a floresta amazônica: Xamanismo e tradução." *Mana* 4 (1): 7–22.
Carneiro da Cunha, Manuela. 2009. *"Culture" and Culture: Traditional Knowledge and Intellectual Rights*. Chicago: Prickly Paradigm Press.
Chapuis, Jean, and Hervé Rivière, eds. 2003. *Wayana eitoponpë: (Une) histoire (orale) des Indiens Wayana*. Matoury: Ibis Rouge.
Chaumeil, Jean-Pierre. 1983. *Voir, savoir, pouvoir: Le chamanisme chez les Yagua du Nord-Est péruvien*. Paris: École des Hautes Études en Sciences Sociales.
Cognat, André. (1967) 1987. *J'ai choisi d'être indien*. Paris: L'Harmattan.
Cognat, André. 1977. *Antécume ou une autre vie*. Ed. Claude Massot. Paris: R. Laffont.
Course, Magnus. 2009. "Why Mapuche Sing." *Journal of the Royal Anthropological Institute* 15 (2): 295–313.
Déléage, Pierre. 2007. "A Yaminahua Autobiographical Song: *Caqui Caqui*." *Tipití* 5 (1): 79–95.
de Léry, Jean. (1578) 2008. *Histoire d'un voyage faict en la terre du Brésil*, ed. Frank Lestringant. Paris: Librairie Générale Française.
Dowdy, Homer E. 1963. *Christ's Witchdoctor: From Savage Sorcerer to Jungle Missionary*. New York: Harper & Row.
Eliade, Mircea. 1964. *Shamanism: Archaic Techniques of Ecstasy*. Princeton, NJ: Princeton University Press.
Fausto, Carlos. 1999. "Of Enemies and Pets: Warfare and Shamanism in Amazonia." *American Ethnologist* 26 (4): 933–956.

Fausto, Carlos. 2012. "Too Many Owners: Mastery and Ownership in Amazonia." In Brightman et al. 2012, 29–47.

Grotti, Vanessa E. 2009. "Protestant Evangelism and the Transformability of Amerindian Bodies in Northeastern Amazonia." In Vilaça and Wright 2009, 109–125.

Grotti, Vanessa E. 2013. "The Wealth of the Body: Trade Relations, Objects and Personhood in Northeastern Amazonia." *Journal of Latin American and Caribbean Anthropology* 18 (1): 14–30.

Grotti, Vanessa E., and Marc Brightman. 2010. "The Other's Other: Nurturing the Bodies of 'Wild' People among the Trio of Southern Suriname." *Etnofoor* 22 (2): 51–70.

Grotti, Vanessa E., and Marc Brightman. 2012. "Humanity, Personhood and Transformability in Northern Amazonia." In Brightman et al. 2012, 162–174.

Harner, Michael, ed. 1973. *Hallucinogens and Shamanism*. Oxford: Oxford University Press.

Hendricks, Janet W. 1993. *To Drink of Death: The Narrative of a Shuar Warrior*. Tucson: University of Arizona Press.

Keane, Webb. 1997. "From Fetishism to Sincerity: On Agency, the Speaking Subject, and Their Historicity in the Context of Religious Conversion." *Comparative Studies in Society and History* 39 (4): 674–693.

Kelly, José Antonio. 2005. "Notas para uma teoria do 'virar branco.'" *Mana* 11 (1): 201–234.

Koelewijn, Cees. 1984. *Tarëno tamu inponopï panpira* [Stories of Trio Elders]. 2 vols. Leusden: Algemeen Diakonaal Bureau.

Koelewijn, Cees, and Peter Rivière. 1987. *Oral Literature of the Trio Indians of Surinam*. Dordrecht: Foris.

Kopenawa, Davi, and Bruce Albert. 2010. *La chute du ciel: Paroles d'un chaman Yanomami*. Paris: Plon.

Miller, Joana. 2007. "As coisas: Os enfeites corporais e a noção de pessoa entre os Mamaindê (Nambiquara)." PhD diss., Universidade Federal do Rio de Janeiro.

Oakdale, Suzanne. 2005. *I Foresee My Life: The Ritual Performance of Autobiography in an Amazonian Community*. Lincoln: University of Nebraska Press.

Oakdale, Suzanne. 2009. "Ritual and the Circulation of Experience: Negotiating Community in the Twentieth-Century Amazon." In Senft and Basso 2009, 153–170.

Ralegh, Walter. (1596) 1997. *The Discoverie of the Large, Rich and Bewtiful Empyre of Guiana*. Transcr., annot., and intro. by Neil L. Whitehead. Manchester: Manchester University Press.

Rivière, Peter. 1969. *Marriage among the Trio: A Principle of Social Organization*. Oxford: Oxford University Press.

Rivière, Peter. 1984. *Individual and Society in Guiana: A Comparative Study of Amerindian Social Organisation*. Cambridge: Cambridge University Press.

Rivière, Peter. 1994. "WYSINWYG in Amazonia." *Journal of the Anthropological Society of Oxford* 25 (3): 255–262.

Rivière, Peter. 1995. "Ambiguous Environments." In *Threatened Peoples and Environments in the Americas*, ed. Magnus Mörner and Mona Rosendahl, 39–50. Stockholm: Institute of Latin American Studies, University of Stockholm.

Rivière, Peter. 1999. "Shamanism and the Unconfined Soul." In *From Soul to Self*, ed. M. James C. Crabbe, 70–88. London: Routledge.

Robbins, Joel. 2004. *Becoming Sinners: Christianity and Moral Torment in a Papua New Guinea Society*. Berkeley: University of California Press.

Robbins, Joel. 2007. "Continuity Thinking and the Problem of Christian Culture: Belief, Time, and the Anthropology of Christianity." *Current Anthropology* 48 (1): 5–38.

Rubenstein, Steven L. 2002. *Alejandro Tsakimp: A Shuar Healer in the Margins of History*. Lincoln: University of Nebraska Press.

Sáez, Oscar Calavia. 2007. "Autobiografia e Liderança Indígena do Brasil." *Tellus* 12: 11–32.

Sahlins, Marshall. 2005. "On the Anthropology of Modernity; or, Some Triumphs of Culture over Despondency Theory." In *Culture and Sustainable Development in the Pacific*, ed. Antony Hooper, 44–61. Canberra: Asia Pacific Press, Australian National University.

Senft, Gunter, and Ellen B. Basso, eds. 2009. *Ritual Communication*. Oxford: Berg.

Staden, Hans. (1557) 2008. *Hans Staden's True History: An Account of Cannibal Captivity in Brazil*. Ed. and trans. Neil L. Whitehead and Michael Harbsmeier. Durham, NC: Duke University Press.

Taylor, Anne C. 1993. "Remembering to Forget: Identity, Mourning and Memory among the Jivaro." *Man* (n.s.) 28: 653–678.

Vilaça, Aparecida. 2000. "Relations between Funerary Cannibalism and Warfare Cannibalism: The Question of Predation." *Ethnos* 65 (1): 83–106.

Vilaça, Aparecida. 2005. "Chronically Unstable Bodies: Reflections on Amazonian Corporalities." *Journal of the Royal Anthropological Institute* 11 (3): 445–464.

Vilaça, Aparecida, and Robin M. Wright, eds. 2009. *Native Christians: Modes and Effects of Christianity among Indigenous Peoples of the Americas*. London: Ashgate.

Viveiros de Castro, Eduardo. 2011. "The Forest of Mirrors: A Few Notes on the Ontology of Amazonian Spirits." Projeto AmaZone, last modified 12 October. http://amazone.wikia.com/wiki/The_Forest_of_Mirrors?oldid = 7019.

Wetaru, Tëmeta, and Cees Koelewijn. 2003. *Tëmeta Inponopïhpë Panpira* [Tëmeta's Testament]. Katwijk: Van den Berg.

Chapter 6

TECHNOLOGICAL ANIMISM
The Uncanny Personhood of Humanoid Machines

Kathleen Richardson

How should animism be understood in the early twenty-first century? From Tylor's description in *Primitive Culture* ([1871] 1920) to Bird-David's (1999) critique of it as the 'failed epistemology' model of animism, anthropologists have shifted tremendously in their vision of animistic phenomena. Descola (1996), Ingold (2006), Corsín-Jiménez and Willerslev (2007), and Viveiros de Castro (1998, 2004), among others, have challenged Western epistemologies in the study of animism, particularly Cartesian dualisms that divide the real from the non-real. Even in these innovative works, however, animism remains associated with processes of personifying nature, especially animals (and sometimes plants or other features of the natural landscape), by attributing thoughts, feelings, and intentions to these entities. Yet the potential for animism in technoscientific settings—the personhood of machines—has hardly been explored in the anthropological literature on animism.

Notes for this chapter begin on page 125.

This chapter examines the role of animism in the creation and production of humanoid robots. I suggest that the concept of animism has broader applications in both 'natural' surroundings and the highly technological and experimental setting of robotics laboratories, where myth, fiction, and scientific exploration are brought to bear on the question of what it means to be human. I propose the term 'technological animism' to describe the conceptual model of personhood that emerges in the interaction between fiction, robotics, and culturally specific models of personhood, which may already include non-human persons.

How, as anthropologists, might we draw on debates related to animism to make sense of a peculiar activity where technologists create human-like robot entities that have been intentionally designed to have specific kinds of human qualities (such as emotions or memory) and then put them with adults and children in order to understand the relational effects of these entities (Richardson 2015)? Corsín-Jiménez and Willerslev (2007) problematize the constructs we use as anthropologists, arguing that modes of reflection are contained within our constructs, as well as within the relations between constructs that provide an analytical architecture. What analytical architecture might be useful in understanding the expansion of the field of humanoid and social robotics? In this chapter, I draw on the psychoanalytic writings of Sigmund Freud and the scientific and theoretical writings of Masahiro Mori, as well as on cognitive science and contemporary anthropological studies of animism, to illuminate the liminal character of both fictional and real robots. In essence, my findings decisively challenge the view of animism as a phenomenon belonging to the 'primitive' and situate it instead as a means of understanding personhood beyond the human—even beyond the 'natural'.

The making of robots is a complex multinational and multicultural scientific enterprise. In US robotics labs, I met North American, Japanese, Indonesian, Irish, Colombian, and Italian roboticists. After a while, the multiplicity of persons of different nationalities, life histories, and lived experiences converged into specific themes. In this chapter, I focus on the theme of technological animism and its roots in popular fiction. The automata of the eighteenth century were an important precursor to the mechanical reproduction of humans and animals, as I discuss below, but what we may call the 'modern robot' began as a character in a play, entering public life not via a laboratory or a factory, but at a theater. *Rossumovi Univerzální Roboti* (Rossum's Universal Robots), an avant-garde play from the early twentieth century by Karel Čapek ([1921] 2006), inaugurated the trend in which fictional representations of androids and other human-like automata directly influenced the development and popular reception of modern robots.

In my fieldwork in American robotics laboratories with international teams of scientists from Japan, the United States, and Europe—and focusing especially on the lab at the Massachusetts Institute of Technology (MIT)—I found that fictional representations of animate beings were pivotal to the emergence of technological animism. In the US, fictional visions of robots as 'uncanny' agents of annihilation have influenced American researchers to carefully manage (and often minimize) the human qualities of robots in order to avoid evoking these destructive qualities. Their creations affirm a vision of robots as secular and non-magical. Yet at the same time, American researchers are unable to 'control' their own narratives about robots as they compete with popular fictions—such as the *Terminator* franchise of films and television series (beginning with the 1984 film of the same name)—that present robots as threatening. US roboticists saw themselves as producing objects in a climate of hostility and frequently blamed Hollywood representations of robots and artificial intelligence (AI) for this.

The Japanese researchers whom I met in US robotics labs contrasted their robot philosophies and practices as distinct, even radically different, from those of their Euro-American counterparts. They drew on animistic elements of Japanese Buddhism and Shintoism to support a distinctive cultural narrative of robots as friends and not foes (Coeckelbergh 2013; Jensen and Blok 2013; Robertson 2007; Sone 2008). These religious beliefs provide a 'principle of equivalence' that can be seized upon to relate humans and non-humans (Mori 1970). While a full discussion of Japanese animism is beyond the scope of this chapter, it is worth briefly discussing what this means for my argument. Based on the interpretations of sociologist John Clammer, Jensen and Blok (2013: 97) suggest that Shintoism can be seen "as a complex and specific form of animism. It is in the shape of a vital animism, within a complex, modernized and advanced techno-scientific country, that Shinto holds interest for us as a vehicle for rethinking relations with the non-human world." In Shinto, a "radical 'personalization'" of everything consists in the presence of spirits (*kami*) in all beings (ibid.).

By drawing on fiction and religion, Japanese and North American robotic scientists do not diminish their scientific credentials, but add to them. For Japanese roboticists, it seems as if Japanese people are ready to welcome robots with open arms, as they step directly into their living rooms from the production lines of Sony, Toshiba, and Honda. A number of social scientists have contrasted the popular understanding of robots in Japan with Euro-American views (Allison 2006; Jensen and Blok 2013; Sone 2008). They have particularly examined how models of non-human personhood, originating in Japanese Shinto and Buddhism, have influenced the development of 'techno-animism', a term first coined by anthropologist Anne Allison (2006) in *Millennial Monsters*. This idea refers to the Japanese conceptualization of technological entities as heterogeneous hybrids (ibid.: 13), blending what Jensen and Blok (2013: 85) describe as "advanced technologies and spiritual capacities." However, I propose that technological animism applies not only to Japan, but also to Euro-American imaginings of robots, as explored below. American roboticists distinguish their technoscientific practice from mainstream (Judeo-Christian) religion, but they rely on fiction as a context for making, designing, and imbuing robots with animistic qualities. Whereas fiction, Japanese Buddhism, and/ or a Judeo-Christian heritage might seem to be at odds, the work of roboticists at MIT indicates that the making of humanoid robots is a practice in which religion and fiction fuse with technological practice. Technological animism thus emerges from the interaction between a religious or cultural context, fictional models, and technoscientific production. I begin by examining the fictional models that have brought robots into the popular imagination.

A Short History of Robots in Europe and North America

The first fictional representation of a 'modern' robot, and indeed, the origin of the term 'robot' itself, was a phantasmagoric tale of revolution set against the backdrop of political turmoil in inter-war Europe. In *Rossum's Universal Robots* (hereafter *R.U.R.*), artificial humans are created out of thousands of individual organic body parts and assembled on a factory production line. The term 'robot' comes from a Slavic term meaning 'to work slavishly', although it can also be a neutral word for 'work' in Slavic languages. In Čapek's ([1921] 2006) play, the factory production line (where robots are produced) and the scientific labora- tory (which creates the formula for robots) merge into one integrated setting in a darkly futuristic vision of modernity: the most important theme in the play is the 'robot revolution', which destroys humanity. Written in a historic moment of worldwide embattlement, when World War I (1914–1918) and the Russian Revolution (1917) were still recent memories, Čapek's play is a political drama, a commentary on the destructiveness of war. It is also a commentary on humanity and the capacity to (re)animate it in alternative ways, since his robots are made with human body parts, echoing themes occurring in a plethora of Euro-American and Judeo-Christian religious and literary texts, from the Jewish myth of the Golem to Mary Shelley's *Frankenstein*. All of these fictions share the leitmotif of a threat to humanity from the remodeled human form.

R.U.R. inaugurated Euro-American robot fiction. In its first phase, spanning the 1920s to the 1950s, this fiction imagined robots as revolutionaries, embed- ded in the political narratives of the era. From the 1950s to the 1990s, revolution- ary robots were reimagined as domestic devices and thus, to a certain extent, neutralized of political energy and force. In the 1960s, robots were extended into a new area when the first industrial robot—the Unimate Robot—entered the production line. Its use on a General Motors assembly line in New Jersey mirrored the factory theme in *R.U.R.* The 1960s also saw the rise of AI as a field that would inspire Stanley Kubrick's (1968) classic film, *2001: A Space Odyssey*.

The third phase of robot fiction began in the 1990s and continues today. Contemporary fictional robots may be social companions, friends, caregivers, and potential lovers. They are sometimes even religious or faith-based beings. At the same time, the theme of annihilation has persisted, and fictional robots are often still frightening agents working for the destruction of humanity. In the new *Battlestar Galactica* (Moore and Eick 2004–2009), a remake of the 1970s television series (Larson 1978), humanoid machines motivated by religious beliefs plant bombs and carry out assassinations, threatening the destruction of humanity in order to protect themselves. The themes of quasi-spirituality, robots, and science fiction also feature in the massively popular *Star Wars* films, beginning with *Star Wars, Episode IV: A New Hope* (Lucas 1977). Other fictions show humans living in an alienating world, as in the film *Surrogates*

(Mostow 2009), where contact is mediated through mechanical avatars, or the film *The Matrix* (Wachowski and Wachowski 1999). The Spike Jonze's (2013) film *Her*, starring Joacquin Phoenix, puts a new twist on the theme of alienation, showing artificially intelligent beings as potentially rescuing people from emotional disengagement. Contemporary robot fiction thus engages with themes of terrorism, religious war, alienation, and the pervasive integration of technology in everyday life.

Euro-American roboticists are intensely aware of popular conceptions of robots as agents of destruction, and this influences their laboratory practice. Although all of the robots I have studied are research platforms (meaning they are experimental prototypes rather than commercial objects), there is still fear among scientists that, should their robots become commercially available, the belief that robots are destructive will make the general population uneasy about buying or using them. Scientists have pre-empted this threat by working to design robots that they perceive to be culturally less threatening. This is why you will see childlike robots in many robotic labs in North America, Europe, and Japan.

Technological Animism and the Rise of Childlike Bodies

In the past 10 years, research to develop 'social' robots, and more particularly childlike robots, has flourished worldwide. Since I conducted fieldwork at MIT in 2003–2005, I have found the child robot to be a recurring laboratory motif. Examples include Kismet and Mertz (MIT), Bandit (University of Southern California), KASPAR (University of Hertfordshire), RobotCub (various labs in Europe), ASIMO (Honda, Japan), and Biomimetic Baby or CB2 (Japan). Even when robots are not intentionally designed to appear childlike, many researchers still incorporate notions of child developmental psychology. During fieldwork in North American and British laboratories, I repeatedly found that robotic labs look more like kindergartens. Even when the US DARPA (Defense Advanced Research Projects Agency) was funding projects, labs were filled with toys, children's books, and machines deliberately designed to look adorable. In the high-tech AI robotic labs of MIT, where scientists craft robots and engage in ongoing experimentation with them, it is common to find brightly colored objects, rattles, and trains. In keeping with this childlike atmosphere, interactions with humanoid robots often take the form of adult-child exchanges.

The Honda robot ASIMO (Advanced Step in Innovative Mobility) is perhaps the world's most well-known robot and provides an illustrative example. ASIMO stands at 4 feet 3 inches tall and is roughly the height of an eight-year-old boy. I say 'boy' because it looks like a boy dressed in an astronaut's suit. ASIMO could easily be a machine imitating an astronaut, or a robot imitating a boy imitating an astronaut. The 'head' of ASIMO is mostly a helmet, and when facing ASIMO close up, I found that its face is significantly 'reduced' in expressive human features, with only a line to mark the mouth and two dots in place of eyes. What exactly are the roboticists at Honda trying to achieve when designing their most significant robot in this way? There are a number of issues to unpack here. Depending on whom you speak to about the Honda robot, you will get a different response. According to the official site, ASIMO was made to provide a platform so that researchers could develop an experimental, sophisticated machine. The robot is envisioned as a supportive assistant to "help people": "In the future, ASIMO may serve as another set of eyes, ears, hands and legs for all kinds of people in need. Someday ASIMO might help with important tasks like assisting the elderly or a person confined to a bed or a wheelchair. ASIMO might also perform certain tasks that are dangerous to humans, such as fighting fires or cleaning up toxic spills."[1] Is ASIMO a child or a small human or something else altogether? Knowing what ASIMO's size is supposed to represent is important. If ASIMO is a child duplicate, then are the manufacturers unintentionally creating all kinds of ethical problems that have to do with child labor?

ASIMO was the first technological robot I had seen that was overtly childlike. I was struck by the explanation that a professor of robotics gave to account for the robot's size: "The child at this approximate height can reach power sockets and light switches." It never occurred to me that an army of childlike domestic robots caring for the elderly or carrying out domestic work might evoke controversy. The shift to childlike robots represents a shift in cultural consciousness in relation to robots in Japan and North America. It should be noted that labs in the US and Japan make a variety of different robots. But even if the robots in these labs are not formally created to resemble children, other aspects of their research, design, and development draw on studies of child development and the field of 'epigenetic robotics' (see Berthouze and Metta 2005; Zlatev and Balkenius 2001). This field sees the development of 'intelligence' as an incremental and experiential process that involves the robot and its relations with others and with its environment (Aryananda 2007; Breazeal 2002; Breazeal and Aryananda 2002; Breazeal and Scassellati 2000; Breazeal and Velásquez 1998).

The robotics professor told me it was necessary to design robots to appear cute and childlike in order to counteract popular notions that robots are threatening to humanity and hyper-sophisticated. He explained that the design and utilization of child development models for his group's robots was effectively a reaction to the threatening images of robots popularized through fiction and film. The robot assassin portrayed by Arnold Schwarzenegger in James Cameron's (1984) film *Terminator* is an example. Roboticists anticipate that a robot designed to look like an infant or young child, or otherwise to look cute, will be less threatening and will elicit more engagement. There are considerable design challenges to making robots small and childlike in form—factors such as hardware flexibility, the machine's function and complexity, and so on. To heighten the attractiveness of their machines, roboticists frequently design their robots to have large eyes, which are common in infants. Evolutionary biologists speculate that children's larger eyes are more attractive to their caregivers, making it less likely that they will be harmed by them. At the former Artificial Intelligence Lab at MIT, roboticist Cynthia Breazeal imaginatively employed the techniques of Disney animators to make her robots cute.

The scientists I spoke to found that childlike and cute robots encourage adults to interact with them, even if the interaction requires extra effort on the part of the adult to maintain it. An adult might linger for a longer period of time if he or she perceives the robot to be funny or appealing, even if the robot is performing behaviors to benefit only itself (e.g., recording data for the researcher from the interaction). I have seen the efforts of adult men and women as they try to engage with Radius, a socially inspired robot head, and other robots at the Maria Stata Center at MIT, which is a perfect environment for securing a stream of passersby. Often adults persist even if the robot moves erratically and repeats a string of scripted sentences that are at odds with the moment. When a robot is childlike, adults tend spontaneously to support the machine and compensate for what it is lacking, altering their expectations as one might with a child, and they may even nurture the machine. The term 'caregiver' is sometimes used to describe the role an adult assumes when interacting with a childlike robot. The exchange between adults and childlike robots results in an asymmetrical social relationality, as between adults and children. For example, I frequently interacted with the robot Radius, using brightly colored toys to help the robotic scientist in the lab better calibrate its facial and color recognition software. I found myself calling the robot's name as it jerkily moved it head in any direction but mine. I persisted in trying to attract the machine's attention until Radius's eyes briefly connected with mine. I had its attention, only to lose it again moments later.

In epigenetic robotics, the robot can be made to learn about its environment in a structured way, mimicking particular stages of child development. However, a robot's configuration of capabilities, learning, and appearance confound the categories that people use when thinking about childhood. Although it may be the size of an eight-year-old boy, a robot may still be used as a research platform to explore baby crawling; thus, age, size, skill, and functions are jumbled up. Interestingly, presenting the robots as children invites their inscription into honorary kinship categories. I know robotic scientists who openly welcome being labeled the 'mother' or 'father' of their robot platforms (Breazeal 2002; Robertson 2007, 2010).

The exchanges described above foster technological animism. The human participants in these interactions are aware that the other party is not human, much less a child. Yet they perceive, and respond to, the 'animation' of the robot as if it were a (partially human) person. This technological animism is not premised on the putative existence of a soul or on other intangible soul-like qualities. On the contrary, it produces an intangible sense of human-like qualities through purely mechanistic (technological) means.

Fictional robots provide further fuel for technological animism. The robot (a copy) is sustained by its relation to the originals (human adult/robot fiction), as roboticists and laypeople interacting with robots draw on fictional representations when projecting intentions, actions, and agency onto robots. In the case of Radius or ASIMO, the robot child (copy) is bolstered by its original (human child) and enlivened further, through technological animism, by the adult's extra effort to support the robot child. Let me stress that I have seen robots do absolutely nothing at all and still impress audiences with their human-like qualities. This is because the adult is not seeing just the physical object in front of him or her, but is perceiving a whole catalogue of cultural references that reinforce the exchange within the ontology of technological animism.

Fictional Animism, Automatons, and the Uncanny (Valley)

In 2001, *AI: Artificial Intelligence* (Spielberg 2001) was released in cinemas across the world. The story focuses on a robot child, David, and his existential crisis at being neglected and abandoned. The movie draws inspiration from the nineteenth-century tale of Pinocchio, in which a childless bachelor crafts a puppet in the shape of a boy because he is lonely and longs to care for a son. In the film, David is programmed to attach to one specific person, and his durability as a robot means that he is doomed to outlive the humans whom he loves and who have abandoned him. David's story is really about love and separation. The film raises questions that are now being played out in robotics laboratories: Can humans develop bonds and attachments to robotic entities? Can this process be facilitated or supported if the robot is childlike? If robots become sophisticated enough to start performing some of their imagined supportive and social companionship roles, will this transform attachment patterns that currently take place almost exclusively between humans or between humans and animals, particularly domesticated pets? Can such patterns be transferred to robots that have both human and mechanical qualities? Recent films such as *Her* echo these questions about love and attachment between humans and animate machines.

Donna Haraway (1991) asserts that technoscience breached the boundary between fact and fiction in the twentieth century. Yet in robotic fiction and robotic science, there has never been a boundary to breach, because the latter has inherited the properties of the former as it took robotics into new territory. Films like *AI: Artificial Intelligence* and *Her* provide imaginative models for the potential future of robotics, while raising social and ethical questions surrounding robots. These questions arguably boil down to the problems of technological animism, that is, the ascription of human-like qualities of personhood to robots, which can easily provoke discomfort and fear. Japanese roboticist Masahiro Mori (1970) explores such reactions in his work on the 'uncanny valley'. Mori placed human-like objects on a grid with appearance at one axis and behavior on another. The highest point in the chart is a healthy human person, and the lowest point is a zombie.[2] Behavior and appearance need to connect; otherwise, Mori argues, the entity is frightening. A robot that appears lifelike but moves with jerky movements in repetitive ways gives rise to a sense of the uncanny, since the expectation is that the more human-like the robot appears, the more it should behave in human-like ways. In Olga Ulturgasheva's description of *djuluchen* (this volume), she cites an Eveny hunter's story in which a wolf has sent his 'forerunner' ahead of him, which appears to the hunter as if it were a "broken machine that repeated itself … over and over again." When an entity is out of synch with some aspect of its being, it begins to resemble a machine. Hence, when the human-like robot fails to act appropriately like a human, it falls into the 'uncanny valley', the lowest point of the graph, where it ostensibly provokes the greatest fear.

The Freudian idea of the uncanny, which inspired Mori's writing, is a psychoanalytical explanation for objects and scenarios that provoke terror, uncertainty, and confusion by challenging our familiar concepts. Freud's ([1919] 2003) essay, *The Uncanny*, deals in part with his theory about the Oedipus complex, but his notion of the uncanny has become a more popular reading. The "uncanny" sensation arises from "the unhomely" (ibid.: 152), "the 'double'" (ibid.: 141), or that which provokes "intellectual uncertainty" (ibid.: 140). It can be a consequence of the difficulty in judging "whether something is animate or inanimate" (ibid.: 141) or the confusion when something not alive "bears an excessive likeness to the living" (ibid.). Freud was interested in the context that facilitates this uncomfortable breaching of boundaries and how it might be explained. Not everything that is ambivalently animate and inanimate triggers the uncanny. In Freud's view: "[T]he fairy tale is quite openly committed to the animistic view that thoughts and wishes are all-powerful, but I cannot cite one genuine fairy tale in which anything uncanny occurs. We are told that it is highly uncanny when inanimate objects—pictures or dolls—come to life, but in Hans Andersen's stories the household utensils, the furniture and the tin soldier are alive, and perhaps nothing is farther removed from the uncanny. Even when Pygmalion's beautiful statue comes to life, this is hardly felt to be uncanny" (ibid.: 153). The uncanny, then, is not triggered by the animation of the inanimate per se, but by the animation of the inanimate in a specific type of context. Freud included psychical and physical states in the uncanny and referred to the numerous fictional, imaginary, physical, and real conditions that might trigger them. But the question remains, when do boundaries become so blurred that they trigger this state of discomfort and fear?

Čapek's *R.U.R.*, which was published two years after *The Uncanny*, would have been an interesting subject for Freud's analysis. Instead of robots, Freud examines the psychic states evoked by human-like objects, such as automata and dolls. At the time, automata were objects that some thought destabilized the boundaries between human and machine, living and dead, animate and inanimate. In the eighteenth and nineteenth centuries in Europe, hundreds of mechanics constructed human and animal automata, such as Jacques de Vaucanson's Digesting Duck, which was exhibited in the 1700s and was said to drink and defecate (Standage 2002). The automata gave rise to the term *androïdé*, defined as "an automation in human form, which by means of well-positioned springs, etc. performs certain functions which externally resemble that of man," as defined in Diderot and d'Alembert's *Encyclopédie* (cited in ibid.: 20). Čapek's term 'robot' later replaced *androïdé* in popular usage to describe a humanoid machine. The making of automatons raised questions about the boundaries between human and machine—and later between the original human and the robot copy—as well as questions about the dialectic transference of potential properties between them.[3]

The Turk, a famous eighteenth-century automaton, encapsulates these themes. The Turk was designed by Wolfgang von Kempelen and exhibited throughout

Europe and the US in the 1700s. Ostensibly an automaton that played chess, the Turk fooled audiences into thinking it was a 'living' machine, as it was perceived to 'think'. "By choosing to make his machine a chess player, a contraption apparently capable of reason, Kempelen sparked a vigorous debate about the extent to which machines could emulate or replicate human faculties," writes Standage (2002: xiv). The immensely popular Turk was later revealed to be a fraud: its abilities came from a man positioned inside, controlling its actions.

The making of automata raised questions about what was human or machine, living or dead, animate or inanimate—the very questions that, I argue, technological animism infuses into our ontological milieu. Automata produced 'uncanny' effects in audiences: many early automata were anthropomorphic mimetic objects that evoked "that species of the frightening that goes back to what was once well known and had long been familiar" (Freud [1919] 2003: 124). As Gaby Wood (2002: xiv) explains: "[T]here was anxiety in the present situation—an anxiety that all androids, from the earliest moving doll to the most sophisticated robots, conjure up." Wood sees this as a perfect example of the uncanny as "the feeling that arises when there is an 'intellectual uncertainty' about the borderline between the lifeless and the living" (ibid.).

So far I have highlighted the potentially uncanny nature of robots and the fictional representations of robots as harbingers of human destruction, which directly parallel Freud's ([1919] 2003) ideas about the animistic doppelgänger, or 'double', and its connection to the fear of death. According to Freud, fear is triggered when persons carry a resemblance to other persons, or when people worry that the psychic contents of their minds are known to another through mental transmission (e.g., telepathy). Freud describes "[t]he invention of such doubling" initially as "a defence against annihilation," an expression of what he sees as the "primordial narcissism that dominates the mental life of both the child and the primitive man" (ibid.: 142). However, the appearance of animism in advanced technological settings directly challenges the paternalistic evolutionism of Freud's theory. Freud describes a psychosocial state in which one's thoughts, fantasies, and feelings become 'doubled' in the other, and he puts 'primitive' thought in a category with the thinking of children. "The double," Freud writes, "becomes an object of terror" when the "ego has not yet clearly set itself off against the world outside and from others" (ibid.: 143). Yet the fear of the double as a harbinger of annihilation and object of terror can also emerge in technological animism and its humanoid robots. This is strong evidence for uncoupling the theory of animism from evolutionist models of thought, and I argue that technological animism is a pervasive part of how we understand new technologies.

Ulturgasheva's fascinating description of *djuluchen* (a spirit that travels ahead) in this book provides a useful contrast to Freud's fearful double. Among the Eveny, peoples of Northeastern Siberia, the *djuluchen* is a double of another kind, one that moves ahead of the person and is perceived not as an annihilating other but as an ongoing aspect of one's personhood. In this sense, the Eveny never catch up with their double as it is always several steps ahead.

The uncanny, then, has been a powerful force in imagining and responding to humanoid robots in fiction as in actual technological development, and it affects both how and when robots are treated as persons. The blissful fantasy of the robot coming to life might also become its beholder's worst nightmare—the double emerges as fact and fiction begin to meld.

Japanese Robots: In the Shadow of Atom Boy

Mori's description of the 'uncanny valley' and the anxiogenic properties of so many robot narratives would seem to define humanoid machines in terms of fear and discomfort. Yet the vision of humanoid robots that I found in Japanese laboratories was very different and may relate to a contrasting 'cosmogenesis' in the story of Atom Boy (Jensen and Blok 2013).

Like Čapek's *R.U.R.* for Euro-American roboticists, the character Tetsuwan Atomu, translated into English as Astro Boy or Atom Boy, is the point of reference for their Japanese counterparts. Created by Osamu Tezuka, the manga (comic book) series *Tetsuwan Atomu* was published from 1952 to 1968 and continues to enjoy cult status in Japan today. It is perhaps surprising that Atom Boy became such a uniquely Japanese portrayal of an intelligent being created from the power of the atom at a time when Japan was still reeling from the nuclear strikes that devastated the people and cities of Hiroshima and Nagasaki. This lent particular salience to the atom as both a scientific and military object in 1950s Japan. In contrast with the robots who foment violent revolution in *R.U.R.*, Atom Boy is a benevolent figure, with a childlike relationship to his human guardians.

The power that manga and anime (movie and television animation) such as Atom Boy have had on the Japanese imagination became apparent in my interviews with Japanese roboticists. When I asked a famous Japanese roboticist about his motivations for engaging in his research, he cited Atom Boy and other cartoons as having had an early influence: "When I was a small kid, maybe 10 years old, and after the end of World War II, Japan ... was totally destroyed. However, many people struggled to recover ... And years later economic prosperity started ... TV programs began broadcasting ... At that time, animation was played only in movie theaters. I believe that the first animation in the world was Astro Boy ... especially made before TV broadcasting. So I watched the TV, and also there are a lot of other types of robot animations all over Japan. So that was so exciting. I was totally imprinted by that kind of movie ... cartoons ... animations" (pers. comm., June 2003). Atom Boy, or Astro Boy, was not in fact the first animation ever made, but it clearly had a strong impact on this professor. In his narrative, an interest in fictional robots eventually gave way to actual research on humanoid robots. His story suggests that his technological activity was an unfolding of his inner desires—a sense that his desire and fantasy could be realized in the form of robots. His childhood fantasies acted as the backdrop to his adult fantasies and informed the direction of his work as an engineer. This echoes the idea of the *djuluchen* described by Ulturgasheva whereby Eveny young people project themselves into the future through their 'forerunners'.

The professor's story reveals the context for a different vision of robots in Japanese society. In this view, humanoid technological creations belonged to a positive futuristic vision that was shaped by post-war reconstruction and an optimistic unfolding of the future in the present. Certainly, Japanese robotic scientists expressed very different sentiments about the public reception of robots than the European and American scientists I interviewed. The Japanese scientists were confident that the public would accept humanoid robots not as terrifying creations but as potential social agents that would take over the roles of live humans. Japan is already ahead of the robot game in many respects, with the highest number of robots per worker of any country in the world. As its elderly population increases and its working-age population shrinks, the Japanese nation invests in robotics as a means to national self-sufficiency (Robertson 2010; Sone 2008). Robots may also benefit from ideas of animation that appear in Japanese Buddhism and Shintoism. In those beliefs, it is possible for non-humans to be animated and possess a soul without threatening the personhood of humans, thus providing a cultural model for the development of a positive technological animism, as described above.

In spite of these positive cultural attitudes toward robots, Japanese roboticists are aware of the potential for their creations to become uncanny. Take, for instance, the humanoid robot Repliee, developed by Osaka University and manufactured by Kokoro Company, whose appearance is that of an attractive Japanese woman in her twenties. The researchers claim that Repliee can interact naturally with people, but on viewing footage of her, one can quickly spot errors in her behavior. She would pass for a human only briefly as her bodily movements are jerky and the whirring sounds of the mechanical motors that make up her system are audible.

In his article on robotics, Mori (1970) believed that when robots' behaviors grew in sophistication, their increased human-like appearance would not be a problem. In fact, Japanese scientists have incorporated his concept of the 'uncanny valley' into their research as a design philosophy. What the Japanese and MIT laboratory (as well as wider social) imaginaries suggest is that the inherent problem of contemporary robotics rests with the making of robots in human form, which is not just a vastly complex technical problem, but a cultural one.

Anthropomorphism, Liminality, and Mimesis

Let us now consider anthropomorphism in relation to technological animism, since the robots I study have a humanoid form. Anthropomorphism is a polyvalent concept that is important to our understanding of animism and also has broader applications, for instance, in the field of animal behavioral studies (de Waal 1996). Although robots are made in labs by experts in the highly specialized fields of electrical engineering, mechanical engineering, and computer science, they are not merely technological objects but cultural ones, with meanings that their makers do not exclusively control. Despite the propensity of humans to attribute human-like qualities to non-humans, anthropomorphism is still arguably a problematic concept in anthropology (Haraway 1991, 2006) and other disciplines (de Waal 1996), because it locates humans as the main agent in relations with materialities and non-humans. Moreover, anthropologically, seeing animal life-worlds from a human perspective can confuse and elide the meanings that underscore these different existences (ibid.). Haraway (1991, 2006) challenges this perception fiercely in her studies of simians, cyborgs, and dogs. Yet, in my view, the emphasis on hybridity (Latour 1993, 2005) and relational nature-culture mixtures (Haraway 1991) does not adequately explain the multiple ways that anthropomorphism operates in everyday Euro-American interactions with non-human animals, machines, and things (Vidal 2007). Moreover, I suggest that the emphasis on hybridity and relationalities between persons and things diminishes human subjectivity in these processes. The human spectator plays a crucial role in the ways that anthropomorphic entities, such as robots, are configured. While humans may interact with things like robots that trigger thoughts, feelings, and behaviors, their interactions are mediated through human socialities (Gell 1998; Guthrie 1995). Much like the 'art of capture' that Swancutt (this volume) describes in relation to spiders and souls, conflicts of description arise, indicating that the same phenomena can have radically different interpretations. It is, then, useful to make an analytical point about what is actually happening and what people think and say is happening: this explains how different persons can draw on radically different ontological frameworks and interpret the same event in different ways (see Swancutt, this volume). This brings us to the efficacy of acts that need to be considered in each specific context. Anthropomorphism is not merely a frame in which to understand human interactions with technologies that have human qualities. It is a means by which to rethink the importance of human sociality in forging interactions with non-humans—especially those interactions that give rise to technological animism.

Anthropomorphism can refer to various processes of attributing human characteristics to non-human animals, things, and, of course, human-like robots. As a concept, anthropomorphism has been discussed widely in anthropology in relation to animals (Miles 1997; Moynihan 1997; Silverman 1997). There is also literature on the cognitive-perceptual bases for ascribing anthropomorphic qualities to other beings. For Guthrie (1995, 2007), anthropomorphism is a cognitive-perceptual process whereby humans 'guess' about the states of others or attribute a theory of mind (ToM) to others, including other humans (see also Baron-Cohen 1995). Is even the scientific ToM an outcome of technological animism? While it is a result of scientific practice, I suggest that the ToM is a kind of animism, wherein one can telepathically understand the intentions of others through reading their minds, as if persons were theatrical scripts.

Cognitive-perceptual reactions to robots are somewhat akin to the Euro-American reactions to dolls, puppets, and automata described above (Freud [1919] 2003: 141–142); Wood 2002). Such items are felt to be uncanny because they have a similar appearance to humans but a different 'materiality'. Robots are not only uncanny; they are even liminal, as they are existentially 'betwixt and between' humans and machines. As George Bernard Shaw (1972: vi) wrote about theatrical puppets: "What really affects us in the theatre is not the muscular activities of the performers, but the feelings they awaken in us by their aspect; for the imagination of the spectator plays a far greater part there than the exertions of the actors." This is not unlike the reaction that people may have to robots through 'technological imagination'. This 'everyday' theatrical dimension of robotics is part and parcel of the roboticists' genealogies (Richardson 2011). And as we saw from the ethnography presented above, roboticists deliberately exploit human cognitive-perceptual intuitions—which form part of technological animism—in the way that they produce robotic creatures through a mimesis of the human form, but also as a mimesis of fictional automatons.

In the process of mimesis, as Michael Taussig (1993) shows, the power of the original (in his case, colonialists in Panama) is transferred and captured by the copy (ritual figurines made of those colonialists by indigenous Cuna). Here, features of the original are detached and inform the copy, so that in acquiring properties of the original, the copy is empowered by its relation to it. Since the original in the case of robots is a fictional character, the fictional setting is a constituent part of the original as well. Given this, the human-like robot is 'enhanced' by virtue of its being a copy that bears within it the power of the original. And it is this co-opted power of the original that produces technological animism. Since these creatures existed as fictions before, albeit in different forms, robot machines are not merely technical entities devoid of cultural properties. They are, in effect, cultural beings.

The robot was never imagined as a pure machine or a pure human. In *R.U.R.*, robots were not made of machine parts; rather, they were made of human parts by machines. But can anthropological theorizing in the field of animism really help us to understand what kind of entity the robot is? Robot systems are designed to be situated and embodied quite deliberately, and the robot is designed to judge and act in its environment from its own perspective. While humans and non-humans come into relation with one another as assemblages in a network (Latour 2005), not all entities have equivalent agency. There is a colonial aspect to actor-network-theory (ANT) that entails speaking on behalf of others, such that scallops, for example, can be understood only when interpreted by the mind of the analyst and presented in human speech and language forms (Callon 1986). In my view, some aspects of Latour's (2005) actor-network-theory echo classical ideas of animism, except that in the animistic imagination, all entities can have subjectivity and agency. In ANT, however, no one has subjectivity of any greater significance than that which is granted to another entity, as one merely analytically describes how multiple agents come into contact and intersect with others (Callon 1986). The robot, then, is not an entity that can be neatly classified. Rather, as Corsín-Jiménez and Willerslev (2007) suggest, we need to reflect on the concepts we are using. The robot is human and non-human, machine and non-machine, real and non-real. Just as they are never pure machines, humanoid robots can never be fully human. Taussig (1993: 11) makes this point about the reproduction of the original, showing that, in the copy, a part is distorted or wholly left out.

Humanoid robots are, then, meant to be odd approximations of the human bodies they are supposed to resemble. Robots have faces, but they may have a nose or mouth missing. Or they may have a full humanoid shape but lack hands or feet.[4] Yet the absence of physical parts is only part of the story of their limitations. It does not matter if robots carry out the acts they have been created to perform, such as 'socially' interacting with a person or navigating along a corridor. It is enough that people can imagine the robots performing the acts for which they were produced. Having watched many robot demonstrations, I witnessed this on several occasions. Let me end with one illustrative example from a demonstration held at MIT's Media Lab that I attended, during which a robot was presented to an excited audience of around 20 people. After the robot was introduced, we waited for it to carry out the actions that had been described by the robotic scientist moments before. The robot could not perform those actions, yet only two people in the audience pointed this out (I was one of them). The other spectators were in awe of the robot despite the fact that it could not do what it was supposed to do. The spectators were filling in the empty spaces of the robot's performance with technological animism.

Conclusion

In this chapter, I suggest that the concept of animism has analytical value even in the highly scientific realm of robotics, where the development of humanoid machines opens up questions of what it means to be human or a non-human 'animate' machine. Moreover, the evidence of technological practices that are, to all intents and purposes, 'animistic' invites us to reframe the discussion of animism as a form of human consciousness that is transcultural and not unique to indigenous cosmologies. If robots can be humanoid and animate—if they offer the possibility of technological animism—what does this mean for animism and its associations with a mythical 'nature'? Humanoid robots invite us to imagine (and, indeed, seem to embody) a form of 'non-human' personhood that is neither 'natural' nor religious in origin. If robots all too easily transport us to the 'uncanny valley', it is because of their animistic potential. This suggests that the term 'animism' should not be limited to 'natural' phenomena, but instead understood as a broader concept underlying the cultural construction of agency and personhood.[5] Technological animism is strong evidence against the enduring association between animism and the social evolutionist idea of the 'primitive'.

Fictional models of robots, along with religious and cultural ideas, merge with laboratory practices in people's understandings of humanoid robots. Fictional tales become places where we can express fears in particular ways; they are often places of horror, destruction, and annihilation. Fictions serve a purpose in allowing an outlet for the unconscious mind without letting it becoming manifested in the lived (and fearful) realities in which the double appears. I have not tried to diminish the cultural differences between robotic practices in Europe, North America, and Japan, but have attempted to show that the theme of robotic fiction encompasses them all. In fiction, as Freud explains, there is experimentation with boundaries, ontological orders, and cosmological meanings. The analogy between fictional representations and robots is not such a superficial contrast, since the work of roboticists is encased in fiction—even as fiction is merged with scientific creation. Perhaps, then, the most uncanny element of the popular fear surrounding a machine-robot takeover is its own strange potential to become a self-fulfilling prophecy, with the real agents of change (humans) lost in their increasingly machine-moderated world of technological animism.

Acknowledgments

I would like to thank Mireille Mazard and Katherine Swancutt for their ongoing and generous support during the development of this book. Their drive, enthusiasm, and passion were a guiding force for me in preparing this chapter. Thanks are extended as well to the publisher's editorial staff.

Kathleen Richardson is a Senior Research Fellow in the Ethics of Robotics at the Centre for Computing and Social Responsibility (CCSR), De Montfort University, Leicester. Her research examines the development of robots as companions, therapists, friends, and sexual partners. She is also part of the Europewide DREAM project (Development of Robot-Enhanced Therapy for Children with Autism Spectrum Disorders), a project developing therapeutic robots for helping children with autism in their social learning. She is the author of *An Anthropology of Robots and AI: Annihilation Anxiety and Machines* (2015) and is currently working on another manuscript.

Notes

1. See Honda, "History of Asimo," http://asimo.honda.com/asimo-history/.
2. Mori uses a zombie as the index for the greatest fear-producing robot design because it transgresses the boundaries between living and dead, while being neither one nor the other.
3. This dialectic transference between machines and humans resonates with the notion of 'hyper-reflexivity' as explained by Katherine Swancutt and Mireille Mazard in the introduction to this book.
4. Elsewhere, I explain further how robot scientists narrowly focus on those parts of the robot's body that human spectators expect to see when robots perform a humanoid function (see Richardson 2015). Because humans spend a great deal of time looking at eyes during social interactions, roboticists who make 'social' robots ensure that there are features on the robot face that act as eyes, even if those features have no practical function—that is, if they do not work like human or animal vision systems.

5. I am not the first to suggest that animism can occur in scientific settings. Allison (2006) refers to 'techno-animism', and Ingold (2006: 9) has extended the discussion of animism to astronomers fascinated with finding animate life forms elsewhere in the universe.

References

Allison, Anne. 2006. *Millennial Monsters: Japanese Toys and the Global Imagination.* Berkeley: University of California Press.

Aryananda, Lijin. 2007. "A Few Days of a Robot's Life in the Human's World: Toward Incremental Individual Recognition." PhD diss., Massachusetts Institute of Technology.

Baron-Cohen, Simon. 1995. *Mindblindness: An Essay on Autism and Theory of Mind.* Cambridge, MA: MIT Press.

Berthouze, Luc, and Giorgio Metta. 2005. "Epigenetic Robotics: Modelling Cognitive Development in Robotic Systems." *Cognitive Systems Research* 6 (3): 189–192.

Bird-David, Nurit. 1999. "'Animism' Revisited: Personhood, Environment, and Relational Epistemology." *Current Anthropology* 40 (S1): S67–S91. Special issue titled "Culture: A Second Chance?"

Breazeal, Cynthia. 2002. *Designing Sociable Robots.* Cambridge, MA: MIT Press.

Breazeal, Cynthia, and Lijin Aryananda. 2002. "Recognition of Affective Communicative Intent in Robot-Directed Speech." *Autonomous Robots* 12: 83–104.

Breazeal, Cynthia, and Brian Scassellati. 2000. "Infant-Like Social Interactions between a Robot and a Human Caregiver." *Adaptive Behavior* 8 (1): 49–74.

Breazeal, Cynthia, and Juan Velásquez. 1998. "Toward Teaching a Robot 'Infant' Using Emotive Communication Acts." MIT Artificial Intelligence Laboratory Publications. http://www.ai.mit.edu/projects/ntt/projects/NTT9904-01/documents/Breazeal-Velasquez-SAB98.pdf.

Callon, Michel. 1986. "Some Elements of a Sociology of Translation: Domestication of the Scallops and the Fishermen of St Brieuc Bay." In *Power, Action and Belief: A New Sociology of Knowledge?* ed. John Law, 196–223. London: Routledge & Kegan Paul.

Cameron, James, dir. 1984. *The Terminator.* Film. Distributed by Orion Pictures.

Čapek, Karel. (1921) 2006. *R.U.R. (Rossum's Universal Robots).* Trans. Claudia Novack; intro. Ivan Klíma. New York: Penguin Books. First published in Prague by Aventinum.

Coeckelbergh, Mark. 2013. "Pervasion of What? Techno-human Ecologies and Their Ubiquitous Spirits." *AI & Society* 28 (1): 55–63.

Corsín-Jiménez, Alberto, and Rane Willerslev. 2007. "'An Anthropological Concept of the Concept': Reversibility among the Siberian Yukaghirs." *Journal of the Royal Anthropological Institute* 13 (3): 527–544.

Descola, Philippe. 1996. *In the Society of Nature: A Native Ecology in Amazonia.* Trans. Nora Scott. Cambridge: Cambridge University Press.

de Waal, Frans. 1996. *Good Natured: The Origins of Right and Wrong in Humans and Other Animals.* Cambridge, MA: Harvard University Press.

Freud, Sigmund. (1919) 2003. *The Uncanny.* Trans. David McLintock; intro. Hugh Haughton. London: Penguin.

Gell, Alfred. 1998. *Art and Agency: An Anthropological Theory.* Oxford: Clarendon Press.

Guthrie, Stewart E. 1995. *Faces in the Clouds: A New Theory of Religion.* Oxford: Oxford University Press.

Guthrie, Stewart E. 2007. "Anthropology and Anthropomorphism in Religion." In *Religion, Anthropology and Cognitive Science*, ed. Harvey Whitehouse and James Laidlaw, 37–62. Durham, NC: Carolina Academic Press.

Haraway, Donna J. 1991. *Simians, Cyborgs, and Women: The Reinvention of Nature*. London: Free Association Books.

Haraway, Donna J. 2006. *The Companion Species Manifesto: Dogs, People, and Significant Otherness*. Chicago: Prickly Paradigm Press.

Ingold, Tim. 2006. "Rethinking the Animate, Re-animating Thought." *Ethnos* 71 (1): 9–20.

Jensen, Casper B., and Anders Blok. 2013. "Techno-animism in Japan: Shinto Cosmograms, Actor-Network Theory, and the Enabling Powers of Non-human Agencies." *Theory Culture & Society* 30 (2): 84–115.

Jonze, Spike, dir. 2013. *Her*. Annapurna Pictures. Distributed by Warner Bros. Pictures.

Kubrick, Stanley, dir. 1968. *2001: A Space Odyssey*. Film. Distributed by Metro-Goldwyn-Mayer.

Larson, Glen A., prod. 1978. *Battlestar Galactica*. Television series. Distributed by MCA/Universal.

Latour, Bruno. 1993. *We Have Never Been Modern*. Trans. Catherine Porter. Cambridge, MA: Harvard University Press.

Latour, Bruno. 2005. *Reassembling the Social: An Introduction to Actor-Network-Theory*. Oxford: Oxford University Press.

Lucas, George, dir. 1977. *Star Wars, Episode IV: A New Hope*. Film. Distributed by Universal Studios.

Miles, H. Lyn. 1997. "Anthropomorphism, Apes, and Language." In Mitchell et al. 1997, 383–404.

Mitchell, Robert M., Nicholas S. Thompson, and H. Lyn Miles, eds. 1997. *Anthropomorphism, Anecdotes, and Animals*. Albany: SUNY Press.

Moore, Ronald D., and David Eick, prod. 2004–2009. *Battlestar Galactica*. Television series. David Eick Productions.

Mori, Masahiro. 1970. "Bukimi no tani." [The Uncanny Valley] *Energy* 7 (4): 33–35.

Mostow, Jonathan, dir. 2009. *Surrogates*. Film. Distributed by Walt Disney Studios Motion Pictures.

Moynihan, Martin H. 1997. "Self-Awareness, with Specific References to Celeoid Cephalopods." In Mitchell et al. 1997, 213–219.

Richardson, Kathleen. 2011. "Are Friends Electric?" Times Higher Educational Supplement, 9 June. https://www.timeshighereducation.com/features/are-friends-electric/416434.article.

Richardson, Kathleen. 2015. *An Anthropology of Robots and AI: Annihilation Anxiety and Machines*. New York: Routledge.

Robertson, Jennifer. 2007. "Robo Sapiens Japanicus: Humanoid Robots and the Posthuman Family." *Critical Asian Studies* 39 (3): 369–398.

Robertson, Jennifer. 2010. "Gendering Humanoid Robots: Robo-Sexism in Japan." *Body & Society* 16 (2): 1–36.

Shaw, George Bernard. 1972. "Note on Puppets." P. vi in Max Von Boehn, *Puppets and Automata*. New York: Dover Publications.

Silverman, Paul S. 1997. "A Pragmatic Approach to the Inference of Animal Mind." In Mitchell et al. 1997, 170–188.

Sone, Yuji. 2008. "Realism of the Unreal: The Japanese Robot and the Performance of Representation." *Visual Communication* 7 (3): 345–362.

Spielberg, Steven, dir. 2001. *AI: Artificial Intelligence*. Film. Distributed by Warner Bros. Pictures and DreamWorks Pictures.

Standage, Tom. 2002. *The Mechanical Turk: The True Story of the Chess-Playing Machine That Fooled the World*. London: Penguin.

Taussig, Michael. 1993. *Mimesis and Alterity: A Particular History of the Senses*. New York: Routledge.

Tylor, Edward B. (1871) 1920. *Primitive Culture: Researches into the Development of Mythology, Philosophy, Religion, Language, Art and Custom*. Vols. 1 and 2. London: John Murray.

Vidal, Denis. 2007. "Anthropomorphism or Sub-anthropomorphism? An Anthropological Approach to Gods and Robots." *Journal of the Royal Anthropological Institute* 13 (4): 917–933.

Viveiros de Castro, Eduardo. 1998. "Cosmological Deixis and Amerindian Perspectivism." *Journal of the Royal Anthropological Institute* 4 (3): 469–488.

Viveiros de Castro, Eduardo. 2004. "Exchanging Perspectives: The Transformation of Objects into Subjects in Amerindian Ontologies." *Common Knowledge* 10 (3): 463–484.

Von Boehn, Max. 1972. *Puppets and Automata*. New York: Dover Publications.

Wachowski, Lana, and Andrew P. Wachowski, dirs. 1999. *The Matrix*. Film. Distributed by Warner Bros Pictures.

Wood, Gaby. 2002. *Living Dolls: A Magical History of the Quest for Mechanical Life*. London: Faber and Faber.

Zlatev, Jordan, and Christian Balkenius. 2001. "Introduction: Why 'Epigenetic Robotics'?" In *Proceedings of the First International Workshop on Epigenetic Robotics* (*Cognitive Studies* series, Vol. 85), 1–4. Lund: Lund University. http://www.lucs.lu.se/LUCS/085/Zlatev.Balkenius.pdf.

POSTSCRIPT

Anthropologists and Healers—Radical Empiricists

Edith Turner

This postscript presents the living ethnography of the work of a 'psychic' individual from northern Alaska who recognized her own gift and was aware of her marked position in society due to her possession of second sight. Such people occur freely among all societies. My study gives the record and the testimony of Claire Sevukaq in 1987 from among the Iñupiaq people.[1] Based on Claire's account, it will be seen that these people spend their whole waking lives deeply aware of spirits, alive to what Jung called their 'collective unconscious', and what Thomas Fowler (2008) refers to as the 'psyche'. Like anthropologists, healers such as Claire are what I call 'radical empiricists': they go by what their hands feel and what they see with their eyes, or their second sight.

Claire Sevukaq in Alaska: Her Own Second Sight

Some 30 years after I had first worked among African ghost doctors with Victor Turner in Zambia in the 1950s, news came through the university of a remarkable culture of healing in a peripheral region of North America on the northern slope of Alaska. It was a land of the Iñupiaq, a people living mainly on sea hunting in a freezing climate.

It was 21 September 1987 when I went to visit the healer, Claire Sevukaq, in the village of Ivakuq. Claire's living room was homey. There was a mop across the sofa. Family photographs crowded the walls. A picture showed the Sevukaq whaling crew busy on an enormous whale, with cuts already made in its side. Nearby was the famous picture of Jesus by Sallman, the Savior's face divine and all-knowing. I saw a milk crate containing neat files holding easily available forms for the village food stamp system. Claire was the organizer.

Claire's face was interesting; she had strong oval features. Now she was looking at me, interested in me. I introduced myself to this healer, thinking, "Come on, Edie, your own dad was a doctor." I started out, "I've heard of your work. I've a great respect for Iñupiat healing."

"What made you interested in it?" she asked.

I told her the most dramatic healing event I knew. "I once saw my husband Vic heal somebody. This man had a heart attack in our living room and his heart stopped. Vic put his hand on the man's heart, and it started again. I still wonder what was going on, if I might learn what's behind it ... I've a lot of respect for what you do."

"I'm very glad. I've been getting discouraged, frustrated." She looked away.

"Are the medical doctors getting you down?"

"Yes."

"Don't let 'em," I said. "It's a good work you're doing."

She and I liked each other. We began to talk about our families and grandchildren. Claire said, "The baby, Jeanie, she's seven. Jeanie wants to be a healer like me. The kid's learning it already." She looked at Jeanie with appreciation. Then she was silent, pondering a minute. "Iñupiat healing is different." She lingered over the word. "Come into the kitchen and talk while I work." But soon a message came over Claire's Citizens band (CB) radio, and she cocked an ear. "Claire, come on in. Claire, come on in," the voice said. "Go to Netta's at once, she's sick. She's throwing up."

Netta was an elder, and she was sick—and healing always comes first. Before leaving, Claire thought for a moment, then went to her refrigerator. In it stood two jars of a blackish fluid made of Iñupiat herbs: *qanganaruaq*, called 'stinkweed', a fragrant plant classified as Artemisia tilesii, and wormwood, which is also related to a traditional medicine of Europe, absinthe. Claire took out some of the boiled infusion and drank a cupful to give her healing strength. She handed me a little to try myself. It was bitter and heartening.

At Netta's house, I peeped into her bedroom. Clem, her grandson, was at the entrance. Netta was lying with Claire at her side and Jeanie, the seven-year-old healing apprentice, sitting between her knees. My housemate Carrie had already found her way there and was helping. Ardell Lowe, another health aide, was sitting apart from Claire. Claire could feel that Netta's stomach was in the wrong position and that it was hard and tight. She could feel air pockets that were stopping the stomach from working, causing Netta to vomit blood. Netta had not been able to eat for three days.

Many people were gathering in the moment of old Netta's danger—her older kin and many grown-up grandchildren. I greeted the elders. They sat like statues on straight chairs. There was silence. I felt a little frightened. Netta vomited, groaning, and lay back; then she vomited again and muttered something in Iñupiat. Claire was working on Netta's stomach with both hands, digging deep into the folds of the old stomach flesh. Claire had 'good hands' that could soothe and take away pain. Ardell, the health aide, said, "We don't know what is wrong. I'm going to phone the hospital and get them to send the Medivac plane. The senior health aide gave Netta some Mylanta. That's all we are allowed to do."

Meanwhile, Claire was softening Netta's stomach to bring it down into the right position. But the air pocket gave trouble. Now standing in the doorway, I saw the old woman's face become contorted, then I saw it blank out to nothing. Claire kept a strong hold on Netta's head and held on, holding Netta to her. I started to pray. Clem looked fearful, as if death impended; perhaps it did. The old lady reared up again in agony to vomit, then fell back. Her body blanked out, and her head sank back. She looked emptied. Claire massaged her stomach, bending her own head very near to Netta's head.

Claire stayed right close to her, head to head, with her hand always on Netta's stomach, a warm, intimate contact with the 'different' knowledge in it. Netta stayed as she was. She did seem to be resting. Claire began to talk cheerfully, gossiping about her grown-up son and his new television. We laughed, subduing our voices. Netta was now drinking 7 Up, talking, and complaining vividly in Iñupiat about her stomach. She stretched out her feet. She asked for some tea. There was a quiet rush to fetch her a cup. Clem began to smile. Gradually, we became aware that the immediate crisis was past. We waited.

The Medivac plane was flying over. Everyone heard it. The people in the living room passed to and fro to look through the windows, telling each other, "There it is." Margie, Clem's wife, fussed over what clothes to send with Netta. Even so, they forgot her dentures.

As we stood waiting, Clem said to me in his slow voice: "Her spirit went out of her body three times. You can see if a person's going to die. The person looks like a still boat on a still sea going far away. You have to bring it back and draw it back, so that the person doesn't die. Three times it went out of her, and Claire brought it back and pulled it down into her again. A spirit—when it leaves it goes up through the hole in the top of the head." I touched my own long-closed fontanel. Clem said, "That's right, there."

There was a stir. The ambulance had arrived and was backed up just by the door. Marvin, the white Medivac pilot, came in, followed by a tall, dark-haired white man, distant of manner, who turned out to be the doctor. The place was full of people milling around in a confused way. I peered into Netta's room. The team became occupied in following the stereotypical conventions of 'medical practice'. They took Netta's blood pressure, pulse, and temperature and asked questions. Then the stretcher men gathered in the bedroom.

Clem went up to the doctor and told him: "She's been spitting out very dark stuff, black, like blood." The doctor came up the passage to the bedroom and looked into the old lady's vomiting can. "A little blood," he said disparagingly. I returned to the living room, and the doctor came and stood by the wall. We grew silent. After a moment, the ambulance men emerged from the passageway with Netta in their stretcher. We saw her wrinkled face lift up to look out of the ambulance, then the doors were shut and they were off to the airstrip.

After several weeks, I saw Netta restored and back in her living room, her little proud head wobbling a bit and her halting words begging me to work on her stomach because of the wind. She had indeed had a huge cyst removed— "as big as a baby"—and after the operation she gradually regained her active, combative temperament.

A few days after we had seen Netta off in the ambulance, Carrie and I were back in Claire's house, helping her with the laundry this time. She began to describe the sense she had of feeling the pain of the sick: "I can feel the sick person's pain, I can feel where it is. Do you get how I mean? A woman in a village 250 miles away called me and said, 'I'm having a miscarriage.' She was four months pregnant. When the woman spoke, I knew what was wrong—it's my second sight. My second sight told me how to advise the woman. I told her what to do. The fetus was saved, and the baby was born full-term."

Claire said again: "My healing is different. The doctors say, 'You're wrong, Claire.' They think I'm trying to do predictions. I don't predict, I know when someone's pregnant and for how long. Then it turns out I'm right. The health aides say 'You must go by what the doctors say'—but I know. One woman at the clinic came to me. She put out her hand and said, 'Don't touch me.'" Claire put out her hand and drew it back. "I didn't touch her. I told her that she was two weeks pregnant. I knew. In a month she took the test, and she was pregnant. She was scared."

I often think of Claire, especially in relation to my early work with Victor Turner in Zambia on the old Tukuka and Wubwangu rituals for spirit affliction that we attended in 1954 (see V. Turner 1969: 44–93). After a long absence, I returned to Zambia in 1985. I visited with Philip Kabwita, a healer whom I had previously come to know well, and sang in his Wubwangu ritual for a new baby (E. Turner 1986). The ritual still had similar features, with Kabwita dressed in his grass skirt and cat skin headdress for the occasion. But this time he also carried a doctor's black bag that contained a rattle and a conch shell—his 'African telephone'—which he used for contacting spirits. From today's perspective, I now see more clearly the influences of the outside world on Philip and how he exhibited a consciousness of that very ritual consciousness of his—that is, a sense of the current types of sociality of his time and a hyper-reflexive awareness of his own skills of alignment with the spirit powers through his African telephone. In Alaska, Claire also has a spiritual telephone—her CB radio—which puts her in a position to answer sickness calls. Reflecting on this in Claire's presence, I told her about Philip Kabwita the African healer, who received a message by spirit telephone from 350 miles away through the African savanna.

The Faculties at Work at the Heart of Iñupiat Healing

During Claire's treatment of Netta, four of us—Claire, Clem, Carrie, and, to a certain extent, myself—perceived Netta's spirit continually parting company from her tortured organs and wandering toward its outlet in her fontanel. Claire freed the blockage in the stomach again and again, bringing the spirit back down into the old lady's body. The activity of Claire's arms and head showed what she was doing.

A healer's hands on the body 'know' what dead or sick tissue feels like. Having found it out, the live tissue is empowered and the hands restore the communication. The bridging, in a sense, enters another level that has to do with the cycling of the cosmos—the level at which it runs.

From that time on, I was deluged with reports of healings, past and present. I observed many of them and participated in some myself. While I was working on language with Claire, the CB radio spoke: "Claire. Claire. Come in, please. Come over and see little Lee, he's hurt." Lee was three years old. Claire seized her jacket and put it on as she strode out to her three-wheeler ATV. She waited an instant for Jeanie and me to get on behind her before whirling off. She entered Lee's house, all gentle, already knowing the trouble because of her preliminary time of clairvoyance. Inside, the child was screaming. He had jumped off a tall, empty stereo shelf and crashed onto his knees. Now he could neither stand nor walk and was on his mother's lap. Claire brought up a chair and sat opposite Lee. Jeanie was kneeling close by to watch; like me, she was very interested. Claire took one foot gently and turned up the pant leg. Lee's crying got worse. Claire turned her hand over the throbbing knee, almost not touching it.

"I can't hurt you, I can't hurt you," she told the boy as an obvious truth, in her most musical voice. "See, I'm making it better." She was seeing inside him. Her seeing was like an X-ray, as she would say—everything inside was as clear as daylight. The mother held Lee, and Claire felt both of his lower legs. The child's crying began to give way. She felt down the muscles of each leg, drawing down the legs neatly and together. She worked each ankle, the flat of the foot, the toes, bending them gently until they were flexible, showing Lee how good they were. Her hands went back to the knees. The right one bore a bruise and a big swelling below the kneecap. It was water on the knee. She placed both kneecaps centrally and pressed them gently into position as if they were jigsaw pieces, completing the action by pressing carefully with her palm. She worked the dimpled areas of the left knee while swiveling the leg back and forth. Then she returned to the swelling on the right knee. I noted that she left the trickiest bit until last. She pressed the swelling slightly here and there, and I saw it diminish a little. She left that work alone for a time and turned down Lee's pant legs. He slid off his mother's lap and tried a few steps, using his legs like little sticks.

Claire chatted to his mother about this and that. Then she turned to Lee: "Auntie Claire's going to make some mukluk boots for you. How about it, eh?" Little Lee had been making eyes at Jeanie. "Come on," Claire told him, "Auntie's going to feel your knee a bit more." She worked on the swelling again, showing me how it was going down. "See? It's simple." As I watched, it went away altogether, leaving the normal muscle curves visible around the kneecap. I was attending carefully, having experienced under Claire's tutelage the same sense in the hands—a kind of misery and mushiness in the damaged tissues— followed by a similar diminution of swelling. And, when I needed healing from others, I myself had experienced how the pain seems to seep away and just not be there anymore.

Claire drew down Lee's pant legs and let him go. He walked easily. She went to the sink and washed, getting rid of whatever it was. "The pain goes into my own arm," she told me. "My hand gets hot. Hot!" Claire went on talking to the mother, who was short of money and awaiting a welfare check. The place was in poor shape, lacking a carpet, with torn vinyl chair seats and only a garishly colored window shade to cheer the place up. Lee was now jumping from the empty stereo shelf to the sofa. "That's how he did it in the first place," said

Claire. "Jumping and falling on his knees. Stop that." Claire went to wash her hands. We left before more treatment might become necessary.

About her treatment method, Claire had kept saying, "See, it's simple," and it was. It only needed the actual doing. It was healing that was empirical in essence because it was so particularized. The hands knew the details of the inner tissues: they were involved deep in the tissues, not just laid on the outside. I compare it to the work of Singleton, an African healer in Zambia, with his mongoose skin pouch and horn, stroking and feeling and coaxing a damaging ihamba tooth out of the back of a sick person into the cupping horn, and being aware of the right place to do it (E. Turner 1992).

In both Claire's and Singleton's kind of healing, what was at work was the kind of practical consciousness that Clem meant when he said that Iñupiaq healing was 'ordinary' or, in a sense, obvious. One could term the practitioners themselves—not just their ethnographers—'radical empiricists' because they knew very well what they were doing. It may be expected that other types of healers, spiritists and the like, will be found to operate in the same way. The practical part of Iñupiat healing is to create a conversation between the two bodies—that of the afflicted and that of the healer—by means of the hands' work. The healers sometimes say: "They are God's hands, not mine." The trouble can enter as far as the elbows, where the healer blocks it off. Then she washes out the bad things she has drawn into her hands, as Claire did after healing Lee.

When Claire talked earlier of 'knowing' (i.e., second sight) and healing at a distance, I realized that healing in this way did not include bodily touch, yet perception might still take place in a bodily way. This was shown in one case in which Claire, while sitting in her house, felt the same pain in her own body that was afflicting someone outside as he approached the house in search of Claire to heal him. The ability to receive that kind of message appeared to be on the same continuum with the fine bodily sense I have just described. However, this sense was able to extend itself until it became visionary, capable of seeing spirit beings from afar, as in the long-distance conversations via African telephone that were made by Philip Kabwita's family. Philip's grandfather Nkomesha taught him many things. The craft can be taught, and there are gifts.

One day later that year, Claire came to my house and asked me seriously what I was doing in Ivakuk. This time I did not have to say "to write a scholarly paper about healing customs" or some such thing. I told her that I wanted to experience healing and spirit perception and know it as a reality. I told her that in Africa I helped at a healing ritual and, at the climax of the drumming, saw a spirit body emerge from the back of the sick woman. That being so, I could not help but believe in Claire's work. What else could be my aim here? Claire considered a minute. Then she said, "I'm tired. I have that pain in my rib. It happened when I had a Honda accident. The handlebar got my rib here. It's still bothering me after four months."

I was checking the oven and turned. "Shall I rub it for you?" She didn't say yes but went to sit down at the table. She put her hand to a back rib on the right. "It's not badly hurt, but …." I put my hand there and followed where her hands showed the spot. Had she broken the rib? I remembered how in 1941 a horse had crunched my body between his cart and a gate, and how the pain had gone on for months. Maybe I had had a broken rib. Yes, there on Claire's rib was a clenched thing, a little over an inch across. "That's it," she said. "Yes," I replied and showed her the size with my finger and thumb. "It's clenched up."

I merely caressed it, as Claire would have done. Around, and on top. The thing seemed to dwell greedily on that rib, scaring the body into believing it was sick. A lump all right. It was body stuff acting up hard in the wrong place. I sighed. My hands knew this thing was sore. Now, astonishingly, Claire was letting the thing go into my hands. She let it go and let it go. The clenched part was mainly softish now, but I could feel within it a small lengthwise section that was still hard, say half an inch long. And I handled it a bit in the place where it was hard, inside. You get a little picture of it inside there. Now there was only the shadow left. "That's better," said Claire, so I went to wash my hands. She told me later that the pain had not recurred. But I had not brought this about. Did it happen from taking the right action? Not exactly. The relief came from an 'X' factor that intervenes when the two necessary elements are there—that is, a person in pain and a person evidently able to transmit it away.

Some time afterward, I began to think that my perception of Claire's trouble was not 'extrasensory perception', outside the senses, but an actual fine sense—existing contrary to expectations—in the fingers, which could somehow result in the transfer of the ailment. This sense perception of the fingers actually seems to exist. There is a knowledge or a certain awareness in the human consciousness of a link between oneself and the sufferer, which is empowered by a kind of rushing of one's own consciousness into that of the other. Whatever it is, this is the concrete meaning of 'sympathy' or 'feeling with' another, and it follows a palpable path, that is, through the fingers' understanding. In this particular experience, it had something to do with the cast of feelings. When the feelings (which cannot be forced) are open, then the channels to the other person are open. Nothing happens if that person is not sick: it is the hands' sympathy with the person's sick tissues that opens the way. Whatever it is, it is the cause of the 'opening' that takes place due to the hands' contact with the sickness. That rushing of one's consciousness into the other person—that sigh, I think—is exactly the spirit in Iñupiat parlance (alternatively, 'the good Lord') to whom the healers pray. It is not one's own doing; rather, it is one's own allowing. It cannot be forced but is prayed for. 'Prayer' is of that nature and is rather mysterious. A non-egoistic intention is necessary, but intention by itself does not heal. It is the allowing of an opening that does so.

The following Thursday, Claire came to visit. Over a cup of herb tea, she began to talk about her childhood: "My mother, grandmother, and great-grandmother were all healers, and I learned from them. I remember healing someone when I was four. This is just like my daughter, who healed my stomach when she was four ... I can't really say I learned it. I feel it. I get the symptoms from those people ... That's the most important part, the feelings, and I know it. I always felt it. I could sense it. I have to pray about it. I don't do the healing myself. I know the good Lord gave it to me so I'm not going to take all the credit for it." Claire's was a life that unfolded its own dynamic. The unitary principle, her consciousness of herself, was very strong.

The Four-Day Black Period

At different stages of Claire's life, she had experienced at least five episodes that psychologists in Euro-American culture might term 'fugue'. Typically lasting four days, they appeared to be the classic irruptions of shamanic experience, just as the ancient Iñupiat knew them. In early times, these experiences were characterized by a meeting with something fearful, such as a spirit of the dead or of an animal—a being that first afflicted the shaman, then changed and became a helper.

An account of Claire's first recorded episode was related to me by a friend of hers, a white woman whom I met in Fairbanks over a cup of coffee. In about 1970, Claire was in Anchorage in an expensive hotel. For reasons unknown, she stayed there alone for four days. "She had there some kind of transformation," said Claire's friend, looking disturbed. "She told me on the phone. I was at the airport. She told me she'd had some kind of revelation about me. There were certain things that would happen. A person who didn't know Claire's powers would think she'd gone crazy. It was a kind of glossolalia. That was a bad time for Claire." Bending over her coffee, she added, "I don't know what Claire went through in that hotel for four days all by herself."

In 1984, when Claire was not doing much healing, she had another episode, a very bad one. Claire would continually see a devil figure in her peripheral vision. At one time during this phase, Claire uttered a whole lot of nonsense words, greatly upsetting her relatives. Claire told them irritably, "Don't be like that. You don't think I am anything, do you? I can't help it, it comes to me." But at the end of this four-day episode, Claire was able to pray to Jesus again, and afterward her healing power was stronger. She appealed to Jesus to be her helper spirit, the opposite of Satan—and indeed, the same switch from dangerous to helpful occurred as in the days before the introduction of Christianity.

In the fall of 1987, Claire and Rebecca, an American Indian school secretary, were studying anthropology together by teleconference. Rebecca used Claire's case to illustrate the experiences of shamans. Rebecca realized that the personality of a shamanic healer was not like that of ordinary people and that Claire's episodes were not necessarily bad.

A further episode occurred on 14 January 1988. I found Claire lying on her couch, very depressed. She shut her eyes and would not speak. I was frightened, thinking she was angry. Four days later she was herself again. When I visited in 1991, yet another episode occurred. I had just arrived for the whaling festival and heard that Claire had returned from a hospital where she had been a patient from 28 May to 2 June. I went to her house and approached the kitchen. A small dark figure was at the kitchen sink, and she did not turn around. "Claire, Claire. Look at this. I've brought you something," I said. She still did not turn. Her gray hair was scrawny, her figure thin. I immediately thought, "An episode again? Isn't this fieldwork pitiful! My dear friend caught up in ... something so mysterious. Okay, I have to try to understand it."

Claire peeped into the shopping bag I had brought and saw peacock blue velvet for a new parka and a peacock blue zipper. She turned convulsively and flung herself into my arms. We were crying. Stroking her wild gray hair and haggard face, I told her, "Dear Claire. You've given me everything, my sweet friend." When we recovered, she told me that the doctor at the hospital had given her the wrong medicine. She was really mad at him. "I'll get an attorney," she said. Now she was off all medicines and was feeling better by the minute. I wondered what the doctor thought he had prescribed the medicine for.

Claire had read my published article, "From Shamans to Healers" (E. Turner 1989). "I liked it," she said. "I liked the comparisons" between shamans and healers. But Claire's four-day periods still puzzled me. An old account survived about an ancestor of Clem's who had been the shaman Kehuq. What it described seemed to be a key to the four-day syndrome. When Kehuq was a young man, he was out on the tundra one day and heard the sound of paddles up in the air. He looked up and saw a boat floating in the sky. It landed, and Kehuq saw in it a shaman with one big eye who danced and gave him pleasure. The boat disappeared, and by the time Kehuq reached home he had forgotten all about it. Late that night, Kehuq started up naked and left his tent for no reason. They brought him back, but for four days he was crazy and could not eat. Yet when he recovered, Kehuq could dance. When he did so, his spirit left him, and he was possessed by the strange shaman's spirit. Kehuq taught his people the shaman's dance and songs and also taught them how to carve the shaman's face in wood. He now had the shaman's power to heal the sick, to speak with the dead, to find lost objects, and to see the future.

There were many accounts about a four-day crazy period, typically followed by a supernaturally successful hunting period and by healing gifts and other benefits. One of Clem's brothers also had four-day episodes during which he would not talk to anyone. Clem himself was familiar with the condition. Furthermore, Jean Briggs (1970: 254–255) mentions that during her fieldwork among the Inuit of Canada, the father of the family with whom she lived appeared to become withdrawn at periods, with the same moodiness and dislike of disturbance as with Claire. The condition called 'Arctic hysteria' (Foulks 1972) may not be a matter of sunlight deprivation so much as the four-day phenomenon.[2]

These four-day episodes come at the will of the spirit beings, who cut off the ordinary person from his or her ordinary life. They cause the person to reassemble differently inside, like a chrysalis. The process has to do not only with the brain but with the body: the 'four-day syndrome' is doing the work of reassembling this person. Mircea Eliade's (1972) book on shamanism has a full section devoted to this experience. It has been called by some the *sparagmos*, part of the spirit initiation of a shaman (see E. Turner 2011). To Claire and the others, the perception of these workings was a familiar thing to them, as they were never tired of telling me. I have found that what I have described was not a hypothesis but a working system.

I recognize that a development of a sense of such processes is the subject of this postscript. Spotting what was going on in the apparently random material of the everyday led me to discriminate as to which were spirit events. So my days were like a divining basket, with the divining implements randomly laid about. One tossed these implements, and they said something that communicated.

Conclusion

My portrait of Claire shows the exigencies under which she suffered. But the haunting she endured during her four-day shaman syndrome was somehow a positive thing, involved in her very make-up. Claire fought the demons. She had an eye—and the gift—for it. The reader will note Claire's reiteration that her healing was 'different'. Yet I do not describe her healing as being 'outside the world' or 'transcendent'. That 'different' world is amenable to our understanding and susceptible to the inquiries of the scholar of natural history. Both worlds are within the purview of the researcher. However, researchers have to have eyes that can accept what they are researching and must use those eyes. At the present time, anthropology itself has changed. The empathy of fieldworkers has taken a step forward so that those whom they study hardly seem to be 'subjects' of cold research at all. Instead, they are simply co-members of the human race—and co-researchers as well.

Edith Turner is on the faculty of the Department of Anthropology at the University of Virginia. She specializes in ritual, healing, and aspects of consciousness. Her numerous publications include *The Spirit and the Drum: A Memoir of Africa* (1987), *Experiencing Ritual: A New Interpretation of African Healing* (1992), and her most recent book, *Communitas: The Anthropology of Collective Joy* (2012). She was for many years the editor of *Anthropology and Humanism*, the journal of the Society for Humanistic Anthropology, and in 2014 she received a lifetime achievement award from that organization. She holds honorary degrees from Kenyon College and the College of Wooster.

Notes

1. I have used pseudonyms in this postscript to protect identities.
2. My own late husband, the anthropologist Victor Turner, had suffered black periods from time to time. We both used to note that they lasted for four days.

References

Briggs, Jean. 1970. *Never in Anger: Portrait of an Eskimo Family.* Cambridge, MA: Harvard University Press.

Eliade, Mircea. 1972. *Shamanism: Archaic Techniques of Ecstasy.* Princeton, NJ: Princeton University Press.

Foulks, Edward F. 1972. *The Arctic Hysterias of the North Alaskan Eskimo.* Washington, DC: American Anthropological Association.

Fowler, Thomas B. 2008. "Sentient Intelligence: Consciousness and Knowing in the Philosophy of Xavier Zubiri." In *Ontology of Consciousness: Percipient Action*, ed. Helmut Wautischer, 549–574. Cambridge, MA: MIT Press.

Turner, Edith. 1986. "Philip Kabwita, Ghost Doctor: The Ndembu in 1985." *The Drama Review* 30 (4): 12–35.

Turner, Edith. 1989. "From Shamans to Healers: The Survival of an Inupiaq Eskimo Skill." *Anthropologica* 31 (1): 3–24.

Turner, Edith. 1992. *Experiencing Ritual: A New Interpretation of African Healing.* Philadelphia: University of Pennsylvania Press.

Turner, Edith. 2011. "The Making of a Shaman: A Comparative Study of Inuit, African, and Nepalese Shaman Initiation." Metanexus Institute. http://metanexus.net/essay/making-shaman-comparative-study-inuit-african-and-nepalese-shaman-initiation.

Turner, Victor W. 1969. *The Ritual Process: Structure and Anti-Structure.* Chicago: Aldine Publishing.

INDEX

www.ingramcontent.com/pod-product-compliance
Lightning Source LLC
Chambersburg PA
CBHW070934030426
42336CB00014BA/2674